GW00727925

War Pensions and Armed Forces Compensation

Law and Practice

War Pensions and Armed Forces Compensation

Law and Practice

Andrew Bano

Visiting Judge of the Upper Tribunal
Formerly President of the War Pensions and
Armed Forces Compensation Chamber
of the First-tier Tribunal

Wildy, Simmonds & Hill Publishing

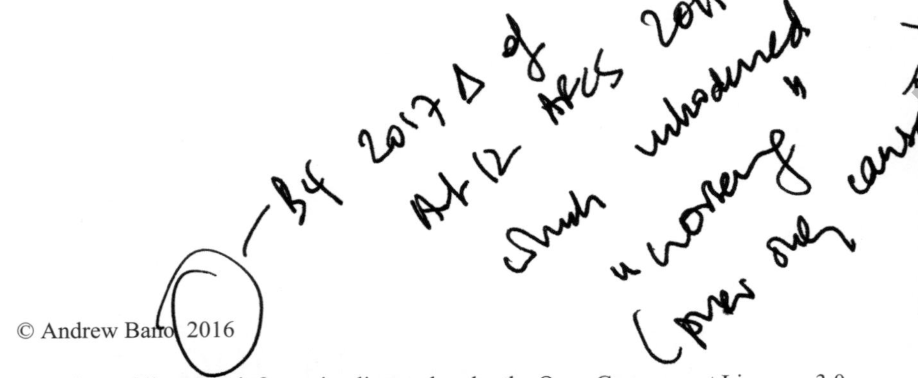

ISBN: 9780854901906

British Library Cataloguing in Publication Data

A catalogue record for this book is available from the British Library

First published in 2016 by

Wildy, Simmonds & Hill Publishing
58 Carey Street
London WC2A 2JF
England
www.wildy.com

Typeset by Heather Jones, North Petherton, Somerset.
Printed in Great Britain by CPI Antony Rowe, Chippenham, Wiltshire.

For Elizabeth

Contents

Appendices

Foreword

Andrew Bano is the quintessential, careful specialist who brings to this book a deep knowledge of and affinity with the war pensions jurisdiction. He has been one of its foremost caretakers. His empathy with and passion for his subject are combined with an admirable attention to detail. His knowledge shines through the history, practice and procedure that he describes. The book is not only an important historical record, but also an eminently readable and encyclopaedic reference work. It will be required reading for specialist judges, practitioners, academics and commentators, and for the armed forces and members of the public whom we serve. Andrew has created the first accessible description of the principles that underpin the jurisdictions that are exercised by the War Pensions and Armed Forces Compensation Chamber of the First-tier Tribunal. We should not underestimate how important that it is to our work. His book will enhance transparency and access to justice for members of the armed forces and their families. That is important to our obligation to maintain the rule of law and to the development of the principles of distributive justice in such an important area.

Sir Ernest Ryder, Senior President of Tribunals
London
August 2016

Preface

The provision of support for injured members of the armed forces and for the families of those killed in military service is one of the oldest ways in which states have provided for their citizens. Societies in every age have recognised the special position of those who have suffered disablement or death in the service of their country by providing veterans and their dependants with benefits that have often been uniquely favourable.

The United Kingdom has been no exception. The War Pensions Scheme, which provided compensation for injury or death suffered by members of the armed forces in the period between the Second World War and 2005, was alone among UK state benefit schemes in placing the onus on the authorities to disprove entitlement to benefit beyond reasonable doubt. Following the report of the Boyce Review in 2010, the Armed Forces Compensation Scheme, which replaced the War Pensions Scheme in 2005, was radically overhauled because it was widely perceived as providing inadequate compensation for wounded members of the armed forces, particularly for combatants who had sustained very serious injuries in Iraq and Afghanistan.

Between 1943 and 2005, armed forces veterans also enjoyed uniquely privileged rights of appeal against tribunal decisions. The Pensions Appeal Tribunals Act 1943 provided for such appeals to go to a nominated High Court judge in England and Wales and to judges of equivalent status in Scotland and Northern Ireland. As a result, the principles of war pensions were developed by some of the most distinguished judges of their day, notably Mr Justice Denning (as he then was), who was the nominated judge in England and Wales in the period after the Second World War.

The lack of a textbook on war pensions and armed forces compensation has, however, meant that much of the case law has been hidden from view. Some of the decisions of the nominated judges found their way into the published law reports, but the majority were reported in the *War Pensions Appeal Reports*, which were available to the public only on request. The decisions of the Upper Tribunal judges, who have now taken over the functions of the nominated judges, are published on the internet, but without a textbook it can be difficult to identify cases which are relevant to a particular issue. The difficulty of accessing the relevant law has meant that judges, lawyers, claimants and their advisers have often had to grapple with the same issues many times over, without being aware of decided cases directly on point. The lack of comprehensive and readily accessible reference sources on war pensions and armed forces compensation has hampered judicial training and, worse still, has increased the risk that similar claims may have different outcomes.

The approaching centenary in 2017 of the establishment of the first pensions appeal tribunals makes this an opportune time to try to remedy this situation. The aim of this book is to explain and to analyse the statute and case law governing entitlement to war pensions and armed forces compensation, and to describe the judicial systems in England and Wales, Scotland and Northern Ireland for resolving disputes. However, it is not intended as a book for the legal profession alone. My hope is that by organising the dense and often complex statutory material into a logical structure, and by explaining the law wherever possible without using technical legal language, this book will meet the needs of all those who need to know about entitlement to war pensions and armed forces compensation benefits, and about the practice and procedure for bringing appeals in each part of the United Kingdom.

The decisions of the nominated judges were often fact-specific and the large number of reported war pensions decisions has made it necessary to make a selection of cases for highlighting. I have therefore concentrated on cases which established key principles of the War Pensions Scheme and which remain relevant today, rather than citing cases which simply applied previously established principles, or which dealt with issues that are now no longer likely to arise in practice.

The Armed Forces Compensation Scheme has presented a contrasting challenge. The Scheme is still in its infancy and many important issues still await judicial consideration. In dealing with the Scheme, my aim has been to analyse the guidance on key concepts that has been given by the Court of Appeal and by the Upper Tribunal to date in the context of the Scheme's objectives, and in particular against the background of the Boyce Review recommendations.

The war pensions tribunals, consisting of a lawyer and medical and service members, were one of the earliest examples of tribunals as we know them today. Their survival nearly 100 years later in almost exactly the same form as when they were established demonstrates their resilience, and testifies to continuing public acceptance of a system of justice in which lawyers and non-lawyers play equal and complementary parts. In describing the reformed tribunal system in

England and Wales under the Tribunals, Courts and Enforcement Act 2007, I have tried to show how the new tribunal system continues to provide an expert tribunal designed to meet the needs of a special body of users, while at the same time forming part of a unified tribunal system with largely common procedures designed to ensure accessibility for users, efficiency and fairness.

My thanks are due to my predecessor as President of the War Pensions and Armed Forces Compensation Chamber, Doctor Harcourt Concannon, for introducing me to the subject and for explaining it with a clarity which I can only strive to match. I am grateful to the current Chamber President, Judge Alison McKenna, for her encouragement and support. I am also indebted to Judge Clare Horrocks, the Chamber's Principal Judge, for giving me the benefit of her advice during our time as colleagues based not only on long experience, but also on practical knowledge of service conditions. I must also record my thanks to Judge Nicholas Wikeley, the temporary President of the War Pensions and Armed Forces Compensation Chamber of the First-tier Tribunal, to Doctor Kenneth Mullan, President of the Pensions Appeal Tribunal in Northern Ireland and to Marion Caldwell QC, President of the Pensions Appeal Tribunal in Scotland, for the help they have given me with regard to procedure in their respective jurisdictions. I am grateful also to Mrs Terry Stewart, who made available to me a valuable collection of documents in Edinburgh.

My thanks are also due to my Upper Tribunal colleagues for their advice and support, but I must single out one name for special mention. Mark Rowland has generously given me the benefit of his unrivalled knowledge of war pensions and armed forces compensation and of the tribunal system by commenting on my drafts. The book has benefitted immeasurably from his contribution, but I must absolve him from blame for any faults which the book may have. The responsibility for those is mine alone.

I have endeavoured to state the law as at 11 April 2016.

Andrew Bano
Easter, 2016

Table of Court and Nominated Judges' Decisions

References are to page numbers.

Table of Commissioners' and Upper Tribunal Decisions

References are to page numbers.

Table of Statutes

References are to page numbers.

Table of Statutory Instruments

References are to page numbers.

Table of Practice Statements

References are to page numbers.

Table of Conventions

References are to page numbers.

Citation of Cases

Some of the many war pensions cases which were decided by nominated High Court judges in England and Wales and by their equivalents in Scotland and Northern Ireland were reported in a series of indexed looseleaf reports originally compiled by the legal adviser to the Ministry of Pensions. The reports are entitled *Reports of Selected War Pensions Appeals*, cited in this book as 'WPAR' (*War Pensions Appeal Reports*), for example, *Giles v Minister of Pensions and National Insurance* (1955) 4 WPAR 445. The year shown in brackets is the year in which the case was decided and the number following the date is the number of the volume which contains the report. The page reference is at the end of the citation.

In 2005, the functions of the High Court nominated judges and their equivalents in Scotland and Northern Ireland were transferred to what were then the Social Security Commissioners. The Social Security Commissioners had a well-established system for reporting important cases. The jurisdiction of the Social Security Commissioners in relation to war pensions and armed forces compensation cases was transferred to the Administrative Appeals Chamber of the Upper Tribunal on the creation of the new tribunal in 2008, except that in Northern Ireland the Social Security Commissioners retained jurisdiction over war pension entitlement appeals.

All Upper Tribunal and Commissioners' cases have file numbers indicating the type of benefit with which the appeal is concerned and the year in which the appeal was registered. In England and Wales, the designation 'CAF' is used to denote an armed forces case, for example, *CAF/3934/2007*. In Scotland, the designation '*CSAF*' is used. In Northern Ireland, the style is slightly different, for example, *C1/06-07(AF)*. Decisions that are unreported and do not have a neutral citation number are cited using the file number, without identifying the parties.

Decisions of the Upper Tribunal that are published on its website are given a neutral citation number, in accordance with the Senior President's Practice Statement 'Form of Decisions and Neutral Citation in the First-tier Tribunal and Upper Tribunal on or after 3 November 2008'. Since 2010, a neutral citation has a 'flag' indicating the subject-matter of the case, for example, *SV v Secretary of State for Defence (AFCS)* [2013] UKUT 201 (AAC), which is an armed forces compensation scheme case, and *ML v Secretary of State for Defence (WP)* [2011] UKUT 511 (AAC), which is a war pensions case. Under current practice, the name of the claimant is normally anonymised. Cases with neutral citation numbers can be found on both the Upper Tribunal[1] and BAILII websites.[2] The Northern Ireland Commissioners have used a similar system of neutral citation since 2010.

Decisions which are selected for reporting in the official series of *Administrative Appeal Chamber Reports* are given a new number. Prior to 2010, this followed the practice for the reported decisions of Commissioners. In Great Britain, it consisted of a prefix followed by letters in brackets denoting the type of case, followed by a number and the year in which the decision was first published as a reported decision, for example, *R(AF) 2/09*. Armed Forces cases were always identified by the letters 'AF'. The Northern Ireland style was similar, but there were no reported armed forces decisions then. Since 2010, the reference for reported cases has been in the form of the year of reporting in square brackets, followed by the number of the case, for example, *EW v Secretary of State for Defence (AFCS)* [2011] UKUT 186 (AAC) is reported as [2012] AACR 3. Reported decisions of Northern Ireland Commissioners are included in the *Administrative Appeals Chamber Reports* using the same style.

---

1 www.gov.uk/courts-tribunals/upper-tribunal-administrative-appeals-chamber.

2 www.bailii.org.

PART I

WAR PENSIONS

Chapter 1

War Pensions – A Historical Introduction

1.1 The provision of pensions for those injured or killed in the service of their country and for their dependants dates back to the earliest times. In Britain, the history of war pensions has been traced back to the reign of King Alfred.[1] The statute 35 Eliz. 1, c.4 (1592–93), which was one of a number of Acts of Parliament passed during the reign of Elizabeth I putting provision for disabled servicemen on a statutory basis, provided for a weekly tax on parishes not to exceed 6d in the pound, so that disabled army veterans 'should at their return be relieved and regarded to the end that they may reap the fruit of their deservings, and others may be encouraged to perform their like endeavours'. In modern times, the obligations of the nation to members of the armed forces and their families have been expressed through the Armed Forces Covenant,[2] the second principle of which is that 'special consideration is appropriate in some cases, especially for those who have given most such as the injured and the bereaved'.

1.2 In 1681, the Royal Hospital Chelsea was built to care for disabled soldiers and in 1705, the Greenwich Hospital was opened to provide for disabled seamen. Up to the beginning of the First World War, the Board of Commissioners of the Royal Hospital Chelsea were responsible for administering army pensions, but at the start of the war responsibility for administering pensions for army officers was given to the War Office. By 1869, injured seamen had been provided with pensions instead of being cared for at the Greenwich Hospital and at the start of the First World War the Admiralty, which had taken over the functions of the Greenwich Hospital, was responsible for administering naval pensions.

1.3 In 1915, a Select Committee under the chairmanship of Lloyd George resulted in a Royal Warrant providing for a weekly pension of £1.25 for injured servicemen who were totally disabled, and for a pension of £1.25 less a claimant's

---

1 *Halsbury's Laws*, Vol 49(1) (4th edn Reissue, LexisNexis), para 665, n 1.

2 Policy Paper, *2010 to 2015 government policy: armed forces covenant* (Ministry of Defence, 2013).

earnings for partial disablement. Children's allowances of 12.5 pence were introduced for total disablement, together with parents' and widows' pensions based on age ranging from 50 pence to 75 pence per week. A Royal Warrant in 1916 provided for compensation for injury aggravated by service, and a further Royal Warrant in 1917 changed the basis of compensation from loss of earnings to the degree of disablement which a claimant had suffered.

1.4 Pensions for widows and orphans were paid by the Royal Patriotic Fund, which was established in 1854 and put on a statutory footing by the Patriotic Fund Reorganisation Act 1903. The Naval and Military War Pensions Act 1915 established the Statutory Committee of the Royal Patriotic Fund Corporation, which could provide supplementary assistance for pensioners and medical treatment in hospital and vocational training and employment for disabled ex-servicemen and their widows, children and other dependants. The Statutory Committee operated through 1,220 local committees, which were replaced by a much smaller number of War Pensions Committees under the War Pensions Act 1921.[3] The Statutory Committee was dissolved by the Naval and Military and War Pensions Act 1917 and replaced by a Special Grants Committee.

1.5 By 1916, the number of war casualties made it necessary to combine the functions of all the various bodies responsible for administering war pensions, and the Ministry of Pensions was formed for that purpose in February 1917. The functions of the Board of Commissioners of the Royal Hospital Chelsea and the Admiralty with regard to disability pensions and grants were transferred to the Ministry of Pensions, which later assumed responsibility for pensions for members of the Royal Naval Air Service and the Royal Flying Corps, and subsequently for the Royal Air Force when it was formed on 1 April 1918. However, responsibility for claims in respect of service after 1921 was transferred back to the authorities previously responsible for them by the War Pensions Act 1920 so as to again make the services responsible for dealing with war pensions claims in peacetime. In 1939,[4] responsibility for administering claims made in respect of service after 2 September 1939 was given back to the Ministry of Pensions.

1.6 Instruments under the Royal Prerogative made at the start of the Second World War provided for disability awards to be made for injury which was directly attributable to, or aggravated by, war service, but there had to be either 'definite evidence' of the wound, injury or disease in contemporary official records, or other definite evidence that left no doubt in the mind of the certifying medical authority that disability was due to war service. The conditions of entitlement were altered slightly in 1940 and 1943, but in response to

[3] See para **23.6**.

[4] By SR & O 1939/1194.

parliamentary and public pressure a White Paper in July 1943 recommended radical changes to the way in which entitlement to benefit was determined. Prerogative Instruments covering each of the armed services were made in December 1943 and January 1944, effective from 14 July 1943, so as to give claimants the benefits of the favourable burden and standard of proof currently provided for by article 4 of the Naval, Military and Air Forces Etc. (Disablement and Death) Service Pensions Order 2006[5] (SPO 2006) (see Chapter 4). Amendments to the legislation in 1947 introduced a more stringent standard of proof for claims made more than 7 years after the termination of service, unless there had been a previous award. In 1949,[6] the requirement for injury or death to have been due to war service was removed, so as to make it sufficient for injury or death to have been caused by service alone. After the Second World War, additional supplementary war pension benefits were created to meet specific needs, and policies providing for payment of a number of discretionary benefits were codified in the legislation.

1.7 Entitlement to war pensions benefits is conferred by instruments made under the Royal Prerogative, reflecting the historical constitutional relationship between the Crown and the armed forces. Prior to 1977, this required the making of separate prerogative instruments for each of the armed services. For the Royal Navy and the Royal Marines, the prerogative instrument was an Order in Council made under section 3 of the Naval and Marine Pay and Pensions Act 1865. For the Army, it was a Royal Warrant made under section 2 of the Pensions and Yeomanry Pay Act 1884. Provision was made for the Royal Air Force by Orders in Council authorised by section 2 of the Air Force (Constitution) Act 1917. However, section 12 of the Social Security (Miscellaneous Provisions) Act 1977 was enacted to allow provision for war pensions to be made by means of Orders in Council covering all three services, issued as statutory instruments and laid before Parliament. The provision of pensions for members of the reserve forces is currently authorised by section 8 of the Reserve Forces Act 1996.

1.8 However, a consequence of the legislation being enacted as Orders in Council is that under section 21(f) of the Human Rights Act 1998, it is classed as 'primary legislation' (see *Secretary of State for Defence v Hopkins*[7]). Although section 3 requires the legislation to be construed in accordance with the European Convention for the Protection of Human Rights and Fundamental Freedoms (European Convention on Human Rights) in so far as it is possible to do so, there is therefore no power under the Act to quash a Service Pensions Order or to declare that any of its provisions are invalid.

---

5 SI 2006/606.

6 RW 1949, Cm 6499.

7 [2004] EWHC 299 (Admin), [2004] ACD 58.

1.9 The current legislative instrument conferring entitlement to war pensions benefits is the SPO 2006, which came into force on 10 April 2006. The SPO 2006 largely consolidated its predecessor, the Naval, Military and Air Forces Etc. (Disablement and Death) Service Pensions Order 1983[8] and its amendments into a single instrument, but SPO 2006 has now itself been extensively amended. The main differences between SPO 2006 and the previous legislation were that the former provisions which prevented a person in receipt of a retirement pension from being eligible for unemployability allowances were revoked, and the power to make deductions from benefits while a person is in a hospital or similar institution is now limited to constant attendance allowance and severe disablement occupational allowance. Provisions were also added allowing the Secretary of State to suspend and cancel benefits in cases where claimants failed to provide evidence or information or failed to attend a medical examination after being required to do so.

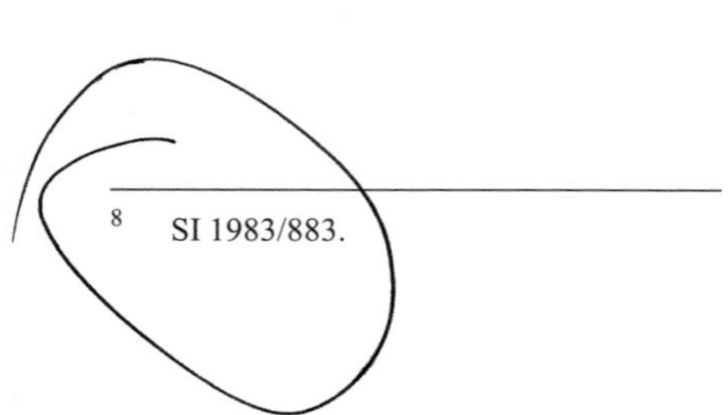

8 SI 1983/883.

Chapter 2

Claiming a War Pension

THE SCOPE OF THE WAR PENSIONS SCHEME

2.1 The War Pensions Scheme covers all regular and reserve[1] ex-service personnel, including the Ulster Defence Regiment[2] (now the Royal Irish Regiment), the Home Guard[3] and nursing and auxiliary services. There are similar schemes covering other personnel including civil defence volunteers, civilians disabled due to enemy action in the Second World War, merchant seamen and members of the naval auxiliary services or coastguard, and members of the Polish Forces under British command or in the Polish Resettlement Forces.

2.2 The scheme applies to disablement or death which is due to service before 6 April 2005.[4] Irrespective of the date when a claimant's service in the armed forces comes to an end, claims in respect of any injury prior to that date must be made under the War Pensions Scheme. Unlike the Armed Forces Compensation Scheme, awards under the War Pensions Scheme cannot be made for any period prior to the termination of service.[5] Claims for disablement or death due to service on or after 6 April 2005 must be made under the Armed Forces Compensation Scheme. Except for a claim for a funeral payment,[6] there is no time limit for making a claim under the War Pensions Scheme, although claims made before the end of the period of 7 years from the termination of service are subject to a burden and standard of proof which is more favourable to the claimant.[7]

---

1 The term 'member of the Reserve or Auxiliary Forces' is defined in SPO 2006, Sch 6, para 38.

2 By Orders made under the Ulster Defence Regiment Act 1969.

3 In relation to injury or death due to service after 27 April 1952, by Orders made under Home Guard Act 1951, s 1(4).

4 SPO 2006, arts 5(1) and 22(1).

5 SPO 2006, art 5(2).

6 See para **10.20**.

7 See Chapter 3.

However, a delay in claiming may result in a loss of benefit due to the limits on backdating awards (see Chapter 7).

MAKING A SERVICE PENSIONS ORDER CLAIM

2.3 Prior to 1997, a claim for war pension did not have to be in any particular form. However, amendments to the Naval, Military and Air Forces Etc. (Disablement and Death) Service Pensions Order 1983[8] (SPO 1983) introduced in that year[9] made it a requirement for claims for war pension benefits to be in a form prescribed by the Secretary of State. Article 34(1) of the SPO 2006 now provides that:

> (1) … it shall be a condition precedent to the making of any pension, allowance, supplement or lump sum payment mentioned in paragraph (2) (including any such award which follows an earlier award or which follows a period, which, had there been an award for that period, would have ended in accordance with article 33(1)[10] that the person making the claim shall have—
>
> (a) completed and signed a form approved by the Secretary of State for the purpose of claiming that pension, allowance or supplement payable under this Order; and
>
> (b) delivered that form either to an appropriate office[11] of the Secretary of State or to an office of an authorised agent.[12]

Under article 34(2A) of the SPO 2006, a claim under article 8(6) for constant attendance allowance for a claimant who is terminally ill[13] can be made on the claimant's behalf without the claimant's knowledge or authority. Claims under article 29[14] for pensions for orphans, or under article 31[15] for unemployability supplement payable in respect of children who are not children of the claimant,

---

8 SI 1983/883.

9 By Naval, Military and Air Forces Etc. (Disablement and Death) Service Pensions Amendment (No. 3) Order 1996 (SI 1996/2882), art 3.

10 I.e. for marriage or cohabitation subsequent to the making of an award (see para **10.17**).

11 The address to which claims should be sent is Veterans UK, Ministry of Defence, Norcross, Thornton Cleveleys, Lancashire FY5 3WP.

12 Defined in SPO 2006, Sch 6, para 22 as including UK consular officials in the territory or place where the claimant is resident at the time the claim is made (the word 'whether' in that paragraph seems to be a misprint for 'where').

13 See para **9.1**.

14 See para **10.14**.

15 See para **9.10**.

must be made by the child's guardian, or other person having parental responsibility for the child within the meaning of the Children Act 1989.[16]

2.4 Claims for war pension[17] should be made on Form AFCSWPS001. This form, together with claim forms for funeral expenses, allowance for lowered standard of occupation, war pensioners' mobility supplement, constant attendance allowance, and unemployability supplement can be downloaded from the Veterans UK website,[18] but there is no provision for making claims electronically. Claim forms for other benefits can be obtained from Veterans UK. There is also a downloadable 'Claim for War Pension (further condition)' form for making a claim in respect of a condition in addition to one which has previously been accepted as attributable to or aggravated by service.[19]

When a claim is not required

2.5 A claim is not required in the following cases (see Chapters 9 and 10 for a description of the benefits referred to):

(i) if a member of the armed services has been medically discharged;[20]

(ii) for a claim for comforts allowance under article 14(1)(a)(ii) of the SPO 2006, or age allowance under article 16, if the claimant is in receipt of war disablement pension (i.e. retired pay or a disablement pension under article 6);[21]

(iii) for a claim for elderly persons allowance under article 26 of the SPO 2006 if the claimant is in receipt of a pension for surviving spouses, or surviving civil partners under article 23, or a pension for dependants who lived as spouses or as civil partners of the deceased under article 24;[22]

(iv) for a claim for exceptionally severe disablement allowance under article 9 of the SPO 2006, severe disablement occupational allowance under article 10, comforts allowance under article 14, or

---

16 SPO 2006, art 34(3).

17 The same form is used for making claims under the Armed Forces Compensation Scheme.

18 The forms can be downloaded from the Veterans UK website at www.gov.uk/government/publications/afcs-and-war-pensions-scheme-claim-form.

19 In *R (Clancy) v Secretary of State for Defence* [2006] EWHC 3333 (Admin), Davies J approved the use of this form in order to avoid uncertainty as to whether a new condition was within the scope of the original claim.

20 See paras **2.11** and **2.12**.

21 SPO 2006, art 35(4).

22 SPO 2006, art 35(5).

a temporary allowance under article 27 if a claim has been made for constant attendance allowance under article 8;[23]

(v) for a claim for invalidity allowance under article 13 of the SPO 2006, comforts allowance under article 14, or a temporary allowance under article 27 if a claim has been made for unemployability allowance under article 12;[24]

(vi) for a claim for an allowance for a child under the child's age limit under article 28 of the SPO 2006, or an award for a child who has attained the child's age limit under article 30 if a claim has been made for a surviving spouse's or surviving civil partner's pension under article 23, or a pension payable to a dependant living as a spouse or a dependant living as a civil partner of the deceased under article 24, and the claim gives sufficient information for the making of the award.[25]

2.6 If a claim for a war pension has been made on the basis of a particular disablement,[26] and a medical examination has been carried out before the claim has been determined, no separate claim is needed for any other disablement found on the medical examination also to have been attributable to or aggravated by service, whether or not the additional disablement is due to the same injury (article 35(6) of the SPO 2006).

WHAT A CLAIM COVERS

2.7 The question of what disablements or injuries are covered by a claim was considered by Judge Rowland in *MF v Secretary of State for Defence (WP)*.[27] Although the case was concerned with how the Secretary of State's powers of review[28] of a previous decision should be exercised, it was necessary to decide at what point in time a claim had been made for injuries to the claimant's right leg, which he alleged were caused by an unnatural gait resulting from an injury to his left leg which had been accepted on a review as being due to service. Judge Rowland held that:

23 SPO 2006, art 35(7).

24 SPO 2006, art 35(8).

25 SPO 2006, art 35(9).

26 See para **3.4** for the meaning of 'disablement'.

27 [2013] UKUT 491 (AAC).

28 Review is considered in Chapter 6.

(i) There are no exceptions to the requirement in article 34(1) of the SPO 2006 that a claim for the benefits to which the article applies must be made in the prescribed form (at [30]).[29]

(ii) It is implicit in article 34(2) of the SPO 2006 that separate claims have to be made for each of the benefits listed in article 34(2)(a) to (p) (although a claim for a gratuity under article 7 is implied). However, there is nothing in article 34 to suggest that a separate claim is required in respect of each injury or each element of consequential disablement (at [41]).

(iii) A claimant cannot be expected to identify a disablement in technical terms, but it is not unreasonable to expect a claimant to be able to identify those parts of the body that do not function properly or that hurt, or to describe impairment in non-technical terms sufficient to alert the Secretary of State to the nature of the medical examination that will need to be carried out (at [54]).

(iv) The practical benefit of article 35(6) of the SPO 2006 is to enable a claimant to draw to the attention of the medical examiner any disablements not identified on the claim form, so as to mitigate the effect of any defects in the form or any difficulty which the claimant has in completing forms (at [55]).

DATE OF CLAIM

2.8 The importance of the 'date of claim' is that it is that date which determines the commencement date of any award (see Chapter 7).

Receipt of claim or enquiry about claiming benefit

2.9 The 'date of claim' is the date on which the claim is received by the Secretary of State (i.e. normally at the Veterans UK offices at Norcross), or by an 'authorised agent' (generally a UK consular official in cases where a claimant is residing abroad) (article 37(1) of the SPO 2006).[30] However, article 37(2) allows a claim to be treated as having been made on an earlier date if an enquiry about claiming benefit has been made before a claim has been submitted. If an enquiry about claiming benefit has been made by the claimant, or by a relative of the

---

29 Judge Rowland contrasted the position in social security cases, where there is power under Social Security (Claims and Payments) Regulations 1987 (SI 1987/1968), reg 4(1) to treat any document as a valid claim.

30 If a claim or enquiry is made by post in the United Kingdom and is delayed by postal disruption caused by industrial action, either within the postal service or elsewhere, the date of claim is treated as the day on which it would have been received in the ordinary course of post (SPO 2006, art 37(6)).

claimant, or by a representative of a charitable organisation,[31] the date of claim is treated as the date when the enquiry was made, provided that a claim in proper form is made no later than 3 months after the date when the enquiry was made.

Date of claim for additional benefits

2.10 If a claimant is awarded war disablement pension[32] and makes a claim for any of the additional benefits listed in article 34(2) of the SPO 2006 within 3 months of the notification of that award being 'given or sent',[33] the date of claim of the additional benefit is treated as being the same as the date of claim for war disablement pension.[34] If the claim for the additional benefit is not made within that time, it is treated as having been made when it is received,[35] subject however to the same rule as for other claims with regard to the date of an enquiry about the benefit being treated as the date of claim.[36]

'DEEMED' CLAIM ON MEDICAL DISCHARGE

2.11 Under article 35 of the SPO 2006, a claim for war disablement pension or for a gratuity is not required if a member of the armed forces is discharged on medical grounds. If a member of the armed services dies while still in service, no claim is required for a surviving spouse's or surviving civil partner's pension under article 23.[37]

Scope of 'deemed' claim

2.12 In *R(AF) 2/07* Judge Jupp held that a 'deemed claim' under these provisions extends only to the conditions covered by the decision made on the claim.[38] If a claimant later wishes to make a claim in respect of any other

---

31 SPO 2006, art 37(7) provides that 'charitable organisation' includes a company limited by guarantee with charitable objects.

32 I.e. disablement pension or retired pay under SPO 2006, art 6.

33 I.e. the date of posting of the notification, not the date of receipt.

34 SPO 2006, art 37(3).

35 SPO 2006, art 37(4).

36 SPO 2006, art 37(5). (The purpose of this provision is not clear as it seems to be already covered by art 37(2).)

37 See para **10.3**.

38 As this case confirms, it was formerly the practice of the authorities not to inform a claimant that a 'deemed claim' had been made, or that such a claim had been refused.

condition, a new claim must be made and any award in respect of that condition can begin only from the date when the new claim is made.[39]

WITHDRAWAL OF CLAIMS

Power to treat claims as withdrawn

2.13 Article 36(1) of the SPO 2006 gives the Secretary of State power to treat a claim as withdrawn if a claimant fails within 3 months to:

(i) comply with a request for information which is reasonably required to determine the claim; or
(ii) give a satisfactory explanation for failure to attend a medical examination of which at least 10 days' notice has been given.

The power extends to cases in which no claim is required under article 35 of the SPO 2006.

Withdrawal by claimant

2.14 A claimant can withdraw a claim at any time before it is determined by giving notice to that effect to the Secretary of State or the authorised agent to whom the claim was delivered, but the withdrawal of the claim does not prejudice a subsequent claim for the same benefit.[40]

---

39 Subject to the provisions for backdating considered in Chapter 7.

40 SPO 2006, art 36(3).

Chapter 3

Entitlement to War Pension – General Principles

DISABLEMENT OR DEATH 'DUE TO SERVICE'

3.1 In order to be entitled to any war pension benefits, a claimant must have suffered disablement or death which is 'due to service'. Articles 40 and 41 of the SPO 2006 prescribe the conditions and burden and standard of proof for establishing entitlement, which depend on whether a claim has been made or death has occurred before (article 40) or after (article 41) the end of the period of 7 years from the termination of service.

3.2 Under both articles 40 and 41 of the SPO 2006, disablement must be accepted as 'due to service' if it is due to an injury which:

(i) is attributable to service; or
(ii) existed before, or arose during, service and has been and remains aggravated thereby.

Death must be accepted as 'due to service' if it was 'due to or hastened by' (article 40) or 'due to or substantially hastened by' (article 41):

(i) an injury which was attributable to service; or
(ii) the aggravation by service of an injury which existed before or arose during service.

Initial burden on the claimant – the Royston principle

3.3 In *Royston v Minister of Pensions*,[1] it was held that under what is now article 40 of the SPO 2006, the burden of establishing the existence of the

---

1 [1948] 1 All ER 778 and (1947) 3 WPAR 773 (there are significant differences between the two reports, see *Secretary of State for Social Security v Bennett*, 17 October 1997 (unreported)).

disablement that is claimed to have been caused by service lies on the claimant. Therefore, under both articles 40 and 41, the burden of establishing the existence of disablement or the fact of death lies on the claimant. However, under article 40 the onus is then on the Secretary of State to show beyond reasonable doubt that the disablement or death was not due to an injury that was either attributable to, or aggravated by, service: there is no legal burden on the claimant to provide reliable evidence supporting the link between the disablement and service. On the other hand, under article 41 the onus is on the claimant to provide reliable evidence supporting that link but, if the claimant does so, he or she is entitled to the benefit of any reasonable doubt. Subject to the *Royston* principle, under article 40 the onus is on the Secretary of State to show beyond reasonable doubt that injury was neither attributable to, nor aggravated by, service. Under article 41, there is an initial burden on the claimant to show that disablement or death was due to service, but article 41(5) provides that the claimant is entitled to the benefit of any reasonable doubt in deciding whether the conditions of entitlement are satisfied. Under both articles, an injury which is attributable to service entitles an applicant to an award for as long as the disability continues, whilst an award for an injury which is aggravated by service lasts only as long as the aggravation remains (see article 41(4)).

'DISABLEMENT' AND 'INJURY'

3.4 'Disablement' is defined in paragraph 27 of Schedule 6 to the SPO 2006 as 'physical or mental injury or damage or loss of physical or mental capacity', and 'injury' is defined in paragraph 32 of Schedule 6 as 'including wound or disease' (subject to exclusions in cases involving the use of alcohol or tobacco).[2] The term 'disablement' therefore covers virtually all forms of physical or mental impairment, including hysterical and neurotic conditions, even if the disablement has not caused any loss of capacity for work or the enjoyment of life, although in such a case a nil assessment of the degree of disablement will be appropriate (see *Harris v Minister of Pensions*[3]). In *R(AF) 1/07*, Mr Commissioner Mesher (as he then was) defined 'disablement' as 'some impairment of the proper functioning of part of the body or mind' and held that 'disablement' should be distinguished from what a person is prevented from or restricted in doing as a result of the disablement (which is taken into account in assessing a person's degree of disablement), as well as from the mere symptoms of a condition. In *CT v Secretary of State for Defence*,[4] Judge Jacobs held that 'disablement' refers to the consequences of a condition or injury, so that in the case of a disfiguring injury

2 See para **8.17**.

3 [1948] 1 KB 422, [1948] 1 All ER 191.

4 [2009] UKUT 167 (AAC).

the relevant disablement consists of the interference with the capacity to enjoy a normally occupied life, rather than to the disfigurement itself.

3.5 Articles 40 and 41 of the SPO 2006 refer to disablement which is 'due to an injury', but the definition of disablement in paragraph 27 of Schedule 6 also includes 'physical or mental injury' as one form of disablement. Even though physical or mental injury can therefore both be a cause of disablement and also form part of the disablement that results from an injury, in *R(AF) 1/07*, Mr Commissioner Mesher (as he then was) held that it is nevertheless necessary to separate the disablement on which a claim is based from the basic 'injurious process' underlying the disablement (often referred to as a claimant's 'condition'). 'Injury' is also to be distinguished from the incident in service that is said to have been the cause of injury. In *CAF/3198/2012*,[5] Judge Levenson summarised the stages which are necessary to establish entitlement as follows:

(i) there must be a disablement – an impairment of proper functioning of mind or body (whether or not it currently involves any loss of capacity to do things), or a loss of capacity to do things;
(ii) the disablement must be due to (caused by) an injury, which is any pathological process that could cause a disablement, but which is distinct from the incident or accident that caused the injury;
(iii) the injury must be attributable to service.

Diagnostic labelling

3.6 Since there is no obligation on a claimant to select a 'diagnostic label' for a claim and claims are often made in non-medical terms, for example, 'bad back', the decision making process generally involves selecting a diagnosis or term that accurately denotes the basic injurious process encompassed by the claim, for example, 'lumbar spondylosis', in order to decide whether death or disablement is due to service.

3.7 In *Secretary of State v Rusling*,[6] the claimant asserted that his disablement was due to 'Gulf War Syndrome'. The Secretary of State accepted the claim on the basis of a diagnostic label of 'Symptoms and signs of Ill-Defined Conditions', but the claimant appealed against the rejection of the diagnostic label of 'Gulf War Syndrome', on which he had based his claim. Section 1 of the Pensions Appeal Tribunals Act 1943 requires the Secretary of State to notify the claimant of the ground for rejecting a claim and gives a right of appeal on the

---

5 Unreported.

6 [2003] EWHC 1359 (QB), [2003] All ER (D) 186 (Jun).

issue of 'whether the claim was rightly rejected on that ground'.[7] Newman J held that there is therefore a right of appeal against the choice of diagnostic label used by the Secretary of State in determining the claim, even though the claim has been accepted on some other basis. However, a different view was taken in *JM v Secretary of State for Defence (AFCS)*[8] (see para **25.5**).

'ATTRIBUTABLE TO SERVICE'

Meaning of 'attributable to service'

3.8 In *JM v Secretary of State for Defence (AFCS)*,[9] a case concerned with liability for bullying under the Armed Forces Compensation Scheme,[10] a three-judge panel of the Upper Tribunal (Charles J, Judge Rowland and Judge Lane) accepted that the underlying purposes of the War Pensions Scheme and of the Armed Forces Compensation Scheme are the same, so that the term 'attributable to service' in the War Pensions Scheme can be read in the same way as 'caused by service' in the Armed Forces Compensation Scheme (although under that Scheme it may also be necessary to decide whether service was the 'predominant cause' of injury[11]). In *EW v Secretary of State for Defence*,[12] Judge Mesher stressed that liability under the Armed Forces Compensation Scheme does not depend on whether injury was intended or foreseen, or on any breach of duty, but solely on whether the terms of the Order are met. In *JM*, the Upper Tribunal expressed the view (at [95]) that while it is therefore permissible to derive assistance from general principles of causation in areas of law such as employment law, social security law or the law of tort, there is no justification for importing into the field of war pensions principles of liability from other areas of law.

3.9 Although the decided cases on attributability often turn on their own facts and are sometimes difficult to reconcile, in *Marshall v Minister of Pensions*,[13] Denning J explained the core principle as follows:

---

7 See para **25.5**.

8 [2015] UKUT 332 (AAC).

9 [2015] UKUT 332 (AAC).

10 See paras **14.4–14.8**.

11 See paras **14.2–14.8**.

12 [2011] UKUT 186, [2012] AACR 3.

13 [1948] 1 KB 106.

> The essential matter, therefore, to justify attributability is that war service[14] should be one of the causes of the disease. As I explained in *Chennel's* case,[15] however, it must be a cause, as distinct from part of the circumstances in or on which the cause operates. Cases often occur when the disease would have arisen in any event, war service or no war service. In such cases it is not attributable to war service. They can best be illustrated by a metaphor. If a rope is weak and on that account breaks when it is carrying a normal load, the cause of the break is not the load but the weakness of the rope. If, however, the rope is weak and breaks when carrying an abnormal load, there are two causes, one the weakness of the rope and the other the abnormally heavy load.

Service cause

3.10 An injury which occurs in the course of service is not necessarily attributable to service, see *Horsfall v Minister of Pensions*,[16] in which Tucker J upheld the decision of a tribunal dismissing an appeal brought by the widow of a Squadron Leader with atherosclerosis and whose duties had included organising fitness activities for service personnel stationed at the airfield, who died of a heart attack shortly after playing a game of squash on Air Ministry premises. In *Wedderspoon v Minister of Pensions*,[17] it was held that the death of a medical officer who took an overdose of a sleeping draught was not attributable to service, and in *Monaghan v Ministry of Pensions*,[18] Denning J held that, in the case of a soldier who died as a result of drinking raw spirits found on a captured barge, service was the circumstance that gave the claimant the opportunity to drink, but that the act which caused his death lay entirely within his personal sphere. *Monaghan* was followed in *Gaffney v Minister of Pensions*,[19] in which Ormerod J upheld the rejection of a claim brought by the widow of a serviceman who died as a consequence of traumatic epilepsy resulting from an assault which occurred while the claimant was returning to barracks after a night out. In *Pillbeam v Minister of Pensions*,[20] Denning J held that complications of surgery are attributable to service if they result from an operation which has become necessary only because a disease has been aggravated by service.

---

14 Denning J was considering a scheme in which injury had to be attributable to war service, rather than to service alone.

15 *Minister of Pensions v Chennel* [1947] KB 250.

16 (1944) 1 WPAR 7.

17 [1947] KB 652.

18 (1947) 1 WPAR 971.

19 (1952) 5 WPAR 97.

20 (1948) 4 WPAR 129.

3.11 On the other hand, an injury which is sustained while a claimant is off duty may still be attributable to service. In *Williams v Minister of Pensions*,[21] injury sustained by a claimant while cleaning a rifle during embarkation leave was held to be due to service, and in *Giles v Minister of Pensions and National Insurance*,[22] Ormerod J held that a claimant who was on leave and who was shot in the back with a blank cartridge fired by a cadet on shooting practice was entitled to a pension because the requirement that the claimant should wear uniform (which may have made him into a target) meant that the accident was not entirely within the claimant's own personal sphere. There must, however, be a sufficiently close causal connection between the injury and some factor of service, and in *Richards v The Minister of Pensions and National Insurance*,[23] the same judge dismissed an appeal brought by a claimant who put his hand through a barrack room window after a fight with another private, on the ground that the claimant had been 'engaged on some personal enterprise of his own', and that the accident 'did not occur in any way by reason of any duty or compulsion of service'.

Injury due to more than one cause

3.12 An important difference between the War Pensions Scheme and the Armed Forces Compensation Scheme is that under the War Pensions Scheme injury can be attributable to service even if service is not the only, or even predominant, cause of the injury. In *Marshall v Minister of Pensions*,[24] the claimant had a weakness of the abdominal wall and consequently suffered a hernia as a result of a cough which was found to have been caused by service conditions. Denning J held that the claimant was entitled to succeed even if the predominant cause of his disease was unrelated to service:

> The task of the Minister and of the tribunal is to ascertain what are the causes of the arising of the disease, not to assess their relative potency. If one of the causes is war service the disease is attributable to war service, even though there may be other causes and, it may be more powerful causes, operating, and to which it is also attributable.

3.13 Applying that principle, it was held in *Hollorn v Minister of Pensions*[25] that acute neurosis could have been caused by service factors, even though there was evidence that the claimant had an unstable personality.

---

21 [1947] 2 All ER 564

22 (1955) 5 WPAR 445.

23 (1956) 5 WPAR 631.

24 [1948] 1 KB 106.

25 [1947] 1 All ER 124.

Self-harm

3.14 The suicide of a former member of the armed forces was held to be unconnected to service and due to supervening causes in *Fuller v Minister of Pensions*[26] and in *Blanchflower v Minister of Pensions*,[27] but in *Freeman v Minister of Pensions and National Insurance*,[28] it was held that each case turns on its own facts and that the deceased's suicide in that case was attributable to service as it resulted from pain and anxiety caused by a disability which was service-related.[29] In *R(AF) 2/08*, the claimant had been the mechanic of an aircraft which had crashed with tragic loss of life while the claimant was serving in the Royal Air Force. He developed post-traumatic stress disorder (PTSD) and a depressive condition which caused him to harm himself, which were accepted as attributable to service. The claimant became agitated by the sound of a low-flying aircraft while he was chopping a vegetable, and injured his finger. Judge Bano allowed the claimant's appeal against the tribunal's decision rejecting the claim in respect of that injury, on the ground that service conditions had 'played a part in producing the general complex of circumstances which led to the injury'.

Bullying

3.15 The principles governing liability for bullying under the SPO 2006 have not been authoritatively decided. Claims in respect of physical or mental injury resulting from bullying are often resisted on the ground that bullying lies within the personal sphere of those concerned, but if factors of service have rendered the victim more vulnerable to bullying or less able to take steps for his or her own protection, it may be relevant to consider whether service was one of the causes of injury.

Medical treatment

3.16 If a surgical operation becomes necessary because of the aggravation by service of a condition and the operation would not have been necessary without the service aggravation, injury resulting from complications of the surgery is attributable to service.[30] Even if the need for an operation is unrelated to service,

26 (1948) 3 WPAR 1617.

27 (1950) 4 WPAR 887.

28 [1966] 1 WLR 456.

29 See also *Duff v Minister of Pensions* (1948) 2 WPAR 753, and *Miers v Minister of Pensions* (1964) 5 WPAR 673.

30 *Pillbeam v Minister of Pensions* (1948) 4 WPAR 129.

injury caused by unskilled surgery in a military hospital may be held to be attributable to service.[31]

INJURY AGGRAVATED BY SERVICE

Difference between injury 'attributable to' and injury 'aggravated by' service

3.17 The question of whether an injury has been aggravated by service arises only if it has been found that injury was not attributable to service (see *Whitehurst v Minister of Pensions*[32]). The differences between an injury which is attributable to service and one which is aggravated by service were described by Denning J in *Marshall v Minister of Pensions*[33] as follows:

> If the disease existed before war service, it cannot be attributable to war service, but may be aggravated by it. If it arose during war service, if war service was one of the causes of it arising, then, it is attributable to war service. But, if war service was not a cause of it arising, it cannot be attributable to war service but may be aggravated by it.
>
> Upon the first question it is often difficult to say when a disease arises, especially in those diseases which are insidious in onset, such as osteoarthritis, or those which exist before symptoms appear, such as infectious diseases, or those which may lie dormant, such as duodenal ulcer. The usual question is whether the disease arose before war service. If the Minister asserts that it did, the burden is on him to prove it, but he may do so by inferences by X-rays or from pre-war symptoms or the like. He must, however, prove that the disease existed before war service as distinct from a susceptibility or predisposition to it. The distinction between the two is this: a disease is an injurious process (including an injurious condition or deformity) which will in its natural progress (unless resisted or cured) operate to cause illness or incapacity even though no other cause may operate; whereas a susceptibility or predisposition contains only the potentiality of an injurious process and may never become injurious unless some other cause operates. Take an analogy: iron is susceptible to rust, but the 'disease' of rust only arises when, on exposure to damp, oxidisation sets in. So, also, certain persons may be predisposed to duodenal ulcer but the disease starts only when on exposure to stress or strain inflammation sets in which is the injurious process leading to ulceration.
>
> If the injurious process exists before war service, the only question is one of aggravation, and that depends on whether the injurious process is accelerated or intensified by war service. If the injurious process arises during war service, the

31 *Buxton v Minister of Pensions* (1948) 1 WPAR 1121.

32 (1947) 1 WPAR 795.

33 [1948] 1 KB 106.

question of attributability depends on whether war service was one of the causes of it arising.[34]

Injury aggravated by service – duration of award

3.18 Under Articles 40(1)(a) and 41(1)(a)(ii) of the SPO 2006, an award can be made for an injury which has been aggravated by service only if it 'remains aggravated thereby', but in *Sanders v Minister of Pensions*,[35] it was held that decision-makers should be slow to conclude that an injury was no longer aggravated by service unless the evidence was clear. In *Shipp v Minister of Pensions*,[36] Denning J held that that provision did not mean that the claimant's condition had to remain aggravated by service at the date when the claim was made or at the date of the decision accepting or rejecting the claim, but as meaning, 'and remains aggravated or remained aggravated during the period of disablement'. Article 41(4) reverses the effect of *Shipp* for claims made more than 7 years after the termination of service, so that in such cases the claimant's condition must remain aggravated at the date when the claim is made, subject however to a possible right in some cases to backdate the claim to a date when the injury was still aggravated by service (see Chapter 7). The provision is expressed to be without prejudice to article 2(5), which makes any condition of entitlement to an award a continuing condition.

DEATH DUE TO OR HASTENED BY SERVICE

3.19 Under both articles 40 and 41 of the SPO 2006, death is due to service if it was due to an injury which was attributable to or aggravated by service. Under article 40, death is due to service if it was hastened by an injury which was attributable to or aggravated by service, but under article 41(1)(b) death must have been 'substantially' hastened by an injury which was attributable to or aggravated by service in order to be due to service. In *Cook v Minister of Pensions*,[37] it was held that death was hastened by service if life was perceptibly shortened, and in *Hall v Minister of Pensions*,[38] it was held that death had been hastened by an injury which was due to service in a case in which there had been delay in diagnosis and treatment which might have prolonged life if it had taken place

---

34 Cases in which this principle was applied include *Baird v Minister of Pensions* (1946) 1 WPAR 169 ('psychoneurosis' in claimant with previous 'defects of temperament'), *O'Neill v Minister of Pensions* (1947) 1 WPAR 839 (weak stomach leading to peptic ulcer), and *Dore v Minister of Pensions* (1947) 1 WPAR 405 (otosclerosis following bomb blast 6 months earlier).

35 (1948) 1 WPAR 31.

36 [1946] KB 386.

37 (1949) 4 WPAR 625.

38 (1948) 3 WPAR 1321.

earlier. In *CAF/1653/2015*,[39] Judge Mitchell held that the question of whether death was 'substantially hastened' by a service injury is not the same as whether the injury was an underlying cause of death. In a case in which impaired mobility due to service was claimed to have substantially hastened the claimant's death, Judge Mitchell held:

> Once the Tribunal had found that [the claimant's] immobility contributed to his death, it needed to go on to address whether the contribution made by immobility amounted to a substantial hastening of death. This called for findings about the way in which [the claimant's] fatal illness progressed and the role played by his service-related disablement (impaired mobility) in that progression. These findings would have given the Tribunal the factual foundation it needed properly to answer the question whether [the claimant's] service injury, and the immobility it generated, substantially hastened his death.

NO NOTE IN OFFICIAL RECORDS

3.20 Articles 40(6) and 41(6) of the SPO 2006 both provide that 'where there is no note in contemporary official records of a material fact on which the claim is based, other reliable[40] corroborative evidence of that fact may be accepted'. Claimants frequently assert that there is no official record of facts giving rise to a claim, for example, emergency medical treatment administered in combat conditions. This provision enables adjudicating authorities to accept other evidence of such facts, although they are of course not bound to do so.

OVERLAPPING AWARD UNDER THE ARMED FORCES COMPENSATION SCHEME

3.21 Under articles 40(2) and 41(2) of the SPO 2006, injury or death in respect of which a claimant is entitled to benefit under the Armed Forces Compensation Scheme cannot be treated as due to service under the Service Pensions Order.[41]

---

39 Unreported.

40 For the meaning of 'reliable', see para **5.2**.

41 Although SPO 2006 refers only to benefits under the Armed Forces and Reserve Forces (Compensation Scheme) Order 2005 (SI 2005/439) (AFCS 2005), presumably benefits under the Armed Forces and Reserve Forces (Compensation Scheme) Order 2011 (SI 2011/517) (AFCS 2011) are intended to be within the scope of the exclusion. Article 41(1)(a) limits relevant service to service before 6 April 2005, but the same limitation is not applied to art 40 or art 41(1)(b). However, only service before 6 April 2005 applies for the purposes of arts 6, 7 and 22, so that the inconsistent qualifications in arts 40 and 41 may not matter.

Chapter 4

Claims for Disablement or Death within 7 Years of Termination of Service – Article 40 of the SPO 2006

ARTICLE 40 BURDEN AND STANDARD OF PROOF

4.1 The Royal Warrant of 4 December 1943 removed the previous requirement for a claimant to show by 'good and sufficient evidence that his disability was in fact attributable to war service'. Article 4(2) of the 1943 Warrant stipulated that 'in no case shall there be an onus on any claimant to prove the fulfilment of the prescribed conditions', and that 'the benefit of any reasonable doubt shall be given to the claimant'. Those provisions are now contained in article 40(3) of the SPO 2006, which applies to all claims in respect of disablement made no later than 7 years after the termination of service and to claims in respect of deaths within that period, whenever the claim in respect of the death is made.[1] It also applies to 'deemed' claims under article 35.[2]

4.2 In *Starr v Minister of Pensions*,[3] Denning J summarised the effect of article 4(2) of the 1943 Warrant[4] as follows:

> There is, therefore, now no burden on any claimant to produce evidence. He must of course make his claim … The claimant may adduce any evidence he wishes, and the Minister may submit any medical question to a medical officer … He may be able to come to a determinate conclusion without reasonable doubt, but, if the evidence leaves him in reasonable doubt, then the claimant must be given the benefit of the doubt. This means that he must not decide against the claimant on a mere balance of probabilities. There must be a real preponderance of probability

---

1 SPO 2006, art 40(1).

2 See para **2.11**.

3 [1946] 1 KB 345, (1945) 1 WPAR 109.

4 Now SPO 2006, art 40(3).

against him such as to exclude reasonable doubt. That is a rule as to the weight of evidence, which applies to all cases.

Despite some authorities[5] indicating that the standard of proof needed to disprove a claim was proof on the balance of probabilities (i.e. the normal civil standard of proof), in *Judd v Minister of Pensions*,[6] Edmund Davies J held that in a claim under what is now article 40 of the SPO 2006 the Secretary of State must show beyond reasonable doubt that injury was neither attributable to, nor aggravated by, service (i.e. proof to the criminal standard). In the Northern Ireland case of *Minister of Pensions v Greer*,[7] Black LJ held that that principle applies in all article 40 cases, and not only when the evidence on both sides is of equal, or nearly equal, weight.[8]

Injury not noted on entry medical

4.3 Article 40(4) of the SPO 2006 provides:

> (4) Subject to the following provisions of this article, where an injury which has led to a member's discharge or death during service was not noted in a medical report made on that member on the commencement of his service, a certificate under paragraph (1) [i.e. that injury is attributable to or aggravated by service] shall be given unless the evidence shows that the conditions set out in that paragraph are not fulfilled.

In *Starr v Minister of Pensions*,[9] Denning J held that the effect of the similar provision in the 1943 Warrant was that in cases where an injury which led to a claimant's discharge or death was not noted in an entry medical, there was an additional element in the claimant's favour. He considered that, in addition to the onus on the Secretary of State to disprove a claim beyond reasonable doubt in cases where a claimant had adduced evidence in support of a claim, there was also a 'compelling presumption' which entitled a claimant who adduced no evidence to succeed in a claim unless there was evidence that established beyond reasonable doubt that injury was not attributable to, nor aggravated by, service. However, in *Judd v Minister of Pensions*,[10] Edmund Davies J held that the absence

---

5 E.g. *Irving v Minister of Pensions* (1944) 2 WPAR 401, and *Miller v Minister of Pensions* [1947] 2 All ER 372.

6 [1966] 2 QB 580.

7 [1958] NI 156.

8 The approach in *Greer* and *Judd* was approved and applied in *Minister of Social Security v Connolly* (1967) *Scots Law Times* 121.

9 [1946] 1 KB 345, (1945) 1 WPAR 109.

10 [1966] 2 QB 580.

of any onus on a claimant to prove the fulfilment of any conditions of entitlement and the claimant's entitlement to the benefit of any reasonable doubt under what is now article 40(3) of the SPO 2006 applies to *all* claims under the article, whether or not the injury leading to disablement or death was noted on an entry medical. As Edmund Davies J observed in *Judd*, the extent of the additional benefit conferred by article 40(4) is therefore perhaps unclear, but it seems that at the very least it must be read as giving the claimant the benefit of any reasonable doubt in relation to any question thrown up by the absence of a record of a relevant injury or disease in a claimant's entry medical.

Article 40 onus of proof

4.4 Although article 40(3) of the SPO 2006 provides that '… in no case shall there be an onus on any claimant under this article to prove the fulfilment of the conditions set out in paragraph (1) …', as Newman J acknowledged in *Secretary of State v Rusling*,[11] this is however subject to the *Royston* principle,[12] under which it is for the claimant to establish the existence of some disablement. In *Rusling*, Newman J added a further requirement that it is for a claimant to establish military service, and on that basis summarised the extent of the onus of proof on a claimant in an article 40 claim as follows (at [22]):

> Although specific provisions exist in connection with the onus of proof which falls upon a claimant they do not relieve a claimant of the duty to establish certain ingredients of his claim. A claimant must establish:
>
> i) military service:- and
> ii) disablement.
>
> These matters, if established on a balance of probabilities, shift the onus of proof in connection with attribution or causation to the Secretary of State. Since disablement is defined as 'physical or mental injury or damage, or loss of physical or mental capacity' and 'injury includes wound or disease', a claimant must establish an 'injury'. Section 1(1) of the 1943 Act refers to this as the 'injury upon which the claim is based'. Put another way it is for the claimant to establish the injurious process upon which he bases his claim. Once he has done so the issue of attribution or causation will fall to be decided in connection with the injurious process upon which he founds his claim.

In *R(AF) 1/07*, Mr Commissioner Mesher (as he then was) held that the requirement for a claimant to establish the 'injurious process upon which he bases his claim' meant that the claimant has to show a causal relationship between

11 [2003] EWHC 1359 (QB), [2003] All ER (D) 186 (Jun).

12 See para **3.3**.

injury and disablement, but the guidance in the *Medical Advisers Manual*[13] which was approved in *Rusling* uses the term 'injurious process' to denote the pathology of a condition, rather than its aetiology. On that interpretation of the term, article 40 of the SPO 2006 would appear to place on the Secretary of State the onus of disproving any causal link between service and any accepted pathological condition.

Diseases of unknown aetiology

4.5 It was formerly the practice of the authorities to keep lists of diseases of unknown aetiology which could not be held to be due to service, but this approach was criticised in Parliament, and in *Coe v Minister of Pensions and National Insurance*[14] Edmund Davies J gave the following guidance to assist decision-makers in such cases:

> *Rule 1.* If the medical evidence is simply to the effect that nothing is known about the cause of the disease, the presumption of entitlement in the applicant's favour created by Articles [40(3) and/or 40(4) of the SPO 2006] is not rebutted, and an application for a pension on the ground of attributability must succeed. See *Brown v Minister of Pensions*;[15] *Miller v Minister of Pensions*;[16] and *Scott v Minister of Pensions*.[17]
> *Rule 2.* But if there is evidence before the Tribunal that, although its aetiology is unknown, the disease is one which arises and progresses independently of service factors and the Tribunal is convinced thereby and accordingly refuses a pension, this Court will not interfere. See *Donovan v Minister of Pensions*[18] and *Docherty and others v Minister of Pensions*.[19]
> *Rule 3.* On the other hand, it will not suffice to rebut the presumption in the applicant's favour to adduce evidence merely to the effect that '… in the light of modern knowledge, it cannot be accepted that service factors are associated in any way with the onset of the disease or that any circumstances of service hastened its course.' For evidence of that nature does not establish that service factors played no part, but merely declines to accept the positive assertion that service factors played a part in causing the disease. In such circumstances there would have to be an award on the basis of attributability. See *King v Minister of Pensions*,[20] a case of leukaemia.

13 Unpublished internal document included with the case papers.
14 [1967] 1 QB 238.
15 (1946) 2 WPAR 461.
16 (1947) 1 WPAR 615.
17 (1947) 2 WPAR 589.
18 (1946) 1 WPAR 609.
19 (1948) 2 WPAR 655.
20 (1947) 1 WPAR 809.

Claims by members of the Reserve or Auxiliary Forces

4.6 Article 40(5) of the SPO 2006 creates a special rule of entitlement for members of the Reserve and Auxiliary Forces.[21] In such cases, article 40(3) and (4) does not apply to disablement which is due to, or death which is due to or hastened by, a disease unless the disease has been caused or aggravated by accident.[22] A claimant who seeks to establish entitlement without the benefit of article 40(3) and (4) is entitled to the benefit of reasonable doubt established by 'reliable evidence'.[23]

21 Defined in SPO 2006, Sch 6, para 38.

22 In *Fenton v Thorley* [1903] AC 443 'accident' was defined for the purposes of the industrial injuries legislation as '… an unlooked for mishap or an untoward event which is neither expected or designed'.

23 See para **5.2** for the meaning of this term.

Chapter 5

Claims for Disablement or Death more than 7 Years after Termination of Service – Article 41 of the SPO 2006

ARTICLE 41 BURDEN AND STANDARD OF PROOF

5.1 Article 41(5) of the SPO 2006, which applies to claims in respect of disablement or death occurring more than 7 years after the termination of service, provides that, 'where, upon reliable evidence, a reasonable doubt exists whether the conditions [of entitlement] are fulfilled, the benefit of that reasonable doubt shall be given to the claimant'. However, there is no provision in article 41 equivalent to article 40(3), which provides that, 'in no case shall there be any onus on any claimant to prove the fulfilment of the conditions [of entitlement]'. In *Dickinson v Minister of Pensions*,[1] Ormerod J held that that difference means that under article 41 there is an onus on a claimant to show that injury or death was due to service:

> … I am satisfied that the intention of the paragraph [article 41(5) of the SPO 2006] is that it is the duty of the claimant to produce reliable evidence to establish his claim, but if (after hearing and considering that reliable evidence, and making a comparison between such evidence and other evidence which is called on behalf of the Ministry to contradict, or to controvert it) the tribunal has a reasonable doubt, then in those circumstances the plain meaning of that paragraph of the article is that the benefit of that doubt shall be given to the claimant.

Dickinson was applied in *R v Department of Social Security ex parte Edwards*[2] in deciding at what point in time a claimant was entitled to rely on emerging medical

---

1 [1953] QB 228.

2 10 July 1992, unreported.

opinion with regard to a possible causal link between schizophrenia and ordinary life events.[3]

'Reliable evidence'

5.2 In *R v Department of Social Security ex parte Edwards*,[4] McCowan J expressed the view that 'reliable' cannot have been intended to mean 'convincing'. He held that:

> At most ['reliable'] can be construed as 'not fanciful'. But in fact I doubt whether the word adds anything to the sentence. The real question is: does the evidence raise a reasonable doubt in the mind of the Secretary of State? If he finds the evidence unreliable, it obviously will not raise a reasonable doubt in his mind.

The same approach was taken in *Busmer v Secretary of State for Defence*[5] (a Christmas Island ionising radiation case), in which Newman J held:

> Like McCowan J. in *ex parte Edwards*, I have some doubt whether the word 'reliable' sheds much light on the correct approach. The real question is whether on all the evidence which has been presented, on both sides, a reasonable doubt arises as to whether all the conditions have been fulfilled. Because the burden of proof is on the claimant, unless a reasonable doubt has been raised, the claim will fail. If a reasonable doubt has been raised, the claim will succeed.

However, in *Roche v Secretary of State for Defence*,[6] Davis J, while agreeing with McCowan J in *Edwards* on the meaning of 'reliable', held that the word was not to be regarded as mere surplusage, but was designed to emphasise that the evidence adduced should not be fanciful or worthless.

Difference in medical opinion

5.3 The fact that there is a difference in medical opinion does not necessarily mean that there is a doubt which must be resolved in a claimant's favour. In *Howard v Minister of Pensions and National Insurance*,[7] Ormerod J held that in such cases 'there is only a doubt if the Tribunal, having considered the whole of the evidence, are left in doubt, in which case the burden of proof has not been

---

3 See para **7.11**.

4 10 July 1992, unreported.

5 [2004] EWHC 29 (Admin), [2004] All ER (D) 143 (Jan).

6 [2004] EWHC 2344 (Admin), [2005] ACD 16.

7 (1955) 5 WPAR 515.

discharged'. In *Abdale and others v Secretary of State for Defence (WP)*,[8] Charles J rejected a fairness challenge in a case in which an expert was not called to give evidence, on the ground that the tribunal could place no reliance on the evidence of the expert concerned where it differed from or was not supported by the evidence of other expert witnesses.

ARTICLE 41 – THE OVERALL APPROACH

5.4 In *Abdale and others v Secretary of State for Defence (WP)*,[9] the appellants made claims under article 41 of the SPO 2006 in respect of disablement and death alleged to have resulted from exposure to ionising radiation as a consequence of the British atomic tests carried out in the South Pacific and Australia in the 1950s and 1960s. In a decision allowing the appeals, Charles J carried out a comprehensive review of the authorities and gave detailed guidance on the overall approach to be taken in article 41 cases. He held that the tribunal had erred in law by applying an approach to the claimants' cases that was based on findings made applying the normal civil standard of proof (on the balance of probabilities) or a similar standard, for example, by preferring the evidence of one expert to another, as opposed to deciding whether the evidence so rejected raised a possibility that needed to be carried forward in the decision making process. He concluded that the civil standard of proof (proof on the balance of probabilities) is not relevant for the purpose of establishing facts as a 'trigger', on the basis of which a reasonable doubt arises under Article 41(5), and held (at [79]):

> That description of what is reliable evidence [i.e. that it is not fanciful or worthless] links it to the standard set by the Article 41(5) test and in my view adds little to it. Rather it confirms that the test is founded on the establishment of possibilities based on evidence that cannot be rejected as being fanciful or worthless and it therefore provides a direct linkage between the quality and nature of the evidence that can be relied on and the criminal 'reasonable doubt' standard.

In summary, the conclusions of Charles J were as follows:

(i) the article 41(5) test places an onus on the claimant to establish by evidence that is not fanciful or worthless (and so reliable) possibilities that the claimant asserts found the existence of a reasonable doubt;

(ii) the decision-maker must carry forward:

a. such possibilities, and

b. matters about which there is no reasonable doubt,

[8] [2014] UKUT 0477 (AAC), [2015] AACR 20.

[9] [2014] UKUT 0477 (AAC), [2015] AACR 20.

and so the ingredients of the claimant's case into the judgmental or weighing exercise of deciding whether the Article 41(5) test is satisfied;

(iii) that judgmental exercise involves an evaluation of the respective cases of the parties by reference to all of the competing evidence and argument and thus on that basis:

a. the relative strength and weakness of those cases,
b. their ingredients and so the possibilities they advance, and the matters they rely on (including those about which they assert the decision-maker can have no reasonable doubt),

(iv) that judgmental exercise may come into play at the first stage of the process as an evaluation of the evidence and arguments advanced by the Respondent may at that stage be taken into account in determining what is or is not a possibility to be carried forward or what matters the decision-maker has no reasonable doubt about, and

(v) this is not a rigid approach but importantly it is based on the identification and evaluation of possibilities and effective certainties and it is not based on findings of fact made on the balance of probabilities that are thereafter treated as established facts (or effective certainties) or an approach based on which expert evidence is preferred.

Chapter 6

Review of War Pensions Decisions and Awards

REVIEW IN THE WAR PENSIONS SCHEME

6.1 The term 'review' is used in the War Pensions Scheme to denote the process whereby decisions, assessments and awards can be reconsidered and changed. The War Pensions Scheme allows decisions made by the Secretary of State accepting or rejecting a claim for pension and assessments of a claimant's degree of disablement to be reviewed at any time and on any ground, although a revised decision will only operate prospectively from the date of the review application[1] unless there are grounds for backdating.[2] Decisions and assessments made by tribunals can also be reviewed, but only on the ground of a relevant change of circumstances.[3]

Review of decisions and assessments

6.2 Article 44(1) of the SPO 2006 provides:

> (1) Subject to the provisions of paragraphs (3), (4) and (5) and to the provisions of paragraph (8)—
>
> (a) any decision accepting or rejecting a claim for pension; or
> (b) any assessment of the degree of disablement of a member of the armed forces; or
> (c) any final decision that there is no disablement or that the disablement has come to an end
>
> may be reviewed at any time on any ground.

---

1 SPO 2006, Sch 3, para 1(2)(c).

2 See Chapter 7.

3 See para **6.7**.

Review of awards

Meaning of 'award'

6.3 The term 'award' is not defined as such, but article 2(1) of the SPO 2006 refers to a person having been 'awarded' retired pay, pension, allowance or other continuing benefit. Under article 44(2), awards which do not require a 'decision' within the scope of article 44(1) can be reviewed on one of the grounds specified in article 44(2)(a), (b) or (c). Such awards include those which depend on entitlement to other awards, such as severe disablement occupational allowance,[4] which is paid to claimants who are in receipt of constant attendance allowance and who are also ordinarily employed in a gainful occupation.[5] If a claimant is in receipt of constant attendance allowance but is refused this additional benefit, the refusal will not constitute a 'decision refusing a claim for pension' within article 44(1), because the claim for war pension (and for constant attendance allowance) will already have been accepted. However, the refusal will be amenable to review under article 44(2)(a).

Grounds for reviewing awards

Ignorance of a material fact or mistake of fact or law

6.4 By article 44(2)(a) of the SPO 2006, an award can be reviewed at any time if 'the award was made in consequence of ignorance of, or a mistake as to, a material fact, or of a mistake as to the law.' In *TL v Secretary of State for Defence*,[6] Judge Rowland held (at [16]) that 'ignorance of, or a mistake as to, a material fact' is a ground upon which a decision may be reviewed because it was wrong at the date it was made. In social security law, a decision can only be altered on the similar ground in regulation 6(2)(b)(i) of the Social Security and Child Support (Decisions and Appeals) Regulations 1999[7] if the ignorance or mistake relates to a primary fact, and not merely to an inference or conclusion of fact. In *R(I) 3/75*, it was held that a claimant must:

> assert and prove that the inference might not have been drawn, if the determining authority had not been ignorant of some specific fact of which it could have been aware, or had not been mistaken as to some specific fact which it took into consideration.

---

4 SPO 2006, art 10.

5 See para **9.4**.

6 [2013] UKUT 0522 (AAC).

7 SI 1999/91.

Relevant change of circumstances

6.5 Under article 44(2)(b) of the SPO 2006, an award can be reviewed at any time if 'there has been a relevant change of circumstances since the award was made'. In *TL v Secretary of State for Defence*,[8] Judge Rowland held (at [16]) that a 'relevant change of circumstances is a ground upon which a decision may be reviewed because it has become wrong as a result of a change since the relevant date'. In the social security case of *Saker v Secretary of State for Social Services*,[9] it was held that a fact is 'material' if it 'would have influenced the judgment of the medical board, although not necessarily affecting the result' (*per* Lloyd LJ) or 'would have called for serious consideration by the board and might well have affected its decision' (*per* Nicholls LJ).[10] However, in the later social security case of *Wood v Secretary of State for Work and Pensions*,[11] it was held that a fact is material only if it would result in a different outcome decision. The difference between the two approaches is largely academic, since a decision will only be revised as a result of a review if the fact which gives rise to the review leads to a different outcome. In *TL*, Judge Rowland followed the approach taken in social security cases that a new medical report cannot in itself amount to a relevant change of circumstances, but can constitute evidence from which it can be inferred that a change of circumstances has occurred (or from which it might be inferred that a decision was based on ignorance of, or a mistake as to, the facts as they stood at the date of the material decision).[12] However, a mere difference of opinion as to the proper level of assessment cannot justify a reduction in an assessment.[13]

Revision of underlying decision or assessment

6.6 If an award is based on a decision or assessment which has been revised as a result of a review under article 44(1) of the SPO 2006, article 44(2)(c) allows the award to be reviewed to reflect the revised decision or assessment.

Review of decisions or assessments by tribunals

6.7 Assessments or decisions made by tribunals on an appeal can also be reviewed, but only on the ground of a relevant change of circumstances since the

8 [2013] UKUT 0522 (AAC).

9 *R(I) 2/88*.

10 *R(I) 2/88*, Appendix.

11 *R(DLA) 1/03* [2003] EWCA Civ 53.

12 See also *TB v Secretary of State for Defence (WP)* [2014] UKUT 357 (AAC) at [11].

13 See *TB v Secretary of State for Defence (WP)* [2014] UKUT 357 (AAC) at [17].

assessment or decision was made,[14] 'including any improvement or deterioration in the disablement in respect of which the assessment was made'.[15] In *TL v Secretary of State for Defence*,[16] Judge Rowland held that the words 'since the assessment or decision was made' should be read as meaning 'since the assessment or decision that was appealed to the tribunal was made by the Secretary of State', since otherwise the rule which prevents tribunals from taking into account changes in circumstances between the date of the Secretary of State's decision and the date of the appeal hearing[17] would result in a different approach in a case where a decision was 'upheld' by a tribunal from that in a case where a decision was 'made' or 'given' by the tribunal.

6.8 Since article 44(3) of the SPO 2006 specifically provides in relation to the power to review decisions of tribunals that a relevant change of circumstances includes any improvement or deterioration in a claimant's condition, any such improvement or deterioration calling for a change in the assessment of the degree of disablement clearly justifies a review, even if the condition in respect of which the assessment was made has not changed in any other respect. In *DAT v Secretary of State for Defence (WP)*,[18] Judge Mesher considered that in the absence of powers to correct decisions of tribunals equivalent to those in social security cases, a somewhat wider approach to what constitutes a change of circumstances might have to be taken under article 44(3). The need for the powers of review of tribunal decisions to be interpreted broadly has been reinforced by the revocation of the previous powers of tribunal Presidents to set aside tribunal decisions where new evidence has come to light.

Review powers

6.9 The powers which can be exercised by the Secretary of State on a review are set out in article 44(6) of the SPO 2006:

> (6) Subject to the provisions of paragraphs (4) and (5), on a review under this article, the Secretary of State may maintain or continue, vary or cancel the decision, assessment or award and any revised decision, assessment or award shall be such as may be appropriate having regard to the provisions of this Order.

---

14 SPO 2006, art 44(3).

15 See *R(AF) 1/08*, at [24] in relation to the scope of the 'assessment or decision' made by a tribunal on an appeal.

16 [2013] UKUT 0522 (AAC).

17 Pensions Appeal Tribunals Act 1943, s 5B(b) (see para **29.5**).

18 [2013] UKUT 533 (AAC).

Review – the general approach

6.10 Article 44 of the SPO 2006 was analysed in detail by a three-judge panel of the Upper Tribunal in *Secretary of State for Defence v RC (WP).*[19] The background to that case was the decision of the Administrative Court in *R (Secretary of State for Defence) v Pensions Appeal Tribunal ('Hornsby'),*[20] in which Underhill J held that there was no right of appeal under the predecessor of article 44(3) against a refusal by the Secretary of State to undertake a review on the ground of a change of circumstances. The claimant in *RC* applied for a review of a final assessment of disablement, which was refused on the basis that there were no grounds for review because it was not medically possible for any deterioration in the claimant's condition to have been due to service. The claimant appealed against that decision and, relying on *Hornsby*, the Secretary of State applied to strike out the appeal. The First-tier Tribunal declined to follow *Hornsby* and dismissed the application. The Secretary of State appealed against that decision and, although the Upper Tribunal disagreed with some aspects of the First-tier Tribunal's analysis of Article 44, it upheld its decision. The majority (Judge Rowland and Judge Mesher) held that:

(i) Article 44(2)(b) applies to an 'award', and not to any other form of decision. If an award is based on a decision or assessment within the scope of article 44(1), the proper approach is for the Secretary of State to review the underlying decision or assessment under article 44(1) and then, if that decision or assessment is revised, to review and, if appropriate to revise, the award under article 44(2)(c) (at [40]).

(ii) There is no 'threshold' for an article 44(1) review. It is therefore not necessary for a claimant seeking a review under article 44(1) to do any more than articulate a view that an existing decision or assessment should be changed, and whether there is a good or even arguable ground for changing the decision or assessment is material only to the question of whether it should be maintained or revised (at [50]).

(iii) Although article 44(6) does not apply if no review has been undertaken (at [42]), the Secretary of State is bound to make a decision under article 44(6) (i.e. a decision to maintain, continue, vary or cancel a previous decision, assessment or award) whenever a claimant applies for a review under article 44(1) (at [43]).

(iv) There is a right of appeal against any decision under article 44(6), including a decision to 'maintain' a previous assessment (at [60]).

---

[19] [2012] UKUT 229 (AAC).

[20] [2008] EWHC 2168 (Admin), (2008) 105(30) LSG 17.

(v) For the purposes of appeal rights, there is no practical difference between a decision under article 44(6) to maintain an assessment or award and a decision that there are no grounds for review (at [70]).

(The minority member (Walker J) considered that the existence of a right of appeal depends solely on whether the substance of the decision meets the requirements of section 5(2) of the Pensions Appeal Tribunals Act 1943 and has to be decided on a case-by-case basis.)

INSTIGATING A REVIEW

6.11 A review can be instigated either by the Secretary of State or by a claimant. If a claimant applies for a review seeking an increased assessment of disablement and the assessment is in fact decreased on review, the review is treated as having been instigated by the Secretary of State (see *JM v Secretary of State for Defence (WP)*[21]).

6.12 Although there is an official form for applying for a review, as Judge Rowland pointed out in *MF v Secretary of State for Defence (WP)*[22] and in *JM v Secretary of State for Defence (WP)*,[23] article 34 of the SPO 2006[24] applies only to claims, and not to review applications.[25] A review application therefore does not have to be in any prescribed form, and as the majority of the Upper Tribunal held in *Secretary of State for Defence v RC (WP)*,[26] all that is required of a claimant seeking a review is to articulate a view that an existing decision or assessment should be changed. There would seem to be no reason not to take a similar approach in cases where a claimant is unaware that there has been a decision rejecting a 'deemed' claim following a medical discharge, but nevertheless expresses disagreement with the decision which resulted from the claim.[27]

21 [2014] UKUT 358 (AAC), [2015] AACR 7.

22 [2013] UKUT 491 (AAC).

23 [2014] UKUT 358 (AAC), [2015] AACR 7.

24 See para **2.3**.

25 In *JM*, Judge Rowland also pointed out that art 37 does not apply to review applications, so that the date on which an enquiry is made about making a review application cannot automatically be treated as the date of the application under that provision.

26 [2012] UKUT 229 (AAC), at [50].

27 See *AW v Secretary of State for Defence* [2014] UKUT 343 (AAC), discussed at para **6.16**.

Treating a claim as a review application

6.13 In *R(AF) 1/07*, Mr Commissioner Mesher (as he then was) held that if a claimant has made a claim in the past in respect of one or more disablements and has been awarded a pension or gratuity, a contention that the claimant has a new disablement operates as a new claim, and not as an application for a review of the past award, although there may be grey areas where cases could fall into either category. A case where a new claim was treated as a review application is *R(AF) 1/08*, in which the claimant suffered gunshot wounds while serving in the Army in 1954, but was not discharged on medical grounds. After moving abroad, he made a claim in 1997 for a war pension, and the conditions 'gunshot wound to chest and abdomen' and 'generalised anxiety disorder' were accepted as attributable to service. The claimant's disablement was assessed at 20%, which was later increased on appeal to 40%. In July 2004, the claimant made a claim in respect of PTSD. That condition was accepted as a further condition which was attributable to service and a new award was made with effect from July 2004, but the claimant's overall assessment of disablement was maintained at 40%. The claimant appealed against the commencement date of the new award, on the ground that the delay in making the new claim resulted from the Secretary of State's failure to make available information about war pension to ex-service personnel living abroad.[28] Although the claim for backdating on that ground was dismissed, Judge Bano held that the July 2004 claim should have been treated as an application for a review of the decision on the 1997 claim, since the claimant was alleging a mis-diagnosis or mis-description of his original disablement, rather than any new or additional disablement.

CARRYING OUT A REVIEW

6.14 The way in which the review powers of article 44 of the SPO 2006 should be exercised will depend on whether the review requires the original decision, assessment or award to be redetermined. In *MF v Secretary of State for Defence (WP)*,[29] Judge Rowland held (at [58]) that on a review of a decision on whether disablement was due to war service, the claim is in effect determined again. On the other hand, a review of an assessment under article 44(1)(b) or article 44(3) does not require the original assessment to have been wrong, but only that it has ceased to be correct in the light of any improvement or deterioration in the claimant's condition. As Judge Rowland pointed out in *MF* (at [58]), it is therefore doubtful whether a review of the assessment of disablement in respect of a previously accepted condition will involve the

---

28 See para **7.16**.

29 [2013] UKUT 491 (AAC).

redetermination of a previous claim, at any rate where the ground of review is a change in the degree of disablement since the original claim was determined. In such cases, it will only be necessary to decide the degree of disablement at the time when the review decision is made.

6.15 If the review requires a redetermination of the original claim, the burden and standard of proof to be applied on the review of the original decision (article 40 or article 41 of the SPO 2006) will depend on the date of the original claim, rather than on the date of the review application. Accordingly, any review of a decision accepting or rejecting a claim for pension which was originally made within 7 years of the termination of service (including a decision on a 'deemed claim' following a medical discharge under article 35) will be governed by article 40 of the SPO 2006 or its predecessor in earlier Orders, irrespective of the date of the review application. Since Service Pensions Orders have been amended frequently, it may also be necessary to ascertain the terms of the legislation as it was at the time when the claim leading to the decision under review was made.

6.16 In *AW v Secretary of State for Defence (WP)*,[30] the claimant's service records had been lost, but it was accepted that he had served in the Royal Navy between 7 May 1947 and 28 May 1949 and that, since the claimant had been medically discharged, a 'deemed' claim for war pension must have been made and rejected. In 2011, the claimant made a claim in respect of Ménière's disease, stating in his application that while at sea he had been unable to keep his balance and had vomited blood, and that he had eventually been medically discharged. The claim was rejected in 2012, on the ground that the claimant's condition was consistent with injuries which he had received as a child during the bombing of Coventry, and because the claimant had not given details of any injury during service which could have caused his condition. The claimant appealed against that decision, but the tribunal dismissed the appeal because it considered that there was insufficient information to establish a link between the claimant's disablement and any conditions of service. In allowing the claimant's appeal, Judge Bano found that the invaliding condition in respect of which the claimant had been medically discharged must have been Ménière's disease, since prior to his discharge the claimant had been receiving hospital treatment for that condition. Although the claimant had in fact been unaware that a deemed claim under the predecessor of article 35 of the SPO 2006 had been made and rejected, and his 2011 claim in respect of Ménière's disease had been in the form of a new claim, the judge held that the claim should be treated as an application for a review of the decision made in 1949 arising out of the claimant's medical discharge. Since that decision had been in respect of a claim made within 7 years of the termination of service, Judge Bano held that the predecessor of article 40 in force

30 [2014] UKUT 343 (AAC).

in 1949 should be applied in carrying out the review, so that the burden was on the Secretary of State to show beyond reasonable doubt that Ménière's disease was neither attributable to, nor aggravated by, service.[31]

RESTRICTIONS ON DETRIMENTAL REVISIONS

6.17 Following a review under article 44(1) of the SPO 2006, article 44(4) restricts the circumstances in which a decision or assessment can be revised to the detriment of a claimant to cases where the decision or assessment can be shown to have been based on a mistake (rather than a mere difference in opinion), or where there has been a change in the degree of disablement which is due to service. A decision accepting a claim for pension or an assessment of the degree of disablement can only be revised to a claimant's detriment if:

(i) the decision or assessment was given or made in consequence of ignorance of, or a mistake as to, a material fact, or of a mistake as to the law; or
(ii) in the case of a decision accepting a claim for pension, the decision was given after it had been certified that the claimant was suffering from a specified disablement and it is subsequently certified that at the date of the earlier decision the claimant was not in fact suffering from the certified condition; or
(iii) there has been a change in the degree of disablement due to service since the assessment was made.

Article 2(5) of the SPO 2006 provides that any condition or requirement laid down by the Order for an award, or the continuance of an award, or relating to the rate or amount of an award, shall, except where the context otherwise requires, be construed as a continuing condition or requirement, and that any award, rate or amount shall cease to have effect if and when the condition or requirement ceases to be fulfilled. However, that provision is expressed to be subject to article 44(7), which gives the Secretary of State a discretion to continue any award based on the decision at the rate in payment immediately prior to the date of the revision even if a decision accepting a claim for pension is revised to a claimant's detriment. The link between article 2(5) and article 44(7) suggests that a review and revision decision is required to remove or alter benefits to a claimant's disadvantage, even in cases where the claimant has ceased to satisfy some condition or requirement of entitlement of the award or rate or amount of the benefit in question.

---

31 The same approach was taken in *R(AF) 5/07*.

6.18 Article 44(5) of the SPO 2006 imposes similar restrictions in relation to the revision of awards following a review under article 44(2). An award can be revised to the detriment of a claimant only if:

(i) the award was made in consequence of ignorance of, or a mistake as to, a material fact, or of a mistake as to the law; or
(ii) there has been any relevant change of circumstances since the award was made; or
(iii) the decision or assessment upon which the award was based has been revised under article 44(4).

6.19 Article 44(9) to (12) of the SPO 2006 provides for the review and revision of pre-1914 and First World War decisions, assessments and awards, but there are now unlikely to be any surviving recipients of those benefits who are liable to be affected by the review provisions.

Chapter 7

Commencing Dates of Awards

NORMAL COMMENCEMENT DATE OF AWARDS

Award of pension following claim or review

7.1 By article 46 of the SPO 2006 the commencing date of awards is governed by Schedule 3. Schedule 3 provides for circumstances (described below) in which an award can be backdated, but in all other cases the earliest date on which an award following the termination of service of a member, or a death benefit following the death of a member, can commence is the latest of the following: 

(i) in the case of a claim, the date of claim;[1]
(ii) in the case of an application for a review by the claimant, the date of the review application;[2]
(iii) in the case of a review instigated by the Secretary of State,[3] the date when the review took place;[4]
(iv) the date of termination of service where a claim or review application or a claim for a death benefit has been made prior to that date.[5]

However, if a claim or an application for a review is made within 3 months of the date of termination of service or death, or within 3 months of the date of notification of a decision on a claim or on a review application, the award is backdated so that the commencement date of the award is the date of termination

---

1 SPO 2006, Sch 3, para 1(1) and (2)(b).

2 SPO 2006, Sch 3, para 1(1) and (2)(c).

3 See para **6.11**.

4 SPO 2006, Sch 3, para 1(6).

5 SPO 2006, Sch 3, para 1(1) and (2)(a). This appears to duplicate the effect of SPO 2006, art 5(2).

of service or death, or the date of notification of the earlier decision, as the case may be.[6]

Award of pension without claim

7.2 It follows that, where an initial award is made without a claim, it is effective from the date of termination of service or death. This is made explicit by paragraph 9 of Schedule 3 to the SPO 2006, subject to a qualification which no longer has any practical effect.[7]

BACKDATING – PREVIOUS DISCRETIONARY POWERS

7.3 Prior to 1997, there was a general discretionary power to backdate awards,[8] which the Secretary of State exercised by backdating awards for up to 6 years if a decision to reject a claim was considered to have been reasonable on the basis of the evidence available to the decision-maker at the time when the decision was made.[9] The practice under the previous discretionary powers has now been codified, although the codified provisions in their original form have since been amended.

Official error

7.4 Paragraph 1(7) of Schedule 3 to the SPO 2006[10] provides:

> (7) Where an award is reviewed as a result of a decision ('the original decision') which arose from an official error, the reviewed decision shall take effect from the date of the original decision and for this

---

6 This appears to be the intention of SPO 2006, Sch 3, para 1(3), (4) and (5), but the wording of these provisions is very unclear.

7 I.e. that backdating could be deferred to the date 3 years before the claimant's service records were delivered to the Secretary of State by the Secretary of State for Defence. This provision reflected the position until 2001, in which claims for war pension were administered by the Department of Health and Social Security and a claimant's service records therefore had to be sent by the Ministry of Defence to the social security authorities to enable a war pension claim to be determined. Since war pension claims are now administered by Veterans UK, which forms part of the Ministry of Defence, a claimant's service records are now always in the possession of the Ministry of Defence, so that the provision is now obsolete (see Chapter 23).

8 The legislative history of these provisions is described in detail in *R(AF) 3/08*.

9 That policy was held to be lawful in *R v Secretary of State for Social Security ex parte Foe*, 7 November 1995, unreported.

10 Introduced in its present form by the Naval, Military and Air Forces Etc. (Disablement and Death) Service Pensions Amendment Order 2001 (SI 2001/409).

> purpose 'official error' means an error by the Secretary of State or any officer of his carrying out functions in connection with war pensions, defence or foreign and commonwealth affairs, to which no other person materially contributed, including reliance on erroneous medical advice but excluding any error of law which is only shown to have been an error by virtue of a subsequent decision of a court.[11]

7.5 In *CAF/1759/2007*,[12] Judge Jacobs held that this provision does not create a separate review ground, but deals with the consequences of the review of an award which has already taken place. In *R(AF) 5/07*, Judge Bano held that in order to apply the backdating provisions in Schedule 3 to the SPO 2006 for the purpose of determining the commencement date of a reviewed decision,[13] it is necessary to identify the factual basis of the review. Since paragraph 6(1) of Schedule 3 makes specific provision for cases in which there has been a development in medical opinion since the decision under review was made, the judge held that paragraph 1(7) of Schedule 3 must be applied on the basis of medical opinion at the time when the original decision was made. In accordance with cases concerning similar provisions in earlier social security legislation, Judge Bano held that there was an official error only if the original decision-maker had made a clear and obvious mistake:

> ... the question of whether the refusal of an award ... resulted from an official error must be decided on the basis of medical knowledge as it was at that time. It will not be sufficient to show merely that there was a misdiagnosis of the appellant's condition. Applying the standards to be expected of a reasonably competent medical practitioner in the light of psychiatric knowledge [at the time when the decision was made], it will be necessary to demonstrate some clear and obvious mistake which resulted in the decision refusing entitlement. For that purpose, the relevant issue will be not so much the actual terms of the appellant's diagnosis, but whether the authorities were correct in excluding conditions of service as a factor in the claimant's disablement.

Contribution to error by another person

7.6 There is no official error if another person materially contributed to the error, so that an award resulting from a review of a previous erroneous decision

---

11 It is not clear whether the term 'court' includes the Upper Tribunal. Tribunals, Courts and Enforcement Act 2007, s 3(5) provides that the Upper Tribunal is to be a 'superior court of record', and SPO 2006, Sch 3, para 7 appears to use the term 'decision of the court' to include the decision of a Commissioner (the Social Security Commissioners were the statutory predecessors of the Upper Tribunal).

12 Unreported.

13 As Judge Jacobs pointed out in CAF/1759/2007, unreported, it would have been more consistent with the language of SPO 2006, art 44 if Sch 3, para 1(7) had referred to the 'reviewed decision' as the 'revising' or 'revised' decision.

will not be backdated if, for example, the claimant was partly to blame for the mistake. In the social security case of *CDLA/393/2006*,[14] it was held that a decision-maker's reliance on the information on a claim form without obtaining further evidence amounted to a failure in the proper standards of administration, but was not an official error because of the contribution to the error resulting from the way in which the claimant's mother had completed the claim form. The Social Security Commissioner held that 'in judging what was a material contribution a common sense approach should be taken, rather than a highly refined analysis of causation'.

Duty to consider backdating

7.7 In *R(AF) 3/08*, Judge Rowland held that the move away from the previous discretionary backdating powers to the present right to have awards backdated if the prescribed conditions are met, has the important consequence that the Secretary of State is now under a duty to consider whether an award should be backdated. A failure by the Secretary of State to investigate whether backdating might be appropriate, coupled with a failure to provide claimants with sufficiently detailed information to enable them to realise that they must raise the backdating issue themselves, with appropriate evidence, is therefore an official error justifying the backdating of an award following a review of the original decision.

Exercise of the review power

7.8 If the commencement date of an assessment of disablement is reviewed on the ground of official error, it is not necessary that the commencement date for each disablement is the same. In *MF v Secretary of State for Defence (WP)*,[15] Judge Rowland held:

> It is implicit that where, for instance, a decision is found to have been flawed for official error, paragraph 1(7) of Schedule 3 applies so as to allow the revised award made on the review to be backdated only to the extent that the review is related to the official error. Otherwise a claimant would be given an unwarranted advantage by comparison with other claimants in relation to other parts of the decision.

---

14 Unreported.

15 [2013] UKUT 0491 (AAC).

'Officer of the Secretary of State'

7.9 In *Secretary of State for Defence v PY (AFCS)*,[16] Judge Lloyd-Davies held that for the purposes of paragraph 10 of Schedule 3 to the SPO 2006[17] the phrase 'an officer of the Secretary of State or any officer of his carrying out functions in connection with war pensions, defence or foreign and commonwealth affairs' covers only civil servants in the relevant government departments, and does not extend to members of the armed forces (in that case, a Chief Petty Officer and a Surgeon Captain who were alleged to have given the claimant erroneous advice).[18]

Award following development of medical opinion

7.10 Paragraph 6 of Schedule 3 to the SPO 2006 provides:

> (1) Where, upon a review of a decision rejecting a claim for pension, the Secretary of State makes an award on the basis that medical opinion has developed since the date of the decision which is the subject of the review, no payment shall be made in respect of any period preceding whichever is the later of—
>
> (a) the date on which the Secretary of State considers that medical opinion had developed to the extent that an award in the claimant's case was justified; and
>
> (b) the date three years before the date of the application for a review or, where the review is instigated by the Secretary of State, the date three years before the date of the Secretary of State's review decision.
>
> (2) Where the Secretary of State accepts a claim and he is satisfied that the claimant would have made a claim at an earlier date but for the advice he gave that a claim would be rejected on the basis of medical opinion, the Secretary of State may make a payment in respect of a period commencing on, but not in respect of any period before, whichever is the later of—
>
> (a) the date on which the Secretary of State considers that medical opinion had developed to the extent that an award in the claimant's case was justified;
>
> (b) the date three years before the date of claim.

---

16 [2012] UKUT 116 (AAC).

17 See paras **7.15–7.18**.

18 However, that view was doubted by Judge Levenson in CAF/2517/2010, unreported.

7.11 This backdating power applies only where a claim has been rejected, and not to assessments. It has been used where there has been a change in medical opinion with regard to the possible causes of mental illness. In *R v Department of Social Security ex parte Edwards*,[19] the claimant originally made a claim in 1957, governed by what is now the article 41 of the SPO 2006 burden and standard of proof,[20] in respect of schizophrenia. That claim was rejected on the basis of the medical understanding of the causes of schizophrenia as it was at that time. In July 1987, the claimant made a further claim in respect of the same condition, resulting in an acceptance of schizophrenia as attributable to service and in an award payable from the date of claim. A study in 1968 had suggested that schizophrenia could be caused by ordinary life events, which by 1980 had become the generally accepted view among medical practitioners. In the exercise of the general discretionary backdating powers then conferred by paragraph 1 of Schedule 3, the Secretary of State subsequently backdated the claimant's award to 1 February 1980, on the basis that that was the date on which a generally accepted consensus was reached among medical practitioners that ordinary life events may present sufficient stress to precipitate schizophrenia. However, a Divisional Court (McCowan LJ and Pill J) held that that was the wrong approach, and that, applying the article 41 burden and standard of proof, the Secretary of State ought to have identified the point in time at which medical opinion had developed to the extent of raising a reasonable doubt with regard to a possible link between schizophrenia and ordinary life events. In subsequent cases, the Secretary of State took 1 February 1976 as the date on which medical opinion had developed to that extent, being the first day of the month on which a paper was published providing confirmation of the hypothesis in the 1968 paper.[21] Nowadays, the 3-year time limit under paragraph 6(2)(b) of Schedule 3 often makes it less important to ascertain the date of development of the relevant medical opinion.

CLAIM OR REVIEW APPLICATION DELAYED BY ILLNESS OR DISABILITY

7.12 Paragraph 5 of Schedule 3 to the SPO 2006 provides:

> 5. Where a claimant satisfies the Secretary of State that—
>
> (a) he would have made a claim or an application for a review on a date ('the earlier date') earlier than that ('the actual date') on which he actually did so but for the fact that he was incapable

19 10 July 1992, unreported.

20 See Chapter 5.

21 See *R(AF) 5/07*. (The date '1976' in the first line of para 9 of the decision should read '1968'.)

of doing so or of instructing someone to act on his behalf by reason of illness or disability; and

(b) that illness or disability continued to be the cause of the delay up to the moment the claim or application was made

any reference in this Schedule to the date of claim or date of application for review shall be treated as a reference to the later of—

(i) the earlier date; and
(ii) the date three years before the actual date.

Although this paragraph allows for backdating by up to 3 years where a claimant is prevented from making a claim or applying for a review as a result of illness or disability, the effect of paragraph (b) is that any delay in making a claim or applying for a review for any reason other than illness or disability will disqualify the claimant from benefitting from this provision. In *R(AF) 3/08*, Judge Rowland upheld the decision of a tribunal that a claimant with manic depressive psychosis could reasonably have made a claim for pension during periods when he was well enough to work and also to instruct solicitors in a personal injury claim against a hospital.

7.13 In *CSAF/834/13*,[22] the claimant had been assessed as 20% disabled in respect of the conditions 'ulcerative colitis' and 'sacroiliac strain'. Following a fall at her home on 7 November 2011, the claimant was found to have advanced ankylosing spondylosis and dementia and was admitted to hospital on 25 November 2011. On 12 April 2012 the claimant's son informed the Service Personnel and Veterans Agency (SPVA) that his mother was totally unable to walk and asked for the assessment of disablement to be reviewed. The claimant's son completed a review application on the claimant's behalf, which he returned on 23 April 2012. Following a medical examination, a decision was made on 21 September 2012 (by which time the claimant had died) increasing the claimant's assessment of disablement to 100%, but with effect from the date of the review application. On 7 January 2013, the claimant's son applied for the increased assessment of disablement to be backdated on the basis that the claimant's illness had made it impossible for her to make a timely claim, but backdating was refused on the grounds that the claimant had managed well on her own despite her dementia, and because in January 2012 the claimant had given consent to an assessment which had found that the claimant had the capacity to make decisions about her welfare needs.

7.14 In allowing the claimant's appeal against the tribunal's decision refusing the backdating claim, Judge Bano held that the words 'but for' in paragraph 5(a)

22 Unreported.

of Schedule 3 to the SPO 2006 indicate that illness or disability need not be the sole cause of the delay in making the claim or review application, provided that the delay would not have occurred if the claimant had not been affected by illness or disability. The judge held that the provision is concerned not so much with a claimant's powers of comprehension or mental capacity, but rather with the causal effect of the claimant's illness or disability on his or her ability to carry out the specific tasks needed to make an effective claim or review application, or to instruct someone else to do so on his or her behalf. The judge held that those tasks include gathering the necessary information and formulating it in a coherent and comprehensible form.

DELAY CAUSED BY ACT OR OMISSION OF THE SECRETARY OF STATE

7.15 Paragraph 10 of Schedule 3 to the SPO 2006 provides:

> 10. ... where a claimant satisfies the Secretary of State that—
>
> (a) he would have made a claim or an application for a review on an earlier date than he did but for an act or omission of the Secretary of State or any officer of his carrying out functions in connection with war pensions, defence or foreign and commonwealth affairs, which wrongly caused him to delay the claim or application and that act or omission was the dominant cause of the delay; and
>
> (b) that act or omission continued to be the dominant cause of the delay up to the moment the claim or application was made
>
> any reference in this Schedule to the date of claim or date of application for a review shall be treated as a reference to the earlier date referred to in this paragraph.

As with backdating for illness or disability, the act or omission of the Secretary of State need not be the sole cause of the delay in making a claim or applying for a review, but under this provision the Secretary of State's act or omission must be the 'dominant' cause of the delay up to the moment the claim or review application is made. In *R(AF) 1/08*, Judge Bano dismissed the claim for backdating under this head because prior to making a claim in respect of PTSD in 2004 the claimant had made a claim in respect of gunshot wounds and generalised anxiety disorder in 1997. The judge held that the claimant must have been aware of the provisions of the War Pensions Scheme when he made his first claim in 1997, so that any failure by the Secretary of State to make ex-servicemen living abroad aware of the Scheme could not be the dominant cause of the delay in making the 2004 claim.

Failure to provide information about the War Pensions Scheme

7.16 In *R (Coull) v Secretary of State for Social Security*,[23] the claimant alleged that he had not been given the information about the War Pensions Scheme which is normally given to service personnel on discharge. In considering whether to exercise the previous discretionary powers of backdating, the Secretary of State concluded that the claimant had, in fact, been given documents relating to war pensions on his discharge, although it was accepted that soldiers might not always read the information which they had been given. On that basis, Carnwath J held that there had been no error of law in the decision not to backdate the claimant's award. However, in *Secretary of State for Defence v Reid*,[24] the claimant was discharged in 1947 and emigrated to Canada. He made a claim for a war pension in 1997, claiming that he had had no knowledge of the War Pensions Scheme prior to that date. The tribunal accepted that evidence, stating that it was:

> impressed with the thorough nature of the enquiries which [the claimant] had made to ascertain whether any leaflets had been issued, press releases had been circulated or broadcasts made, or correspondence entered into by the Secretary of State or those acting on his behalf to inform the Royal Canadian Legion and Regimental Association of the scheme under the SPO.

7.17 Newman J dismissed the Secretary of State's appeal against the tribunal's decision upholding the claimant's backdating claim and granted a declaration that the Secretary of State was under a duty to take reasonable steps to make available war pensions information to ex-service personnel abroad. The judge held that the operating framework of the Service Pensions Order 'exists in a continuum commencing with service and continuing until death', and that 'the purpose of the legislation will be facilitated if those entitled to claim know of their right to make a claim'. The judge continued (at [46] and [47]):

> I am satisfied that the relationship and proximity of ex-service personnel to the Crown places them in connection with the SPO in a different situation from that which exists in connection with general social welfare legislation. By their service, armed service personnel acquire a legitimate basis for being provided for in accordance with the legislation and the Secretary of State has a duty to take reasonable steps to inform them of the existence of the scheme under the SPO. The duty is not legally enforceable. There is nothing in the SPO to contradict the existence of a duty. Indeed, [article 34 of the SPO 2006] which makes a claim a condition precedent to entitlement, heightens the need for a duty to exist in order to further the purpose of the legislation to maintain the balance of responsibility resting upon personnel and the Crown.

---

23 [2000] All ER (D) 1723.

24 [2004] EWHC 1271 (Admin), [2004] All ER (D) 444 (May).

> I regard the duty as being reasonably incidental to the Secretary of State's overall responsibility for the due and proper administration of the scheme ... Mere ignorance on the part of a claimant will not suffice. Where reasonable steps have been taken an assertion of ignorance will be subject to scrutiny. Even if ignorance is proved that will not, in itself, demonstrate that the steps taken were insufficient.

On the basis of that duty, the judge held (at [50]):

> Having regard to the recognition, recorded in *Coull*, that 'at the time of discharge soldiers may not elect to read the information', there may be a need to consider whether giving information at discharge is sufficient. That said, the fact that Mr Reid did not receive any information does not of itself establish that reasonable steps to provide him with it were not taken. But Mr Reid's case demonstrates how significant the passage of time can be between discharge and disability. The role played in the United Kingdom by Regimental Associations, combined with the greater potential for claims from within the United Kingdom, the frequency of publicity and the consideration to which the claims will be subjected, creates an environment quite unlike that which prevailed for Mr Reid in Canada from 1954 onwards. These factors are highly material.

7.18 With regard to the position of members of the armed forces as officers of the Secretary of State, see para **7.9**.

OTHER CASES

7.19 Schedule 3 to the SPO 2006 contains further commencing date provisions with regard to the suspension and cancellation of awards, termination of marriage and civil partnerships. These provisions are considered below in conjunction with the topics to which they relate. There are also provisions relating to the review and setting aside of tribunal decisions by tribunal Presidents, but the powers in question have now been revoked. Schedule 3 also deals with the commencing date of awards resulting from the review of decisions made before 16 August 1943, but it is unlikely that there are still any claimants liable to be affected by these provisions.

Chapter 8

The Basic Award and the Assessment of Disablement

THE BASIC AWARD

8.1 The basic award in respect of disablement under the SPO 2006 is an annual amount called 'retired pay' for officers[1] or a weekly amount called a 'pension' for other ranks.[2] Article 5(2) provides that an award in respect of the disablement of a claimant cannot take effect prior to the termination of a claimant's service, or in the case of an officer, while the claimant is on the Active List.[3]

Amount of the basic award

8.2 The amount of a war pension depends on the rank or status and the degree of disablement of the claimant.[4] A claimant whose degree of disablement is less than 20% receives a gratuity, but no pension.[5] Under article 5(1) of the SPO 2006, awards can be made 'provisionally or upon any other basis', but the review provisions in the current Scheme[6] would appear to make provisional awards unnecessary.

8.3 Part 1 of Schedule 1 to the SPO 2006 consists of a table of equivalent rank and status in each of the armed services, arranged into 15 Groups. However, the retirement pay rates for all claimants in Groups 1 to 9 and the pension pay

1 Under SPO 2006, Sch 6, para 53, 'retired pay' also includes severe disablement occupational allowance paid to warrant officer members of the naval forces.

2 These terms also apply to benefits payable under earlier schemes.

3 The actual commencement dates of awards are governed by SPO 2006, Sch 3 (see Chapter 7).

4 SPO 2006, art 6.

5 SPO 2006, art 7.

6 See Chapter 6.

rates for all claimants in Groups 10 to 15 are the same. The amount of any gratuity payable under article 6 is determined by a claimant's degree of disablement, but is the same for all claimants irrespective of rank.

ASSESSING DISABLEMENT

8.4 A claimant's degree of disablement is assessed in percentage terms in accordance with article 42(2) and (5) of the SPO 2006. Article 42(2) provides:

> (2) Subject to the following provisions of this article—
>
> (a) the degree of the disablement due to service of a member of the armed forces shall be assessed by making a comparison between the condition of the member as so disabled and the condition of a normal healthy person of the same age and sex, without taking into account the earning capacity of the member in his disabled condition in his own or any other specific trade or occupation, and without taking into account the effect of any individual factors or extraneous circumstances;
>
> (b) for the purpose of assessing the degree of disablement due to an injury which existed before or arose during service and has been and remains aggravated thereby—
>
> 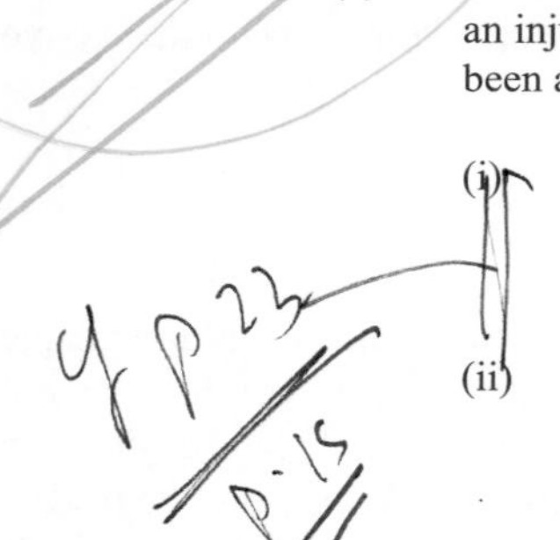
>
> (i) in assessing the degree of disablement existing at the date of the termination of the service of the member, account shall be taken of the total disablement due to that injury and existing at that date, and
>
> (ii) in assessing the degree of disablement existing at any date subsequent to the date of the termination of his service, any increase in the degree of disablement which has occurred since the said date of termination shall only be taken into account in so far as that increase is due to the aggravation by service of that injury;
>
> (c) where such disablement is due to more than one injury, a composite assessment of the degree of disablement shall be made by reference to the combined effect of all such injuries;
>
> (d) the degree of disablement shall be assessed on an interim basis unless the member's condition permits a final assessment of the extent, if any, of that disablement.

Under Article 42(5) of the SPO 2006, disablement of 20% or more must be assessed in 10% bands, up to a maximum of 100%. Disablement of less than 20%

is generally assessed using the percentage bands used to determine the amount of a gratuity, i.e. 1%–5%, 6%–14% and 15%–19%.[7]

Prescribed assessments

8.5 Parts III and V of Schedule 1 to the SPO 2006 set out in tabular form fixed percentage assessments of disablement for particular types of injury and disablement, for example 'loss of 3 fingers', for which the table prescribes an assessment of disablement of 30%. The scheduled assessments were approved by the Hancock Committee in 1947 and the McCorquodale Committee in 1966. Article 42(6) provides that where a disablement is due to a specified injury, or is itself a specified disablement, and the injury or disablement has reached a settled condition, in the absence of any special features, the assessment of disablement must be in accordance with the table. In *NH v Secretary of State for Defenc*e *(WP and AFCS)*,[8] Judge Rowland held that, despite the absence of any provision in the War Pensions Scheme equivalent to regulation 11(8) of the Social Security (General Benefit) Regulations 1982,[9] it is implicit in the Scheme that the prescribed degrees of disablement in Part V of Schedule 1 should be taken into account when making an assessment of disablement under article 42(5). In *DS v Secretary of State for Defence (WP)*,[10] the same judge approved evidence provided by the medical adviser to the Deputy Chief of Defence Staff (Personnel) to the effect that the prescribed degrees of disablement are important in acting as signposts for all other assessments in the Scheme, although the judge held that a failure to refer specifically to the Schedule is not by itself an error of law.

Assessing disablement – general principles

8.6 In *CT v Secretary of State for Defence*,[11] Judge Jacobs gave the following guidance to tribunals on the assessment of disablement:

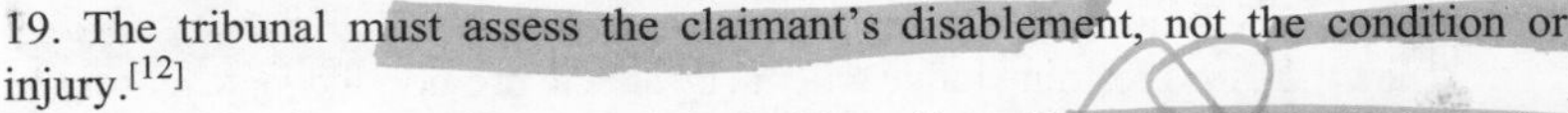

> 19. The tribunal must assess the claimant's disablement, not the condition or injury.[12]

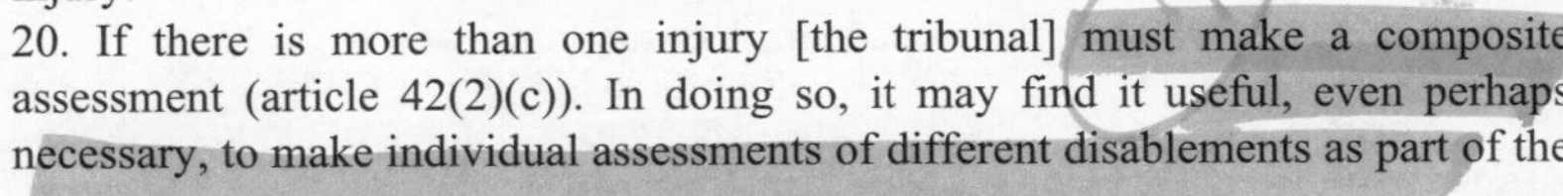

> 20. If there is more than one injury [the tribunal] must make a composite assessment (article 42(2)(c)). In doing so, it may find it useful, even perhaps necessary, to make individual assessments of different disablements as part of the

---

7 See SPO 2006, Sch 1, Pt III, Table 2.

8 [2015] UKUT 35 (AAC).

9 SI 1982/1408.

10 [2016] UKUT 51 (AAC).

11 [2009] UKUT 167 (AAC).

12 The difference between 'disablement' and 'injury' is discussed in para **3.4**.

process of determining the claimant's overall disablement. That will depend in part on the nature of the disablement. For example: if all the claimant's injuries affect his mobility, it would be pointless to identify the contribution of each injury. But if the claimant has a variety of disablements affecting various parts of his physical and mental functioning, it may be helpful to consider them separately before making a composite assessment …

21. Disablement can only be identified by comparison with 'the condition of a normal healthy person of the same age and sex' (article 42(2)(a)). The tribunal must make findings of fact on the claimant's disablement that are sufficient to allow it to apply that test. It must identify the different types of disablement and make findings on their nature, severity and extent. If there is variation, it must make findings on frequency and range of the variation. If there is medication or other treatment, the tribunal must find what effect that has. Treatment may be relevant in three ways. It may alleviate the disablement. It may produce side-effects. And it may itself be a disablement. For example: the need to rely on regular medication may have a mental effect.

22. Having made its findings on disablement and undertaken the comparison, the tribunal has to translate the comparison into a percentage. Article 42(5) provides that 100% represents total disablement. However, that does not mean that 100% is the assessment only for a claimant who is wholly unable to function in any respect whatsoever. The assessments in [Part V of Schedule 1] show that that is not correct. An assessment of 100% is appropriate for someone who may have a considerable degree of function. The result is that the assessment is based on a conventional scale that can only be fixed by reference in general terms to the assessments given in the Schedule. They can give an indication of the level of disablement appropriate for different percentages.

23. It may also be helpful, at least as a check on the assessment that is made, to have regard to particular assessments in Schedule 1 [Part V] …

24. The making of an assessment cannot be done with precision and does not have to be. For assessments over 20%, it is only necessary to assess within 10% bands (article 42(5)). Even choosing between those bands involves deciding in relatively broad terms. And the assessment may involve an element of impression. However, the tribunal must avoid the temptation to decide solely on its impression without appropriate findings of fact and analysis of all relevant aspects of the claimant's disablement. It must approach its task methodically and in a structured way. If it does not, the presiding judge will not be able to provide adequate reasons to explain how and why the tribunal made its decision.

Interacting or overlapping disablements

8.7 In *AM v Secretary of State for Defence (WP)*,[13] Judge Rowland gave guidance on the assessment of disablement in cases where there are interacting or overlapping disablements, also drawing attention to the value of the prescribed assessments in Part V of Schedule 1 to the SPO 2006 as providing an overall check on the accuracy of a composite assessment:

---

13 [2013] UKUT 097 (AAC).

17. It is also important to remember that disabilities may interact or overlap with each other so that a composite assessment may be either greater than, or less than, the sum of the assessments that would be made in respect of the individual conditions were they to be assessed separately, as is recognised in Part V of Schedule 1. Thus, for instance, the loss of two eyes is obviously more than twice as disabling as the loss of one eye. On the other hand, the additional effect of a condition that affects a part of the body that has already been affected by another condition may be less than the effect of the first condition alone would be. Moreover, additional assessments of 20% or more must be certified as a percentage which is a multiple of 10 (article 42(5)) which may involve an element of rounding up and assessments of less than 20% are usually expressed as assessments of 1–5%, 8–14% or 15–19% and this practice is generally applied to the assessments of individual conditions in respect of which a composite assessment is made. Adding together assessments that might more precisely have been expressed at the lower end of the range covered by figures for the individual assessments may well produce a total assessment of less than the total of the figures for the individual assessments.

18. It is not compulsory to make an assessment in respect of disablement that is not due to service, but doing so may again help to explain a decision, because it will show what proportion of a claimant's disablement has been accepted as due to service. Moreover, it is important to remember that, because a 100% assessment does not in fact represent total disablement, the fact that a claimant is suffering from a disabling condition that is not due to service does not necessarily have the effect that the assessment of disablement due to service must be less than 100%.[14]

19. Part V of Schedule 1 also provides useful comparators, enabling medical officers and the First-tier Tribunal to carry out a quick reality check of an assessment by asking themselves whether, taken in the round, the claimant in any particular case is more disabled or less disabled than a person suffering from one of the injuries in respect of which an assessment of the same percentage is prescribed.

Disablement due to injury aggravated by service

8.8 In cases of disablement due to injury which has been aggravated by service (as distinct from injury which is attributable to service), article 42(2)(b) of the SPO 2006 limits the deterioration in a claimant's condition which can be taken into account in the assessment of disablement. Although article 42(2)(b)(i) provides that account must be taken of the total disablement due to the relevant injury at the date of the claimant's discharge, article 42(2)(b)(ii) stipulates that

[14] The evidence approved by Judge Rowland in *DS v Secretary of State for Defence (DP)* [2016] UKUT 51 (AAC) included a statement that 'The clinical picture and disabling effects of 100% disabled pensioners are therefore very variable and at the individual level an assessment of 100% simply implies that as a result of accepted disorder/s the person meets the minimum disablement to attract the maximum award'.

any increase in disablement after that date can be taken into account only in so far as it is due to the aggravation by service of the relevant injury.

8.9 There has been a practice in 'aggravation' cases for medical advisers to issue 'certificates of limitation' where it has been expected that any post-service deterioration would not be due to a condition accepted as aggravated by service, but in *Secretary of State for Defence v RC (WP)*,[15] Judge Rowland and Judge Mesher held that such a certificate is of no legal effect.

HEARING LOSS

Awards for sensorineural hearing loss and related conditions – minimum degree of disablement

8.10 In order to reduce the very large number of claims in respect of hearing loss which were made in the late 1980s and early 1990s, the Service Pensions Order which was then in force was amended in 1992[16] so as to prevent the making of an award in any except the most severe cases of noise-induced sensorineural hearing loss.[17] Under article 5(3) of the SPO 2006, no award can be made in respect of noise-induced sensorineural hearing loss, or such hearing loss accompanied by a related condition or symptom, unless the degree of disablement from that loss alone is assessed as being at least 20%, or unless an award in respect of such disablement resulted from a claim made prior to 7 January 1993. Further restrictions were introduced in 1996, preventing any increase in the assessment of disablement resulting from age-related hearing loss. Note, however, that these restrictions apply only to noise-induced sensorineural hearing loss, and not to hearing loss resulting from other causes, for example blast damage.

Measurement of hearing loss

8.11 Article 42(8) of the SPO 2006 stipulates that noise-induced sensorineural hearing loss is to be measured by means of audiometric tests conducted at or about the termination of service. If no such tests were conducted or the test results are not available, article 42(9) provides for the degree of disablement due to service to be informed by reference to the earliest available post-service evidence, whether or not in the form of audiometric tests, thereby

15 [2012] UKUT 229 (AAC).

16 By the Naval, Military and Air Forces Etc. (Disablement and Death) Service Pensions Amendment (No. 2) Order (SI 1992/3208).

17 The term 'noise-induced sensorineural hearing loss' is defined in SPO 2006, Sch 6, para 39.

allowing decision-makers to 'work backwards' in order to assess the extent of a claimant's hearing loss at the date of termination of service.

Assessment of disablement in respect of noise-induced sensorineural hearing loss

8.12 Under article 42(10) of the SPO 2006, the degree of disablement in respect of noise-induced sensorineural hearing loss due to service is to be assessed by determining the average hearing loss for each ear at 1 kHz, 2 kHz and 3 kHz frequencies (thus excluding the effect of hearing loss at higher frequencies) by reference to the prescribed percentages of disablement for given levels of hearing loss set out in the table in Part VI of Schedule 1. For example, if the average hearing loss at 1 kHz, 2 kHz and 3 kHz in one ear is 73–79 dB, the percentage degree of disablement for that ear is the figure given in the table, i.e. 60%. Article 42(12) provides that any fraction of an average of hearing loss over 50 dB is to be rounded down to the next whole figure.

8.13 Having determined the percentage of disablement for each ear, article 42(10)(c) of the SPO 2006 requires the average percentage binaural hearing disablement to be established as follows:

(i) multiply the degree of disablement in the better ear by 4;
(ii) add the degree of disablement in the worse ear to (i);
(iii) divide the amount arrived at in (ii) by 5.

For example, if the degree of disablement for the left ear in accordance with the table in Part VI of Schedule 1 to the SPO 2006 is 60% and the percentage degree of disablement of the right ear in accordance with that table is 80%, the average percentage binaural hearing disablement is ((60 x 4) + 80)/5%, i.e. (240 + 80)/5 = 320/5, or 64%.

8.14 Under article 42(3) of the SPO 2006, where the average hearing loss at frequencies of 1 kHz, 2 kHz and 3 kHz is not more than 50 dB in each ear, the degree of disablement in respect of hearing loss must be assessed at less than 20%. Article 42(4) provides that neither noise-induced sensorineural hearing loss nor a related condition or symptom (e.g. tinnitus) shall be taken into account in determining a claimant's total degree of disablement if the degree of disablement in respect of that loss alone is less than 20%. The combined effect of these provisions is that unless the average hearing loss in each ear at frequencies of 1 kHz, 2 kHz and 3 kHz exceeds 50 dB, no award can be made in respect of noise-induced sensorineural hearing loss or related conditions or symptoms, either alone or in combination with other forms of disablement.

Hearing loss – age-related and other non-service-related factors

8.15 Further restrictions in respect of hearing loss are imposed by article 42(7) of the SPO 2006, which provides that:

> (7) An assessment of the degree of disablement due to service in respect of noise-induced sensorineural hearing loss shall be based solely on hearing loss due to service and shall not include any hearing loss due to age or other factors which are not related to service as a member of the armed forces and which arise after service.

Deterioration in hearing which is age-related (presbycusis) cannot therefore be taken into account, either to increase an award which has previously been made in respect of hearing loss, or to bring the degree of disablement resulting from hearing loss above the threshold beyond which an award can be made.

8.16 In order to protect some claimants with awards in respect of hearing loss made under the less restrictive provisions previously in force, article 42(11) of the SPO 2006 provides that the method of assessing noise-induced sensorineural hearing loss prescribed by article 42(8), (9) and (10) shall not be applied so as to reduce any award made prior to 12 April 2004.

ALCOHOL AND TOBACCO

8.17 Although the definition of 'injury' in paragraph 32 of Schedule 6 to the SPO 2006 includes 'wound or disease' and alcohol dependency is a 'disease',[18] the definition excludes any injury due to the use or effects of tobacco or the consumption of alcohol unless:

(i) the claimant suffers from a mental condition which is attributable to service;
(ii) the degree of disablement in respect of that condition has been assessed at 50% or more;
(iii) the claimant started or continued to use tobacco or to consume or continue to consume alcohol due to that condition.[19]

In *PR v Secretary of State for Defence*,[20] Judge Wright held that as a matter of statutory construction the issue of whether an alcohol-related condition is

---

18 See *Secretary of State for Social Security v McLean* (Northern Ireland), 17 November 2000, unreported.

19 SPO 2006, Sch 6, para 32.

20 [2013] UKUT 0397 (AAC).

excluded from the definition of injury by this provision should be approached before consideration of any issues of attributability or aggravation. Excessive alcohol which is consumed by a claimant to provide relief from the effects of another condition such as PTSD cannot be treated as 'part and parcel' of that other condition so as to take the effects of alcohol consumption in those circumstances out of the exclusionary provisions in the definition of injury in Schedule 6 to the SPO 2006 (see *CSAF/493/2010*[21]).

INTERIM AND FINAL ASSESSMENTS

8.18 Article 42(2)(d) of the SPO 2006 provides that 'the degree of disablement shall be assessed on an interim basis unless the [claimant's] condition permits a final assessment of the extent, if any, of that disablement'. The practical difference between an interim and a final assessment is that a further assessment of disablement will be made automatically when an interim assessment comes to an end. A final assessment can only be altered following a review, although an interim assessment of disablement can also be reviewed before the end of the assessment period.

8.19 As Judge Rowland explained in *TL v Secretary of State for Defence (WP)*,[22] interim assessments were originally made in the mid-1940s for periods of up to 2 years, which was increased to periods of up to 5 years in the late 1940s or early 1950s. However, a practice developed later of making open-ended interim assessments in cases where a claimant's condition was expected to deteriorate, but not for some considerable time. In such cases, a further medical examination to assess the degree of disablement normally only takes place if there is a review, either as a result of an application by the claimant, or on the Secretary of State's initiative. In *ML v Secretary of State for Defence*,[23] Judge Lloyd-Davies concluded that, in the absence of any provision to the contrary, open-ended interim assessments were lawful. In *TL*, Judge Rowland did not dissent from that view, pointing out that it gave tribunals the flexibility to make open-ended interim awards in cases where the tribunal was satisfied that there is likely to be a significant change in the degree of a claimant's disablement in the foreseeable future.[24] In the light of the review powers currently conferred by article 44 of the SPO 2006,[25] applicable to both interim and final assessments of disablement,

---

21 Unreported.

22 [2013] UKUT 0522 (AAC).

23 [2011] UKUT 511 (AAC).

24 Pensions Appeal Tribunals Act 1943, s 5(2) empowers a tribunal to substitute an interim assessment for a final assessment, but limits the period of such an assessment to 2 years from the date when it is made (see para **25.17**).

25 See Chapter 6.

there would now appear to be no practical difference between an open-ended interim assessment and a final assessment for an unlimited period. As Judge Rowland observed in *TL*, the concept of a final assessment may therefore have outlived its usefulness, particularly since the term 'final assessment' may wrongly suggest to claimants that the assessment cannot be reviewed.

Chapter 9

Other Awards in Respect of Disablement

CONSTANT ATTENDANCE ALLOWANCE AND ASSOCIATED BENEFITS

Constant attendance allowance

Entitlement and rates of allowance

9.1 Prior to 2001, the SPO 1983 provided for entitlement to constant attendance allowance at two rates, but in the exercise of his discretion the Secretary of State paid the benefit at one of four rates, depending on the level of attendance which was required. Following consultation, the position was formalised by amendments to the SPO 1983[1] providing for payment of constant attendance allowance at four rates, thus giving a right of appeal in respect of any decision concerning the allowance. Article 8 of the SPO 2006 now provides that a claimant whose disablement has been assessed at 80% or more and who requires constant attendance on account of the disablement is entitled to constant attendance allowance[2] at one of four rates:[3]

(i) the part day rate where the necessary attendance consists of frequent or regular attendance for periods during the daytime which total not less than 4 and not more than 8 hours per day;

(ii) the full day rate where the necessary attendance consists of:

(a) frequent or regular attendance for periods during the daytime which total not less than 8 and not more than 16 hours per day; or

---

1 By the Naval, Military and Air Forces Etc. (Disablement and Death) Service Pensions Amendment Order 2001 (SI 2001/409).

2 SPO 2006, art 8.

3 The amount of each rate of constant attendance allowance is set out in SPO 2006, Sch 1, Pt IV.

(b) frequent or regular attendance for periods during the daytime which total less than 8 hours per day and attendance on two or more occasions per night;

(iii) the intermediate rate where the necessary attendance consists of:

(a) frequent or regular attendance for periods during the daytime which total not less than 8 hours per day and attendance on two or more occasions per night; or
(b) frequent or regular attendance for periods at night which total not less than 8 hours and during the daytime for periods which total not less than 4 hours per day;

(iv) the exceptional rate where the necessary attendance consists of continual attendance throughout the day and night.

By an amendment to the SPO 2006 introduced in 2009,[4] a claimant with a terminal illness[5] is deemed to satisfy the conditions of entitlement to constant attendance allowance at the intermediate rate for any period of the illness after the date of claim.

Satisfying the attendance requirements

9.2 In *MC v Secretary of State for Defence*,[6] Judge Levenson held that for the purposes of constant attendance allowance, 'attendance' can include supervision which is precautionary or anticipatory, as well as actual attention to a claimant and, following the leading social security case of *Secretary of State v Fairey*,[7] the judge held that attention is 'necessary' if it is reasonably required to enable a severely disabled person to lead as far as reasonably possible a normal life. Neither the word 'constant' nor the word 'continual' means literally non-stop or uninterrupted, and 'constant' is not an independent condition, but a reference to the more detailed provisions in the conditions of entitlement to each of the various rates of constant attendance allowance. The same judge held in *CAF/1268/2011*,[8] that an award of constant attendance allowance cannot be based on problems other than those accepted for the purposes of the war pension

---

4 By Naval, Military and Air Forces Etc. (Disablement and Death) Service Pensions (Amendment) Order 2009 (SI 2009/706), art 3(b).

5 Defined in SPO 2006, Sch 6, para 58A as 'a progressive disease where, in consequence of that disease, death can reasonably be expected within 6 months'.

6 [2009] UKUT 173 (AAC).

7 [1997] 1 WLR 799 at 806.

8 Unreported.

disablement assessment. In *WS v Secretary of State for Defence (WP)*,[9] Judge Knowles held that point (iii) (a) in para **9.1** is only satisfied if a claimant requires attendance on two or more occasions each night, together with frequent or regular attendance for periods during the daytime totalling not less than 8 hours each day, i.e. that attendance which is required on two or more occasions on some nights is not enough.

Exceptionally severe disablement allowance

9.3 Claimants with a permanent disablement who are in receipt of constant attendance allowance at either the intermediate rate or the exceptional rate, or would be if they were not in a hospital or similar institution,[10] are entitled to exceptionally severe disablement allowance,[11] payable at the same rate as the full day rate.

Severe disablement occupational allowance

9.4 Claimants who receive constant attendance allowance at either the intermediate rate or the exceptional rate and who are ordinarily employed in a gainful occupation are entitled to severe disablement occupational allowance[12] except during periods when they are:

- (i) eligible to receive a personal unemployability allowance;[13]
- (ii) in receipt of a 'personal benefit' under Part 2 or Part 3 of the Social Security Contributions and Benefits Act 1992 or the corresponding benefits in Northern Ireland, i.e. retirement pension and certain other category A or B retirement pensions,[14] incapacity benefit, severe disablement allowance, carer's allowance, and employment and support contributory allowance;[15]
- (iii) in receipt of a state pension under Part 1 of the Pensions Act 2014;[16]
- (iv) in receipt of a non-UK benefit similar to a personal benefit.

---

9 [2015] UKUT 0557 (AAC).

10 See para **11.9** regarding the suspension of benefit during periods while a claimant is in hospital or in an institution.

11 SPO 2006, art 9.

12 SPO 2006, art 10.

13 See para **9.7**.

14 I.e. those falling within Social Security (Widow's Benefit, Retirement Pensions and Other Benefits) (Transitional) Regulations 1979 (SI 1979/643), reg 18, or corresponding provisions in Northern Ireland.

15 As defined in SPO 2006, art 10(4).

16 As a result of an amendment by the Naval, Military and Air Forces Etc. (Disablement and Death) Service Pensions (Amendment) Order 2016 (SI 2016/374).

Constant attendance allowance under earlier schemes

9.5 Article 71(4) of the SPO 2006 provides for recipients of constant attendance allowance under previous schemes to be paid at the rates specified by Part IV of Schedule 1.

CLOTHING ALLOWANCE

9.6 Recipients of retired pay or a pension are entitled to clothing allowance[17] if either:

(i) they are in receipt of retired pay or pension in respect of an amputation and regularly wear an artificial limb; or
(ii) as a result of the disablement which gives rise to an award there is exceptional wear and tear of the claimant's clothing.

In *CAF/656/2006*,[18] Judge Bano held that the matters for the tribunal to decide in considering a claim for clothing allowance under article 11(2) of the SPO 2006 were: (i) whether an accepted disablement and any other condition which resulted from that disablement gives rise to wear and tear to the claimant's clothing, and (ii) if so, whether such wear and tear is 'exceptional'.

UNEMPLOYABILITY ALLOWANCES

9.7 Under article 12 of the SPO 2006, claimants who are in receipt of retired pay or a pension in respect of a disablement which is so serious as to make them unemployable are entitled to a personal unemployability allowance.[19] In *CAF/962/2014*,[20] it was held that unemployability has to arise out of the disabling conditions on the basis of which a pension has been awarded. The term 'unemployable' encompasses not just whether the claimant is fit for work or capable of work, but also whether realistically there is any work which the claimant could do. Since the claimant's service-related disablements must be so serious as to make the claimant unemployable in any job, the threshold of entitlement for this allowance is therefore high.

9.8 Since 1997, the allowance has not been payable to claimants aged 65 or over or whose disablement is less than 60%, but article 12(2) and (3) of the SPO

---

17 SPO 2006, art 11.

18 Unreported.

19 The rate payable is prescribed by SPO 2006, Sch 1, Pt IV, para 5(a).

20 Unreported.

2006 gives transitional protection to some former recipients of the allowance who do not satisfy the current conditions of entitlement and whose degree of disablement is 20% or more. Therapeutic earnings[21] which are unlikely to exceed the amount specified in paragraph 5(c) of Part IV to Schedule 1 do not disqualify a claimant from receiving unemployability allowance,[22] and therapeutic earnings received before 9 April 2001 continue to be treated as such until the claimant permanently ceases to do the work in respect of which the therapeutic earnings are paid.[23]

Additional unemployability allowances for dependants

Dependants other than children

9.9 Under article 12(6) of the SPO 2006, there is a discretion to pay an additional unemployability allowance for no more than one adult dependant of a claimant[24] if the dependant's weekly income does not exceed the amount specified in paragraph 5(d) of Part IV of Schedule 1, depending on the dependant's financial circumstances, including any earnings,[25] occupational pension and social security benefits. The additional allowance can be paid for a claimant's spouse, civil partner, adult dependant,[26] or a dependant living with the claimant as a spouse or civil partner.[27]

Child dependants

9.10 An additional unemployability allowance is also payable in respect of any child[28] of the claimant at the rate specified in paragraph 5(b)(ii) of Part IV of Schedule 1 to the SPO 2006, including a child who is not a child of the claimant but who 'in the opinion of the Secretary of State, having regard to the child's relationship to or connection with the member and the other circumstances of the case … should be treated as the [claimant's] child'.[29] This additional allowance is not payable in respect of a child aged 16 or over, unless the child is a student or apprentice, or incapable of self-support by reason of an infirmity which arose

---

21 Defined in SPO 2006, Sch 6, para 60 as 'earnings from work for no more than 16 hours per week and which in the Secretary of State's view is not detrimental to the health of the member'.

22 SPO 2006, art 12(4).

23 SPO 2006, art 12(5).

24 SPO 2006, art 12(7).

25 Defined in SPO 2006, Sch 6, para 28.

26 Defined in SPO 2006, Sch 6, para 19.

27 These terms are defined in SPO 2006, Sch 6, paras 25 and 26.

28 There is an extensive definition of 'child' in SPO 2006, Sch 6, para 23.

29 SPO 2006, art 12(6)(c).

before the child attained the age of 16 and the Secretary of State considers that the circumstances are such as justify the award. Under article 12(9), the Secretary of State has a discretion whether to make or continue an award of unemployability allowance in respect of a child who is living apart from the claimant and to decide the amount of any such award.

Discretion to take into account state pension benefits and equivalent non-UK benefits

9.11 Article 12(10) of the SPO 2006 gives the Secretary of State a discretion to take into account the state pension benefits listed in article 12(10)(a)[30] and equivalent non-UK benefits in order to reduce the amount of a claimant's personal unemployability allowance, or to reduce an additional unemployability allowance payable in respect of a claimant's dependant or child. Note also that entitlement to non-means-tested social security benefits may be affected by an award of either personal unemployability allowance or additional allowances.[31]

Invalidity allowance

9.12 A claimant who has been awarded a personal unemployability allowance and who is aged under 60 at the commencement date of the award is entitled to invalidity allowance at the rate specified in paragraph 6 of Part IV of Schedule 1 to the SPO 2006.[32] If the claimant has received a personal unemployability allowance for two or more periods, the claimant must have been aged under 60 at the commencement date of the last such period, but periods separated by a break of 8 weeks or less, or during which the claimant was engaged in remunerative work[33] and to whom article 12(3)(b) to (f) applies, are treated as a single period. If the personal unemployability allowance is for a period which forms part of a period of 'interruption of employment' for social security purposes[34] in Great Britain or Northern Ireland, or under equivalent provisions in the case of non-UK benefits, in order to qualify for this allowance the claimant must be aged under 60 on the first day of incapacity for work for social security purposes.[35]

---

30 Including a state pension under Pensions Act 2014, Pt 1 as a result of amendments to SPO 2006 made by the Naval, Military and Air Forces Etc. (Disablement and Death) Service Pensions (Amendment) Order 2016 (SI 2016/374).

31 The Social Security (Overlapping Benefits) Regulations 1979 (SI 1979/597).

32 SPO 2006, art 13.

33 Defined in SPO 2006, Sch 6, para 52.

34 The Social Security Act 1975, referred to in SPO 2006, art 13(4), was in fact repealed in 1992 and the concept of a period of interruption of employment disappeared from social security law in 1996. The equivalent concept of a 'period of incapacity for work' has itself been superseded as the result of the replacement of incapacity benefit by employment and support allowance.

35 SPO 2006, art 13(4) and (5).

COMFORTS ALLOWANCE

9.13 Comforts allowance is payable in the most severe cases of disablement at the rate specified in paragraph 7(a) of Part IV of Schedule 1 to the SPO 2006 to claimants who receive both constant attendance allowance and unemployability allowance and to recipients of constant attendance allowance at the intermediate or exceptional rate whose degree of disablement is 100%.[36] Comforts allowance is payable at the lower rate specified by paragraph 7(b) of Schedule IV to all other recipients of constant attendance allowance and unemployability allowance. Article 14(2) provides that claimants who are not receiving constant attendance allowance because they are in a hospital or similar institution are to be treated as if they were in receipt of the allowance.

ALLOWANCE FOR LOWERED STANDARD OF OCCUPATION

Entitlement and rates of allowance

9.14 A claimant in receipt of retired pay or pension whose degree of disablement is less than 100% is entitled to an allowance for lowered standard of occupation at the rates specified in paragraph 8 of Part IV of Schedule 1 to the SPO 2006 if:

> (b) the disablement is such as to render him incapable, and likely to remain permanently incapable, of following his regular occupation and incapable of following any other occupation with equivalent gross income which is suitable in his case taking into account his education, training and experience.[37]

In *R(AF) 4/07*, Judge Mesher held that the comparison which should be made between a claimant's gross pay in his regular occupation and the gross pay in his current occupation should take into account the London weighting allowance which the claimant received in his current occupation because the allowance formed a normal part of the claimant's income.

'Regular occupation'

9.15 For claimants whose disablement was due to service between 2 September 1939 and 1 August 1973, 'regular occupation' means their regular occupation before the commencement of service. For claimants whose disablement was due to injury between those dates who had no regular pre-service

---

36 SPO 2006, art 14.

37 SPO 2006, art 15(1)(b).

occupation and for all other claimants, 'regular occupation' means the claimant's trade or profession in the services on the date that the claimant sustained the wound or injury, or was removed from duty on account of the disease on which the award was based, or if there was no such occurrence, the date of termination of service.[38]

Restrictions on entitlement

9.16 Entitlement to allowance for lowered standard of occupation has been progressively restricted and for claims made on or after 7 April 1997 the allowance is not payable to claimants not already in receipt of the allowance whose disablement has been assessed as less than 40%, or after the age of 65.[39] For claims made on or after 6 April 2009, the allowance is not payable to claimants who are not already in receipt of the allowance if the claimant is in receipt of:

- (i) incapacity benefit in Great Britain or Northern Ireland;
- (ii) employment and support allowance in Great Britain or Northern Ireland;
- (iii) equivalent non-UK benefits;
- (iv) Universal Credit which includes an amount in respect of limited capability for work or for work-related activity, or would include such an amount but for regulation 27(4) or regulation 29(4) of the Universal Credit Regulations 2013.[40]

9.17 Under article 15(4) of the SPO 2006, allowance for lowered standard of occupation cannot be paid if a claimant is in receipt of a personal unemployability allowance or treatment allowance,[41] except that a claimant who is already in receipt of allowance for lowered standard of occupation may continue to receive it if the claimant subsequently becomes eligible for an unemployability allowance.[42] The aggregate of retired pay or pension together with allowance for lowered standard of occupation cannot exceed the rate of retired pay or pension which the claimant would receive if disablement were assessed at 100%.[43]

---

38 SPO 2006, art 15(6).

39 SPO 2006, art 15(2)(a).

40 SI 2013/376. SPO 2006, art 15(2)(b).

41 See para **9.19**.

42 SPO 2006, art 15(5).

43 SPO 2006, art 15(3).

AGE ALLOWANCE

9.18 Under article 16 of the SPO 2006, a claimant who has attained the age of 65 whose degree of disablement is 40% or more is entitled to an age allowance at the rate specified by paragraph 9 of Part IV of Schedule 1. The article gives the Secretary of State power to award an equivalent age allowance to claimants who are in receipt of retired pay or pension and who also receive benefits from other schemes, provided that it is to the claimant's advantage and does not result in duplication of benefits for the same period.[44]

MEDICAL TREATMENT

9.19 A claimant in receipt of war pension under the SPO 2006 or previous schemes who incurs a loss of earnings as a result of treatment as an in-patient in a hospital or similar institution, or as a result of a course of medical, surgical or rehabilitative treatment of a remedial nature,[45] is entitled to a treatment allowance at the rate of retired pay or pension which would be payable if the claimant's degree of disablement were 100%[46] instead of a pension at the claimant's normal rate. Claimants who are not normally in employment or who have retired will not be entitled to the allowance for treatment which would involve no, or only occasional, interruptions in employment if they were normally employed.[47]

9.20 Treatment allowance is not payable if the treatment involves no, or only occasional, interruptions in the claimant's employment, but in such cases article 19 of the SPO 2006 provides for the payment of a part-time treatment allowance based on loss of remunerative time resulting from any interruptions, up to the amount specified by paragraph 10 of Part IV of Schedule 1, but subject to a maximum weekly payment of three times that amount.

9.21 Under article 18 of the SPO 2006, an allowance at the same rate as treatment allowance is payable if the Secretary of State is satisfied that on completion of a course of treatment a claimant should abstain from work in consequence of the condition which necessitated the treatment, and as a result of the abstention from work the claimant incurs a loss of earnings. The allowance is not payable to a claimant who is in receipt of a personal unemployability allowance.[48]

---

44 SPO 2006, art 16(2) and (3).

45 See the definition of 'treatment' in SPO 2006, Sch 6, para 61.

46 SPO 2006, art 17(1).

47 SPO 2006, art 17(2).

48 See para **9.7**.

9.22 Article 21 of the SPO 2006 gives the Secretary of State power, under such conditions and up to such amounts as the Secretary of State may determine, to defray the expenses of medical, surgical or rehabilitative treatment, or aids and adaptations for disabled living, arising wholly or mainly as a result of the claimant's disablement, provided that treatment or aids or adaptations are not provided free of charge under any other UK legislative scheme.

MOBILITY SUPPLEMENT

Conditions of entitlement

Impaired mobility

9.23 Under article 20(1) of the SPO 2006, mobility supplement at the rate specified by paragraph 11 of Part IV of Schedule 1 is payable to recipients of retired pay or pension with the following disablements:

> (a) disablement as a result of the amputation of both legs, at levels which are either through or above the ankle; or
>
> (b) disablement, where the degree of disablement is assessed at 40 per cent or more, due to any other injury which is, and is likely to remain for at least 6 months from the decision date (on a claim or review) wholly or mainly responsible for—
>
> > (i) rendering the claimant unable to walk (including with any suitable prosthesis or artificial aid which the claimant habitually wears or uses, or which the claimant might reasonably be expected to wear or use),
> >
> > (ii) restricting the claimant's leg movements to such an extent that the claimant's ability to walk (with any such prosthesis or artificial aid) without severe discomfort is of little or no practical use to him,
> >
> > (iii) restricting by physical pain or breathlessness the claimant's ability to walk to such an extent that it is of little or no practical use to him, or
> >
> > (iv) rendering the exertion required to walk a danger to the claimant's life or a likely cause of serious deterioration in the claimant's health …

To qualify under point (b), a claimant must be assessed as 40% disabled in respect of the injury which affects the claimant's mobility, so that an aggregate assessment of 40% in respect of that injury and some other injury, for example depression, would not satisfy the conditions of entitlement. The words 'unable to walk' require the disablement in question to be wholly or mainly responsible for rendering the claimant physically unable to walk, and do not extend to problems with walking resulting from limited eyesight (see *Secretary of State for Defence v RC (WP)*[49] (Judge Lloyd-Davies)). In *CS v Secretary of State for Defence (WP)*,[50] Judge Powell held that, since article 20(1)(b)(iv) of the SPO 2006 is concerned with disablement that renders the exertion required to walk a danger to a person's life, or a likely cause of a serious deterioration in health, vertigo brought on by walking cannot be taken into account.

Other grounds of entitlement

9.24 Under article 20(1)(c) of the SPO 2006, for claims considered after 9 April 2001, mobility supplement is also payable if, immediately before the first consideration of the claim, the claimant:

(i) had the use of an invalid carriage or similar vehicle provided by the Secretary of State, or a grant towards the cost of running a private car, under the relevant legislation in England, Scotland or Northern Ireland; or
(ii) was in receipt of the mobility component of Disability Living Allowance (DLA); or
(iii) was in receipt of the mobility component of Personal Independence Payment (PIP) at the enhanced rate under section 79(2) of the Welfare Reform Act 2012.[51]
(iv) had disablement as a result of being both blind (with a loss of vision assessed as amounting to more than 80% disablement) and deaf (with a loss of hearing assessed as amounting to not less than 80% disablement) where by reason of the effects of those conditions in combination with each other the claimant is unable, without the assistance of another person, to walk to any intended or required destination while out of doors.

Loss of payment if vehicle provided by the National Health Service

9.25 Under article 20(2) of the SPO 2006, mobility supplement is not payable to claimants while they have the use of an invalid carriage or other petrol or electric powered vehicle provided for them under the relevant National Health Service legislation in England and Wales, Scotland or Northern Ireland, although the Secretary of State may pay mobility supplement for such period as is considered reasonable beginning with the date when a claimant acquires a car if

49 [2009] UKUT 297 (AAC).

50 [2011] UKUT 514 (AAC).

51 SPO 2006, art 20(1)(c).

the claimant is paying for the vehicle with the intention of learning to drive it and will use the mobility supplement in whole or in part to meet the expenses of acquiring the car.[52]

DIFFUSE MESOTHELIOMA LUMP SUMS

Entitlement to diffuse mesothelioma lump sum

9.26 The SPO 2006 was amended with effect from 11 April 2016[53] by the addition of a new article 21A and a new Schedule 1A to allow claimants with diffuse mesothelioma to claim a lump sum amounting to £140,000 in lieu of other SPO benefits if the following conditions are satisfied:

(i) a consultant respiratory physician or consultant oncologist makes or has made a diagnosis that the claimant has diffuse mesothelioma;
(ii) the claimant makes or has made a claim under article 34(1) and (2)[54] of the SPO 2006 in respect of disablement due to diffuse mesothelioma which was caused by service before 6 April 2005;
(iii) the claim is or has been accepted as attributable to or aggravated by service under article 40 or article 41 of the SPO 2006;
(iv) the claimant elects or has elected to receive a diffuse mesothelioma lump sum after acceptance of the claim.[55]

Election to receive diffuse mesothelioma lump sum

9.27 By paragraph 3 of Schedule 1A to the SPO 2006, an election to receive a diffuse mesothelioma lump sum is made by completing and signing an approved form and delivering it to the Secretary of State or an authorised agent in the same way as a claim form.[56] The provisions relating to the date of claims and to the withdrawal of claims applicable to normal claims[57] also apply to elections to receive a diffuse mesothelioma lump sum.[58]

52 SPO 2006, art 20(3).

53 By the Naval, Military and Air Forces Etc. (Disablement and Death) Service Pensions (Amendment) Order 2016 (SI 2016/374).

54 See para **2.3**.

55 SPO 2006, Sch 1A, para 2.

56 See para **2.3**.

57 See paras **2.9** and **2.14**.

58 SPO 2006, art 21A(3)(c).

Period for electing to receive a diffuse mesothelioma lump sum

9.28 Under paragraph 4 of Schedule 1A to the SPO 2006, a person who did not make an election to receive a diffuse mesothelioma lump sum prior to 11 April 2016 must have done so within 3 months beginning with that date, or within 3 months beginning with the date on which the claimant was notified of acceptance of a Service Pensions Order claim, whichever is the later. If a claimant was in receipt of disablement benefit on 11 April 2016 due to diffuse mesothelioma, the election to receive a diffuse mesothelioma lump sum payment must have been made within 3 months beginning on that date, or within 3 months beginning on the date on which the claimant was provided with a written estimate of the lump sum to which the claimant would be entitled if he or she made an election, if later.

Amount of diffuse mesothelioma lump sum

9.29 Under paragraph 5 of Schedule 1A to the SPO 2006, the amount of a mesothelioma lump sum is £140,000 less:

(i) the total amount of any disablement benefits in respect of diffuse mesothelioma paid prior to the date on which payment of the diffuse mesothelioma lump sum is made;

(ii) the total amount of any death benefits paid prior to the date on which the diffuse mesothelioma lump sum payment is made, except for an award for funeral expenses under article 32.

Effect of a diffuse mesothelioma lump sum

9.30 Under article 21A of the SPO 2006, entitlement to a diffuse mesothelioma lump sum brings to an end entitlement to all other Service Pensions Order disablement and death benefits, except for an award for funeral expenses under article 32.

Repayment of diffuse mesothelioma lump sum

9.31 Paragraph 7 of Schedule 1A to the SPO 2006 contains provisions providing for the recovery of a diffuse mesothelioma lump sum from a claimant or a 'designated person'[59] if payment of the lump sum was made in error, or as a result of a misrepresentation or failure to disclose a material fact, or if there was no entitlement to receive the payment for any other reason, or if the member or

---

59 See Chapter 26, n 18.

designated person has received or may receive compensation[60] which will benefit the member or designated person. Since a claimant is entitled to a diffuse mesothelioma lump payment only if the disease has been diagnosed by a consultant respiratory physician or oncologist,[61] it would seem that these provisions will seldom be applied.

60 It is not apparent why the abatement provisions in SPO 2006, art 52 should not be applied in such cases, particularly since the definition of 'pension' in the article has been expanded by amendments to art 51 made by Naval, Military and Air Forces Etc. (Disablement and Death) Service Pensions (Amendment) Order 2016 (SI 2016/374), art 8 to include a lump sum payment.

61 See para **9.26**.

Chapter 10

Awards in Respect of Death

ENTITLEMENT TO DEATH BENEFITS

Conditions of entitlement

10.1 Awards in respect of death under Part V of the SPO 2006 are payable where death is 'due to service'.[1] Whether article 40 or article 41 applies to the claim depends on the date of death, rather than on the date of claim, so that article 40 applies in all cases where death occurs within 7 years of the date of termination of service, and article 41 applies in all cases where death occurs after the end of that period.

10.2 Awards in respect of death are also payable in the following cases:

(i) where death has been accepted as due to service under earlier schemes;[2]
(ii) where death occurs after 22 November 1916 and constant attendance allowance was payable to the scheme member at the date of death, or would have been payable if the claimant had not been in a hospital or other institution;[3]
(iii) where the member's degree of disablement was 80% or more and unemployability allowance[4] was payable to the member at the date of death, or the member was engaged in remunerative work for a period not exceeding 104 weeks and article 12(3)(b), (c) and (f) of the SPO 2006 applied to the member.[5]

---

1 See Chapters 3, 4 and 5.

2 SPO 2006, art 22(2).

3 SPO 2006, art 22(3).

4 See para **9.7**.

5 SPO 2006, para 22(4).

Under article 22(6) of the SPO 2006, only the amount by which a death benefit exceeds the amount of any allowance, grant or other payment out of public funds payable during the lifetime of a member is payable if the payment continues after the member's death.

SURVIVING SPOUSES AND CIVIL PARTNERS

Rates of pension

Basic pension

10.3 The rates of pension payable to surviving spouses and to surviving civil partners of members of the armed forces whose death was due to service are set out in Tables 1 to 5 of Part II of Schedule 2 to the SPO 2006.[6] Within each table, the amount of pension payable is determined by which of the Groups in Part I of Schedule 1 is applicable to the member's rank or status at the date of death, although the rates are the same for the spouses and civil partners of all members in Groups 12 to 17 (non-commissioned ranks). Tables 1 to 3 apply in the following cases:

- (i) where a surviving spouse or civil partner has attained the age of 40 years (or is the surviving spouse or surviving civil partner of an officer who was a member of the armed forces between 14 August 1914 and 30 September 1921); or
- (ii) where a surviving spouse or civil partner is in receipt of an allowance awarded in respect of a child under article 28, 30 or 31[7] (allowance for children under the child's age limit, award for children who have attained the child's age limit and awards to or in respect of ineligible members of the families of unemployable pensioners); or
- (iii) where a surviving spouse or civil partner was in receipt of an allowance awarded under article 28 in respect of a child of whom that person is the parent[8] until the date on which the child attains the age of 16 years, or where, in the opinion of the Secretary of State in any other case, that person should be treated as having been in receipt of such an allowance until that date; or
- (iv) a child in respect of whom the surviving spouse or civil partner was awarded an allowance under article 28 or article 31[9] dies before

6 SPO 2006, art 23(1).

7 See paras 10.13 and 10.15–10.16.

8 'Parent' is defined in SPO 2006, Sch 6, para 44.

9 See para **10.13**.

attaining the age of 16 years, for a period of 13 weeks beginning with the date of the child's death; or

(v) the surviving spouse or civil partner is incapable of self-support.

In all other cases, the rates of pension payable are those set out in Tables 4 and 5 of Part II of Schedule 2 to the SPO 2006.

Supplementary pension

10.4 A supplementary pension at the rate specified in Tables 6 and 7 of Part II of Schedule 2 to the SPO 2006 is payable in all the above cases if the member's service terminated before April 1973.

PENSIONS TO DEPENDANTS WHO LIVED AS SPOUSES AND DEPENDANTS WHO LIVED AS CIVIL PARTNERS

Entitlement

10.5 Under article 24 of the SPO 2006, an unmarried dependant of a member of the armed forces who lived with the member as a spouse[10] or civil partner[11] may be awarded a pension if the member had a child who was in the care of the dependant and the dependant was in receipt of a Service Pensions Order allowance in respect of the child. The amount of the payment is at the discretion of the Secretary of State, but may not exceed the amount specified in paragraph 1 of Part II of Schedule 2. The allowance continues for a period of 13 weeks if the child dies before reaching the age of 16.

RENT ALLOWANCE

Entitlement

10.6 Under article 25 of the SPO 2006, recipients of a surviving spouse's or surviving civil partner's pension (and of equivalent benefits under earlier Schemes) will be eligible for a rent allowance based on their weekly rent, rates[12] and council tax, up to the maximum specified by paragraph 2 of Part III of

10 'Dependant living as a spouse' is defined in SPO 2006, Sch 6, para 25.

11 'Dependant living as a civil partner' is defined in SPO 2006, Sch 6, para 26.

12 'Weekly rent and rates' is defined in SPO 2006, art 25(4)(b) and (c).

Schedule 2 to the SPO 2006, if their household includes a child.[13] Recipients of a pension to dependants who lived as spouses or who lived as civil partners of a member will be eligible for rent allowance on the same terms if their household includes a child who is a child of the member. Unless payment of benefit has ceased under article 33,[14] rent allowance may continue to be paid for a maximum of 26 weeks after the household ceases to include a child, even if a surviving spouse or civil partner has ceased to receive a pension.[15]

ELDERLY PERSONS ALLOWANCE

Entitlement

10.7 Recipients of pensions to surviving spouses or civil partners, or of pensions to dependants who lived as a member's spouse or civil partner, are entitled to elderly persons allowances at the rates set out in paragraph 3 of Part III of Schedule 2 to the SPO 2006 on attaining the ages of 65, 70 and 80.

TEMPORARY ALLOWANCES

Entitlement

10.8 Under article 27 of the SPO 2006, surviving spouses or civil partners, or dependants who lived as spouses or civil partners, of a member who dies after 2 December 1963 are entitled to a personal allowance and additional allowances for children if immediately prior to death the member was in receipt of constant attendance allowance,[16] personal unemployability allowance[17] or allowance for lowered standard of occupation.[18] Temporary allowances are also payable if the death of the member occurred within 13 weeks of constant attendance allowance ceasing to be payable as a result of the member entering a hospital or other institution as an in-patient. Under article 27(2), members who were entitled to a

---

13 For the purposes of this provision, SPO 2006, art 25(4)(a) defines 'child' as 'a child who has not attained [the age of 16], or who, having attained [that age], is a student or an apprentice or is incapable of self-support by reason of an infirmity which arose before he attained [the age of 16], and includes any person fulfilling those conditions who should, in the opinion of the Secretary of State, having regard to his relationship or to connection with the member and the other circumstances of the case, be treated as covered by the provisions of this article'.

14 See para **10.17**.

15 SPO 2006, art 25(2).

16 See para **9.1**.

17 See para **9.7**.

18 See para **9.14**.

personal unemployability allowance and who were engaged in remunerative work at the time of their death are treated as having been in receipt of the allowance if the period of remunerative work did not exceed 52 weeks and the conditions in article 12(3)(b), (c) and (f) were satisfied.

Duration of allowances

10.9 Personal allowances are payable for a period of 26 weeks commencing on the day following the member's death in the case of an officer, or on the Wednesday following the member's death in the case of other ranks.[19] The amount of the allowance is the same as the amount of the retired pay, pension and other allowances to which the member was entitled in the 7 days preceding the member's death, excluding clothing allowance, additional unemployability allowances for dependants, or mobility supplement.[20] Article 27(3)(d) of the SPO 2006 contains provisions for calculating the rate of retired pay, pension and allowances of members of earlier schemes. A personal allowance is not payable for any period after the death of a surviving spouse or surviving civil partner.[21]

Temporary allowances in respect of children

10.10 The amount of any temporary allowance also leaves out of account any allowance paid to the member in respect of a child,[22] but under article 27(5) of the SPO 2006 an additional personal allowance may be awarded to a surviving spouse, civil partner or dependant in respect of any child for whom the member was receiving an allowance in the 7 days immediately preceding the member's death. The additional allowance is at the same rate as the allowance which the member was receiving and is payable for so long as the child remains alive and is under the age of 16, or if the child is over that age, is a student, apprentice, or incapable of self-support by reason of an infirmity which arose before the child attained the age of 16, and the circumstances are such as to justify the continuance of the award.

10.11 If a member whose death was due to service had a child who was in the member's charge at the date of death, a dependant of the member will be eligible to receive a personal allowance as if he or she were the member's surviving spouse or civil partner, but the award and the amount of the allowance are

19 SPO 2006, art 27(3)(a).

20 SPO 2006, art 27(3)(b).

21 SPO 2006, art 27(3)(c).

22 SPO 2006, art 27(3)(b).

discretionary and cannot in any case exceed the amount which would be payable to a surviving spouse or surviving civil partner.[23]

Aggregation and power to vary payments

10.12 Article 27(6) and (7) of the SPO 2006 contains provisions dealing with the aggregation of temporary allowances and other pensions and allowances, and giving the Secretary of State power to vary the conditions and amount of a personal allowance in exceptional circumstances during periods when constant attendance allowance or personal unemployability allowance are in payment.

CHILDREN'S ALLOWANCES

Entitlement

10.13 Under article 28 of the SPO 2006, a children's allowance is payable in respect of a child[24] of a member whose death is due to service who is aged under 16 and who is not eligible for the award of an orphan's allowance. The allowance is payable at the rate specified in paragraph 4(a) of Part III of Schedule 2 if the child lives with a parent, and at a rate not exceeding the amount specified in paragraph 4(b) of that Part if the child does not live with a parent, or with a person who is or has been in receipt of a pension to surviving spouses or surviving civil partners, or dependants who lived as spouses or civil partners, or had an award under article 31.[25]

Orphans

10.14 Under article 29 of the SPO 2006, an orphan's pension at the rate specified in paragraph 2 of Part III of Schedule 2 is payable in respect of a child of a member whose death was due to service if the child is aged under 16 and has no parents living.

Children aged 16 or over

10.15 Under article 30 of the SPO 2006, an allowance for a child who has attained the age of 16 can be awarded or continued if the child is a student or apprentice, or is incapable of self-support by reason of an infirmity which arose

---

23 SPO 2006, art 27(4).

24 See the definition of 'child' in SPO 2006, Sch 6, para 23.

25 See para **10.16**.

before the child attained the age of 16 and the making or continuing of the award is justified in all the circumstances of the case.

Ineligible children of members in receipt of unemployability allowances

10.16 If at the date of death a member was in receipt of additional unemployability allowance in respect of a child under article 12(6)(b) and (c) of the SPO 2006[26] (discretionary unemployability allowance for children who are not children of the member), a child's pension or allowance can be awarded on the same basis as if the child were an eligible member of the claimant's family.[27] This provision does not appear to require death to have been due to service.

RELATIONSHIPS SUBSEQUENT TO THE AWARD OF A PENSION

Forfeiture of pensions

10.17 Until 2015, article 33(1) of the SPO 2006 stipulated that any award under the SPO 2006, or under Part II of the 1919 to 1921 Schemes, which had been made in respect of a member's death to a person other than a parent[28] should cease 'if that person marries or lives with another person as the spouse of that person or forms a civil partnership or lives with another person as the civil partner of that person'. Under article 33(3) of the SPO 2006, a pension awarded under articles 23 to 26 did not cease if: (i) the member in respect of whom the pension was awarded died or left service before 31 March 1973; and (ii) the date on which the recipient of the pension entered into one of the relationships referred to in article 33(1) was after 5 April 2005. Allowances awarded in respect of children were not affected by the cessation of a pension awarded to another person under these provisions,[29] and the Secretary of State had a discretion to maintain the payment of children's pensions and allowances under articles 28, 29 and 30 in special circumstances.[30]

Restoration of benefits

10.18 If an award ceased because the recipient of a pension had another person living with him or her as a spouse, or formed a civil partnership, or lived with

---

26 See para **9.10**.

27 SPO 2006, art 31.

28 Death benefits for parents were awarded under some earlier schemes.

29 SPO 2006, art 33(5).

30 SPO 2006, art 33(5).

another person as his or her civil partner, the pension could be re-awarded 'as though the relationship had never existed'.[31] However, that provision did not apply if the recipient of the pension married, except that after 19 July 1995 a pension could be restored if the marriage had come to an end as a result of death, dissolution or annulment, or if the parties to the marriage became judicially separated.[32] Paragraph 2 of Schedule 3 to the SPO 2006 is apparently designed to allow a 3-month grace period for applying for the restoration of a pension with effect from the date on which the relationship ended.[33]

Abolition of forfeiture provisions

10.19 These provisions were strongly criticised and were revoked with effect from 1 April 2015 by the Naval, Military and Air Forces Etc. (Disablement and Death) Service Pensions (Amendment) Order 2015,[34] although not with retrospective effect. The 2015 amendments have, however, altered the position with regard to the restoration of benefits when a relationship subsequent to the award of a pension comes to an end. Under the 2015 amendments, all relationships, including marriage, which led to the forfeiture of a pension under article 33(1) of the SPO 2006 before 1 April 2015 are treated as if they never existed if the relationship comes to an end.

FUNERAL EXPENSES

10.20 Article 32 of the SPO 2006 provides for an award of £2,200 in respect of the expenses of the funeral of a member of the armed forces who dies on or after 6 April 2009 whose death was due to service before 6 April 2005. The claim must be made within 3 months after the date of the funeral, unless a written or oral inquiry about claiming funeral expenses is made to the Secretary of State or to an authorised agent within that period and a claim is made within 3 months of the date on which a claim form is issued in response to the inquiry.[35] This time limit cannot be extended and a claim made after the due date will be refused.

---

31 SPO 2006, art 33(2).

32 See SPO 2006, art 33(7) for the position with regard to foreign divorces, annulments and judicial separations.

33 SPO 2006, Sch 3, para 2(2) contains definitions for determining the date on which different forms of relationship come to an end.

34 SI 2015/208.

35 See para **2.3** with regard to the procedure for making claims.

Chapter 11

Reduction and Cancellation of Awards

ABATEMENT

Abatement in respect of third party compensation

11.1 In order to prevent duplication of benefits for the same injury, article 52(1) of the SPO 2006 allows the Secretary of State to take into account against any pension or gratuity[1] 'in such manner and to such extent as the Secretary of State thinks fit' any compensation which has been or will be paid to a war pension beneficiary, so as to extinguish or reduce the war pension benefits which would otherwise be payable. Under article 52(2), any compensation which has not been recovered because of an 'unreasonable act or omission' can also be taken into account. 'Compensation' is defined in article 52(3) as:

(a) any periodical or lump sum payment in respect of the disablement or death of any person, or in respect of any injury, disease or incapacity sustained or suffered by any person, being a payment—

(i) for which provision is made by or under any enactment, Order in Council (including this Order), Warrant, Order, scheme, ordinance, regulation or other instrument; or
(ii) which is recoverable as damages at common law; or

(b) any periodical or lump sum payment which, in the opinion of the Secretary of State, is recoverable or payable—

(i) under any enactment, scheme, ordinance, regulation or other instrument whatsoever promulgated or made in any place outside the United Kingdom, or
(ii) under the law of any such place

1 Defined in SPO 2006, art 51(1)(a).

and is analogous to any payment falling within subparagraph (a) of this paragraph; or

(c) any periodical or lump sum payment made in settlement or composition of, or to avoid the making of, any claim to any payment falling within subparagraph (a) or (b) of this paragraph, whether liability on any such claim is or is not admitted.

11.2 These provisions are used to abate the amount of war pension which would otherwise be payable to a beneficiary to take into account damages recovered in a civil claim arising out of the accident which has caused the injury in respect of which compensation is payable. However, because of the complex interaction between war pension benefits, social security benefits and common law damages, the application of the abatement provisions is often complicated and difficult.

Ministry of Defence policy

11.3 The relevant paragraphs of the former Ministry of Defence policy on abatement in respect of third party compensation are set out in the decision of Judge Rowland in *AL v Secretary of State for Defence* (at [10]).[2]

11.4 On the basis of an analysis of the relevant statutory regimes, Judge Rowland doubted in *AL v Secretary of State for Defence*[3] whether the provisions in the policy for the partial disregards of general damages and special damages for loss of earnings in fact achieved the stated aim of treating war pensioners on a par with civilian counterparts who sustained an industrial accident for which a third party was to blame and for which industrial injuries benefit was payable, and it is understood that the policy has been amended in the light of Judge Rowland's observations. Social security law provides for the recovery of social security benefits from defendants in personal injury claims for a maximum period of 5 years,[4] and Judge Rowland accepted (at [42] and [43]) that the policy was correct in treating the amount of abatement of war pension in respect of damages for personal injury as no greater than the relevant elements of a war pension received in respect of the relevant injury over a 5-year period. The judge considered, however, that the relevant period of 5 years need not be the 5-year period since the date of the accident (since payment of a pension cannot commence until a claimant leaves service) and need not coincide with the period over which abatement is carried out, provided that the total amount of war pension recovered does not exceed the relevant amount paid in a 5-year period.

---

2 [2014] UKUT 0524 (AAC).

3 [2014] UKUT 0524 (AAC).

4 Social Security (Recovery of Benefits) Act 1997, s 3.

11.5 Judge Rowland held (at [45] and [46]) that the amount of abatement should be calculated by taking account of each element of war pension to the extent to which it is duplicated by the relevant part of the payment of compensation:

> 45. I would consider that [the basic disablement pension] should be taken into account against compensation for loss of earnings – as under [the Social Security (Recovery of Benefits) Act 1997] and for the same reason: this approach protects awards of general damages when there is no award for loss of earnings. I agree … that only the amount payable in respect of an assessment of 40% would be taken into account in this case. As the First-tier Tribunal decided, unemployability supplement and invalidity allowance would also be taken into account against compensation for loss of earnings, as would an allowance for lowered standard of occupation. Constant attendance allowance would be taken into account against damages in respect of care and a mobility supplement would be taken into account against damages in respect of loss of mobility. At this stage of the calculation, those elements would all be taken into account in full if they were exceeded by the amount paid under the relevant head of damages; there would be no need to protect any element equivalent to civilian social security benefit or a Motability agreement.
>
> 46. Calculation of the appropriate proportion of a payment of compensation to be allocated to each head of compensation is always likely to be difficult where a case has been settled without any agreement as to the precise basis of the settlement. However, as in this case, it will often be possible to obtain from a claimant documents sufficient to show whether the claim included elements in respect of loss of earnings, the cost of care and loss of mobility and to make an informed judgement as to whether the likely basis of any settlement can be determined or whether all heads of claim should be taken to have been reduced by the same proportion … The calculation … is to determine the amount of compensation under the relevant head that it is reasonable to attribute to the relevant period of five years.
>
> 47. Having done that calculation, it might be necessary to make adjustments to take account of, for instance, the recovery under the 1997 Act of civilian social security benefits awarded before the claim for war pension was made, if otherwise there would have been recovery of benefits over a period of more than five years or there would be some other unfairness to the claimant.

11.6 Lastly, Judge Rowland held (at [48]) that, once the total amount of abatement has been established, the rate at which it should be abated should take account of the claimant's current circumstances, so that, for example, there might be a need to leave a claimant entitled to constant attendance allowance or mobility supplement if that might make a claim for PIP unnecessary, or protect a motability agreement. Although it would be essential not to calculate the amount to be abated by reference to any part of the award not attributable to the relevant accident, it would be permissible to abate other parts of the award where, say, an allowance taken into account in calculating the amount of the abatement was not to be abated.

Abatement in respect of benefits under other schemes

11.7 Article 52 of the SPO 2006 is also used to prevent duplication of Service Pensions Order benefits with benefits payable under other service pension schemes. In *R(AF) 4/09*, Judge Jacobs held that a Service Attributable Pension payable under the Reserve Forces (Attributable Benefits) Etc. Regulations 2001[5] was 'compensation' under article 52(3) of the SPO 2006 which was paid in respect of reduced earning capacity, so that the Secretary of State was entitled to set off the benefit against the claimant's Service Pensions Order award for lowered standard of occupation.

Pension abated by gratuity

11.8 The power in article 52 of the SPO 2006 is also used in cases where a gratuity has been paid to a claimant, but the percentage of disablement is later increased so as to attract a pension. The Secretary of State's policy in such cases is that where an assessment of disablement increases to 20% or more within 6 years of a gratuity being paid, the gratuity, or part of it, is taken as advance payment of pension when calculating pension commencement dates. In *R(AF) 3/07*, Judge Rowland held that policy to be lawful.

MAINTENANCE IN HOSPITAL OR OTHER INSTITUTION

11.9 Under article 53 of the SPO 2006, constant attendance allowance[6] and severe disablement occupational allowance[7] are withheld from a claimant who is receiving free treatment under the National Health Service Act 1977,[8] or under corresponding provisions in Scotland and Northern Ireland, after 4 weeks following admission to a hospital as an in-patient. Periods of time separated by less than 28 days are treated as continuous for these purposes.[9] These provisions also apply to a claimant who is being maintained in an institution which is supported wholly or mainly out of public funds, or in which the claimant is being

---

5 Available on the Ministry of Defence website at www.gov.uk/government/organisations/ministry-of-defence.

6 See para **9.1**.

7 See para **9.4**.

8 Now replaced by the National Health Service Act 2006 and the National Health Service (Wales) Act 2006.

9 SPO 2006, art 53(3).

maintained under arrangements made by the Secretary of State, otherwise than for the purpose of undergoing medical or other treatment.[10] The provisions do not apply to claimants who are receiving private treatment or who are paying for the cost of their accommodation and other services in National Health Service hospitals.[11]

CHELSEA PENSIONERS

11.10 Chelsea Pensioners are not entitled to any war pension, but claimants' pensions may be restored if they leave the Royal Hospital Chelsea.[12]

SOCIAL SECURITY BENEFITS

11.11 Where an award of a war pension is made for any past period during which social security benefits[13] have been paid, the amount of the pension may be abated by the amount by which the total of benefit paid during the period exceeds the amount which would have been paid if the social security benefit and the war pension had both been paid at the same time.[14]

FORFEITURE

11.12 Under article 57 of the SPO 2006, a pension or gratuity can be withheld or forfeited if the beneficiary or person in respect of whom it has, or may be, awarded is found guilty of an offence and is imprisoned, sent to a young offender institution[15] or deported.[16] Where a dependant would suffer hardship, there is a discretion to pay up to half of the amount of the basic pension to a pensioner's spouse, civil partner, unmarried dependant or dependant who has not formed a civil partnership, or any other person who is entitled to receive money on behalf of the dependant. On the ground for forfeiture ceasing to apply, a claimant whose pension has been forfeited under these provisions may be awarded the pension

---

10 SPO 2006, art 53(2)(b).

11 SPO 2006, art 53(5).

12 SPO 2006, art 54.

13 I.e. contributory benefits, non-contributory benefits, increases for dependants, industrial injuries benefits, income-related benefits, Jobseeker's Allowance and employment and support allowance in Great Britain and Northern Ireland.

14 SPO 2006, art 56.

15 'Young offenders centre' in Northern Ireland.

16 Including being required to leave or being prohibited from entering the United Kingdom or Isle of Man, or having a certificate of naturalisation revoked.

which has been withheld up to a maximum of 52 weeks, less any amounts paid to dependants.[17]

REFUSAL OF TREATMENT

11.13 Under article 58 of the SPO 2006, a reduction of up to one half can be made in the pension of a member who unreasonably refuses to receive medical, surgical or rehabilitative treatment if the treatment is in the member's own interests and is for a disablement which is due to service and for which a pension has been, or may be, awarded. The provision also applies where misconduct by the member makes it necessary for such treatment to be discontinued.[18]

SERIOUS NEGLIGENCE OR MISCONDUCT

11.14 Under article 59 of the SPO 2006, an award which has been, or may be, made in respect of the disablement or death of a member may be withheld, cancelled or reduced if 'the injury or death on which the claim is based was caused or contributed to by the serious negligence or misconduct of the member'. In *Robertson v Minister of Pensions*,[19] Ormerod J held that 'serious negligence' was 'negligence of a quality that would certainly call for some criminal action if it were done in civil life', but in *Minister of Pensions v Griseti*,[20] the judge qualified that definition, holding that it should be applied to the facts of the particular case and holding that a claimant had been guilty of serious negligence in disobeying an order not to handle enemy ammunition. It appears that this provision is very rarely applied.

FAILURE TO DRAW PENSION

11.15 Article 60 of the SPO 2006 provides that an award of a pension can be cancelled and any arrears withheld if a person fails to draw a pension for a continuous period of 12 months or more, but a further award can be made and the arrears paid in whole or in part.

---

17 SPO 2006, art 57(3).

18 This provision also applies to pensions under previous schemes.

19 (1952) WPAR 245.

20 (1955) WPAR 457.

SUSPENSION OF BENEFITS PENDING APPEALS

11.16 Articles 61, 62 and 63 of the SPO 2006 give the Secretary of State power to suspend the payment of a pension or gratuity pending a decision on whether to appeal against a decision of a tribunal, a Social Security Commissioner or the Upper Tribunal, or a court. The suspension will lapse unless the Secretary of State gives notice to the claimant that an application for permission to appeal has been made within 6 weeks of the date when the decision and the reasons for the decision are received by the Secretary of State, but if the requisite notice is given the suspension will continue until the application for permission to appeal and any resulting appeal have been determined. In the case of an application for permission to appeal against the decision of a tribunal or of a Social Security Commissioner[21] or the Upper Tribunal, the suspension may continue if permission to appeal is refused and the Secretary of State makes a further application for permission to appeal within 28 days of the date on which the Secretary of State receives notice that permission to appeal has been refused. If the renewed application for permission to appeal is successful, the suspension will continue until the appeal has been determined. In cases where a Social Security Commissioner or the Upper Tribunal remits a case for rehearing, the appeal is not treated as determined until the rehearing has been completed.

11.17 Article 64 of the SPO 2006 gives the Secretary of State power to suspend payment of any pension or gratuity in 'look-alike' cases where the award of a pension or gratuity might have to be reviewed if an appeal was allowed in another case where an appeal has been brought or is under consideration.

FAILURE TO COMPLY WITH REQUEST OR PENSIONER NOT AT LAST KNOWN ADDRESS

11.18 If it appears that a decision should be reviewed under article 44 of the SPO 2006, article 65 allows the Secretary of State to give the claimant notice to provide within 3 months any evidence or information which is required in order to determine whether the award should be revised, or to attend for a medical examination at an appointed time and place. If it appears that a claimant is no longer resident at his or her last known address, the claimant may be required to provide evidence of his or her current address within 3 months. Failure to comply with these requirements without a satisfactory explanation entitles the Secretary of State to suspend the award, but the claimant must be informed of the suspension

---

21 Appeals in war pensions cases are dealt with by Social Security Commissioners only in Northern Ireland (called Pensions Appeal Commissioners when dealing with these appeals, see Chapter 33).

and of the reasons for it. The claimant must also be informed that the award may be cancelled under article 66 (see para **11.21**).

Restoration of suspended benefits

11.19 Suspension of an award under these provisions will cease if the claimant complies with the requirement within 12 months of the date on which the original notice was sent, or if the claimant is given notice that it is no longer necessary to comply with the requirement. The date on which the suspension ceases will be the date on which the claimant complies with the requirement or is sent notice that compliance is no longer required.

11.20 If an award has been suspended under these provisions but the claimant has later complied with the relevant requirement and the award has been revised following a review, the adjusted award takes effect from the date of the review decision, but the claimant is entitled to a backdating payment of the award at the previous rate, covering the period from the commencement of the suspension to the date of the review decision.[22]

Cancellation of suspended benefits

11.21 An award to a claimant who does not comply with the relevant requirements within 12 months of the original notice may be cancelled,[23] but a new claim can be made for the same award. The claimant must be informed of the cancellation of the award and of the right to make a new claim.[24]

11.22 If a new claim is made following cancellation of an award and the claimant complies with the requirements which led to the original award being suspended, or is informed that compliance with the requirements is no longer necessary, any new award takes effect from the date of the suspension and is 'at such rate as the Secretary of State determines to be appropriate when making the further award'.[25]

---

22 SPO 2006, Sch 3, para 1(8).

23 SPO 2006, art 66(1).

24 SPO 2006, art 66(3).

25 SPO 2006, Sch 3, para 1(9).

PART II

ARMED FORCES COMPENSATION

Chapter 12

The Armed Forces Compensation Scheme

12.1 In March 2001, the government published a consultation paper[1] proposing new schemes to replace both the War Pensions Scheme and the Armed Forces Pensions Scheme.[2] Although the Defence Select Committee criticised the consultation process,[3] the government announced in 2002[4] that it intended to maintain the broad principles of its proposals. On 15 September 2003, the Parliamentary Under Secretary of State for Defence announced that the review process had been completed and that legislation would introduce a new Armed Forces Pension and Compensation Scheme in April 2005. A further report of the Defence Select Committee published in December 2003 recognised that the final proposals had taken account of many of the criticisms made during the consultation process, but expressed concerns about compensation awards being decided on the balance of probabilities and about the appropriateness of using tariff bands to determine the level of compensation payments.

12.2 The March 2001 *Joint Compensation Review* recommended that the War Pensions Scheme and the attributable benefits of the Armed Forces Pensions Scheme should be merged into a single scheme providing lump sum payments for pain and suffering based on a tariff of awards, with further payments for loss of earnings, calculated as a lump sum but paid in instalments as a guaranteed income stream. The time limit for submitting claims would be cut to 3 years, and claimants would have to prove on the 'balance of probabilities' that their

---

1 Ministry of Defence, *Joint Compensation Review: A Consultation Document* (2001).

2 For the background to the consultation, see Social Security Committee, *War Pensions Agency Business Plan 1999–2000*, Sixth Report of Session 1998–99, HC 377 (23 June 1999), paras 25–27.

3 Defence Select Committee, *The Ministry of Defence Reviews of Armed Forces' Pension and Compensation Arrangements*, Third Report of Session 2001–02, HC 666 (1 May 2002).

4 Defence Select Committee, *The Ministry of Defence Reviews of Armed Forces' Pension and Compensation Arrangements: Government Response*, Fifth Special Report of Session 2001–02, HC 1115 (17 July 2002).

condition was due to service. The Review described the core principles which the government considered should be central to the new arrangements as follows:

> Fairness. The arrangements should guarantee a fair deal for all those who are entitled to compensation, and should in particular give due recognition to the needs of those most seriously disabled.
> Simplicity. The arrangements should be simpler to apply and to administer, and easier for claimants to understand, the aim being that decisions on claims should in most cases be taken within a few weeks of their submission.
> Modernity. The arrangements should as far as possible meet the best modern standards for compensation schemes.
> Security. Compensation should be fixed at realistic levels, and for those most seriously injured who may be unable to work again should provide lifetime financial support.
> Employability. Awards should not act as a disincentive to those who are able to work, but should support those who could not do so.
> Human Rights and Fairness at Work. The arrangements should be consistent with the Government's commitment to human rights and to being a modern and fair employer.
> Affordability. The arrangements should be cost effective, affordable, and fair also to the taxpayer.

12.3 Following a further period of consultation with service charities, the government announced its final proposals on 15 September 2003. The Ministry of Defence summarised the key features of the new Scheme as follows:

(i) All Service personnel injured on or after introduction would be covered (even if an individual remained in the then current Armed Forces Pensions Scheme), replacing the current War Pensions Scheme and Armed Forces Pensions Scheme attributable benefits.

(ii) The Scheme would provide a tariff-based lump sum award for pain and suffering. The tariff would have 15 levels of award, based on the Judicial Studies Board, *Guidelines for the Assessment of General Damages in Personal Injury Cases*[5] and would be reviewed periodically.

(iii) It would offer a Guaranteed Income Stream (GIS) for life for those at higher levels of tariff (1 to 11) to compensate for loss of earnings capacity. The value of the income stream would be set at different levels, dependent on the degree of loss of earnings capacity caused by the disablement.

(iv) For an attributable death, a Guaranteed Widows' Income Stream (GWIS) would be awarded. An additional attributable Widows' Compensation lump sum would be paid for death in retirement. For

---

5 Oxford University Press (edition unknown).

deaths in service, the estate would receive a lump sum of four times pensionable pay from the pension scheme but, if three times pensionable pay plus £20,000 was a greater amount, the balance of that amount would be paid from the injury scheme. For children there would also be a children's income stream.

(v) With immediate effect, provision would be made for registered unmarried partners (including same-sex partners) for all deaths resulting from service.

(vi) For the first time, in-service awards for injury for all would be paid for pain and suffering, including for injuries arising from warlike acts and terrorism.

(vii) The scheme would be designed to be administratively straightforward for the majority of claims and would be run by administrators with access to specialist medical and legal advice where needed.

(viii) The scheme would use the 'balance of probabilities' standard of proof, in line with civil claims.

(ix) There would be a time limit to claim of 5 years[6] from the event or after retirement where no particular incident caused the condition, but there would be an exceptions list for late-onset conditions and discretion within the scheme for exceptional cases.

(x) There would be no regular review mechanism. Awards would generally be final with provision for interim awards where the long-term prognosis is unclear and for review in exceptional cases where significant unexpected complications arise.

(xi) There would be an internal disputes resolution procedure and an independent appeals process using the Pensions Appeal Tribunal and the Social Security Commissioners, compliant with the European Convention on Human Rights.

(xii) The scheme would be supported by a welfare support service.

(xiii) It would be a no-fault scheme; a claim against the scheme would not prevent individuals making a claim for negligence against the Ministry of Defence.

(xiv) The attributable benefits would be in addition to those non-attributable benefits under the Armed Forces Pensions Scheme on medical discharge or death-in-service, but there would be a netting off to avoid double compensation (e.g. for loss of earnings capacity).

(xv) The new scheme would be broadly cost-neutral, although there would be some increase in up-front costs due to the payment of lump sums for pain and suffering.

---

6 Increased to 7 years by the AFCS 2011 (see para **13.7**).

12.4 Concerns about the new proposals continued to be expressed by the Defence Select Committee and by service charities, particularly with regard to the time limits on claims, the burden and standard of proof under the new scheme, the handling of claims where service records were inadequate or incomplete, over-rigid application of the tariff, and the mechanism for appeals. The Armed Forces (Pensions and Compensation) Act 2004 did not set out any details of the new Armed Forces Compensation Scheme, but empowered the Secretary of State to establish schemes 'which provide for benefits to be payable to or in respect of a person by reason of his illness or injury (whether physical or mental), or his death, which is attributable (wholly or partly) to his service in the armed forces or reserve forces'.[7] The 2004 Act amended the Pensions Appeal Tribunals Act 1943 to allow armed forces compensation decisions to be designated as specified decisions so as to give rights of appeal against such decisions[8] and created rights of appeal against decisions of Pensions Appeal Tribunals to the Social Security Commissioners.[9]

12.5 The Armed Forces and Reserve Forces (Compensation Scheme) Order 2005[10] (AFCS 2005) came into force on 6 April 2005. Against the background of very serious injuries sustained in hostilities in Afghanistan, awards made under the Scheme were compared unfavourably to civilian awards for lesser injuries, although such criticism did not always take account of the full range of benefits provided by the Scheme. Compensation awards for the most seriously injured were increased from February 2008, and in December 2008 lump sum payments for the most seriously injured claimants were doubled and all injured service personnel received an increase in their awards of between 10% and 100%.

12.6 The decision of the Ministry of Defence to appeal against the decision of the Upper Tribunal in *Secretary of State for Defence v Duncan and McWilliams*[11] in 2009 was widely criticised, although Carnwath LJ expressed the view that the appeal was entirely justified, at least from a legal point of view.[12] In September 2009, in the aftermath of the decision of the Court of Appeal, it was announced that Lord Boyce, the former Chief of the Defence Staff, would chair a review of the Armed Forces Compensation Scheme.

---

7 Section 1(2).

8 See para **25.1**.

9 See para **24.6**.

10 SI 2005/439.

11 [2009] EWCA Civ 1043, [2009] All ER (D) 121 (Oct). See para **18.4**.

12 [2009] EWCA Civ 1043, [116].

12.7 The Boyce Review reported in February 2010.[13] The Review concluded that the Scheme was fundamentally sound, but made a number of important recommendations:

(i) increases in lump sum payments at all levels, except the highest;
(ii) increased awards for mental health conditions;
(iii) a new system of interim payments;
(iv) changes in the method for compensating for multiple injuries;
(v) changes in the method for calculating Guaranteed Income Payments (GIPs), to take account of promotion prospects;
(vi) an increase in the time limits for making claims;
(vii) a different approach to the burden of proof in cases where records were lost or missing;
(viii) better communications to improve awareness of the Scheme and support for those claiming under it;
(ix) the establishment of an expert medical group to advise on compensation for those claiming.

The Boyce Review also recommended the introduction of a further right of review after 10 years for cases of further substantial and unexpected deterioration where to maintain an award would be manifestly unjust.

12.8 The government announced its acceptance of all the Boyce Review recommendations, and in *The Review of the Armed Forces Compensation Scheme – One Year On*,[14] the new government reported on the steps that had been taken to implement the Boyce Review recommendations. These included emphasising that the most compensation should be paid to those with the most severe injuries and examining the relationship between armed forces compensation and other state benefits. The Boyce Review identified specific types of injury, including hearing loss, where the Scheme was not operating as intended, and the newly created Independent Medical Expert Group's recommendations in respect of these conditions were incorporated into the new Scheme.[15]

12.9 The Armed Forces and Reserve Forces (Compensation Scheme) Order 2011[16] (AFCS 2011), which implemented the amendments to the Scheme resulting from the Boyce Review, came into force on 9 May 2011. In the light of

13 Ministry of Defence, *The Review of the Armed Forces Compensation Scheme*, Cm 7798 (The Stationery Office, 2010) (the Boyce Review).

14 Ministry of Defence, 2011.

15 Independent Medical Expert Group, *The Boyce Review of the Armed Forces Compensation Scheme: The Independent Medical Expert Group report and recommendations on medical aspects* (Ministry of Defence, 19 January 2011).

16 SI 2011/517.

the judgment of the Court of Appeal in *Secretary of State for Defence v Duncan and McWilliams*,[17] the new Scheme clarified that descriptors were intended to encompass the expected effects of the primary injury and its appropriate clinical management, and that a separate Armed Forces Compensation Scheme award could be made for an injury consequential on the original injury for which there was a tariff descriptor. Provisions were included dealing with the burden and standard of proof in cases where official records had been lost or destroyed.[18] The new Scheme also implemented the Boyce Review recommendations in respect of multiple injuries by introducing a system for increased compensation for injuries in different body zones.[19] Part 11 of the AFCS 2011 provided for additional benefits to be paid to recipients of awards under the AFCS 2005 to give retrospective effect to the Boyce Review recommendations and for supplementary awards[20] to be awarded retrospectively.

12.10 The AFCS 2011 is subject to frequent amendments, partly as a result of changes to the Scheme resulting from the making of temporary awards and partly as a result of up-rating of benefits.

12.11 The AFCS 2011 will undergo a quinquennial review in 2016.

---

17 [2009] EWCA Civ 1043, [2009] All ER (D) 121 (Oct). See para **18.4**.

18 See paras **16.4** and **16.5**.

19 See para **19.7**.

20 See para **19.3**.

Chapter 13

Claiming Armed Forces Compensation

WHO CAN CLAIM

13.1 The Armed Forces Compensation Scheme covers all serving and former members of the regular and reserve armed forces.[1] Unlike war pensions claims, claims for armed forces compensation can be made whilst a claimant is still serving in the forces, but there are time limits for making a claim. The Armed Forces Compensation Scheme applies to:

(i) injury caused wholly or partly by service where the cause of the injury occurred on or after 6 April 2005, provided that service was the predominant cause of the injury;[2]

(ii) injury made worse by service if the conditions specified in article 9 of the AFCS 2011 are satisfied[3] and service on or after 6 April 2005 was the predominant cause[4] of the worsening of the injury;

(iii) death caused wholly or partly by service if the conditions in article 10 of the AFCS 2011 are satisfied[5] and the cause of death occurred on or after 6 April 2005.

The SPO 2006 contains provisions preventing the making of an award of a war pension for injury or death in respect of which the claimant is entitled to an Armed Forces Compensation Scheme benefit.[6] Prior to 7 April 2014, the AFCS 2011 did not contain any corresponding provisions preventing an award of an Armed Forces Compensation Scheme benefit for injury or death in respect of which a claimant is entitled to a war pension, and in *JN v Secretary of State for Defence*

---

1 See the definitions of 'member' and 'former member' in AFCS 2011, art 2.

2 See Chapter 14.

3 See para **14.9**.

4 See para **14.2**.

5 See para **14.15**.

6 SPO 2006, arts 40(2) and 41(2).

(AFCS),[7] Judge Mesher held that there could be an award under both Schemes if the Armed Forces Compensation Scheme conditions of entitlement were met in respect of a condition for which the claimant was also entitled to a war pension. However, the Armed Forces Compensation Scheme was amended with effect from 7 April 2014[8] by the addition of article 12(2) of the AFCS 2011, which provides that where a person is in receipt of any form of war pension under the SPO 2006 in respect of disablement or death, that disablement or death shall not be accepted as an injury or death caused (wholly or partly) by service for the purposes of the AFCS 2011.

'Spanning' cases

13.2 Under the AFCS 2005, a claim by a person who was injured by service prior to 6 April 2005 and who was still in service at that date had in addition to be considered as a claim for injury made worse by service under the Armed Forces Compensation Scheme, even if an award of a war pension was made. The Boyce Review recommended the abolition of this requirement,[9] and it has not been included in the AFCS 2011. However, it is still open to a claimant to ask for a pre-6 April 2005 injury to be treated as a claim for injury made worse by service under the AFCS 2011.

MAKING A CLAIM UNDER THE ARMED FORCES COMPENSATION SCHEME

Claim a condition of entitlement

13.3 Under articles 43 and 44 of the AFCS 2011, unless one of the specified exceptions applies, it is a condition of entitlement to any Armed Forces Compensation Scheme benefit that a written and signed[10] claim in the prescribed form[11] is given or sent[12] to Veterans UK[13] within the specified time limit. Article

---

7 [2012] UKUT 479 (AAC).

8 By the Armed Forces and Reserve Forces (Compensation Scheme) (Amendment) Order 2014 (SI 2014/412), arts 1(1) and 2(3).

9 Boyce Review, para 2.102.

10 The claim form can be signed on behalf of the claimant.

11 Claims should be made on Form AFCSWPS001, which can be downloaded from the Veterans UK website at www.gov.uk/government/publications/afcs-and-war-pensions-scheme-claim-form.

12 AFCS 2011, art 7(1) provides that a document is 'given or sent' to Veterans UK on the date when it is received by Veterans UK.

13 The address of Veterans UK is Ministry of Defence, Norcross, Thornton Cleveleys, Lancashire FY5 3WP.

43(2) allows for a claim under the SPO 2006 to be treated as an Armed Forces Compensation Scheme claim if the claim was made by a claimant who is in service on or after 6 April 2005, or by a surviving spouse, civil partner, or adult dependant of such a claimant.

When a claim is not required

Discharge on medical grounds

13.4 A claim is not required if a claimant is discharged on medical grounds.[14] By article 2(3) of the AFCS 2011, a person is 'discharged on medical grounds' if the discharge is on the grounds that the person is medically unfit to continue in service, and as a result is entitled to an ill-health pension. In such cases, Veterans UK will automatically consider whether the principal medical condition leading to the medical discharge has been caused by service. If it is decided that the injury was not caused by service, Veterans UK will consider whether the condition is a pre-existing or non-service-related injury that has been made worse by service, entitling the claimant to an award under the Armed Forces Compensation Scheme.[15] The injury is not considered for compensation under the Armed Forces Compensation Scheme if there has already been a successful or unsuccessful Scheme claim in respect of the injury.[16] A 'deemed claim' for injury benefit[17] under this provision applies only to injury benefit in respect of the injury that caused the discharge and any injuries arising from that injury, or from the incident that caused the injury.[18]

Death in service

13.5 A claim for death benefit is not required if a person dies whilst serving in the forces. If a claimant dies whilst serving in the forces leaving an eligible child,[19] but leaving no surviving spouse, civil partner or surviving adult dependant[20] on the date of death, a claim for a child's payment must be made on the child's behalf.[21]

14 AFCS 2011, art 45(1)(a).

15 I.e. under AFCS 2011, art 9 (see para **14.10**).

16 Ministry of Defence, *Armed Forces Compensation Scheme Statement of Policy*, JSP 765 (December 2015), para 5.3.

17 Defined in AFCS 2011, art 2 as a lump sum, a supplementary award and a GIP.

18 AFCS 2011, art 45(5).

19 Defined in AFCS 2011, art 31; see para **20.10**.

20 Defined in AFCS 2011 art 30; see para **20.4**.

21 AFCS 2011, art 45(6).

Additional benefit

13.6 No claim is required for additional benefit[22] and the provisions in article 46 of the AFCS 2011 for determining when a claim is deemed to have been made do not apply in these cases.

TIME LIMIT FOR BRINGING A CLAIM

13.7 The AFCS 2011 increased the AFCS 2005 time limit for bringing a claim from 5 to 7 years. Under article 47 of the AFCS 2011, subject to exceptions in exceptional circumstances[23] and in cases of physical or mental incapacity,[24] the latest date for making a claim for injury benefit is now 7 years beginning with the earliest of the following:

- (i) the day on which the injury occurs;
- (ii) the day on which an injury which is not caused by service is made worse by service;[25]
- (iii) the day on which the claimant's service ends;
- (iv) if the claim is in respect of an illness, the day on which the claimant first seeks medical advice about the illness.[26]

Since injury must be assessed on the basis of the claimant's condition at the date on which a decision on the claim is made,[27] and not at the date when the injury is sustained, and in view of the limited powers of review under the Armed Forces Compensation Scheme, careful consideration may need to be given to the timing of a claim in order to minimise the risk of a deterioration in a claimant's condition after an award on the claim has been made. However, it must also be borne in mind that, except where expressly provided for, there is no power to extend the time limits for bringing an Armed Forces Compensation Scheme claim.

---

22 I.e. an additional award under AFCS 2011, art 75 in respect of an award paid before 9 May 2011 as a result of the retrospective implementation of the Boyce Review recommendations.

23 See para **13.10**.

24 See para **13.11**.

25 Since AFCS 2011, art 9 does not allow a claim for worsening to be made during service, it is not clear how this provision is intended to operate if a claimant's service ends more than 7 years after worsening of an injury occurs.

26 AFCS 2011, art 2 defines 'illness' as 'a physical or mental disorder included either in the International Statistical Classification of Diseases and Related Health Problems or in the Diagnostic and Statistical Manual of Mental Health Disorders'.

27 See *Secretary of State for Defence v Duncan and McWilliams* [2009] EWCA Civ 1043, [2009] All ER (D) 121 (Oct), discussed in Chapter 18.

13.8 The time limit for bringing a claim for injury benefit is extended by 3 years from the date of diagnosis if an illness first presents within the normal 7-year period for bringing the claim, but the diagnosis is made less than 1 year before the end of the period. In the case of a claim for death benefit where a claim is required because death occurs after the end of service, the time limit for bringing a claim in respect of a death which occurs within 7 years from the end of service is 3 years beginning with the date of death.

Claims for fast payments and medical expenses

13.9 A claim for a fast payment[28] must be made within 6 months beginning on the date on which the injury occurs and a claim for medical expenses[29] must be made before the expenses are incurred, unless prior approval was not reasonably practicable due to a medical emergency.

Late onset illness

13.10 The above time limits do not apply to a claim for a late onset illness which has been diagnosed by an accredited medical specialist,[30] or where the death of a claimant has been caused by a late onset illness, or the predominant cause of the death is an injury for which an award of injury benefit has been made at tariff levels 1 to 9 (inclusive).[31] 'Late onset illness' is defined in article 3 of the AFCS 2011 as:

(a) a malignancy, or other physical disorder which is capable of being caused by an occupational exposure occurring 7 or more years before the onset of the illness or the date of death as the case may be;
(b) a mental disorder which is capable of being caused by an incident occurring 7 or more years before the onset of the illness; or
(c) a mental disorder capable of being caused by an incident occurring less than 7 years before the date of onset of the illness, which disorder is capable of causing the person suffering from it to be unable to seek medical help for the disorder within 7 years of the date of onset of the illness.

In such cases, the time limit for bringing a claim is 3 years beginning with the date on which the late onset illness was first diagnosed, or the date of death.

---

28 Under AFCS 2011, art 27 (see para **19.30**).

29 Under AFCS 2011, art 28 (see para **19.35**).

30 Defined in AFCS 2011, art 2 as 'a medical practitioner whose name is included in the specialist register kept and published by the General Medical Council as required by section 34D of the Medical Act 1983'.

31 AFCS 2011, art 48.

Claimant physically or mentally incapable of making claim

13.11 If a claimant is physically or mentally incapable of making a claim for injury or death benefit, or instructing another person to make a claim on his or her behalf, throughout the period in which a claim can be made, there is power to extend the period for bringing the claim for such further period as is reasonable in all the circumstances of the case. In cases where the incapacity has existed for only part of the period, but there has been insufficient time for a claimant to make a claim, or instruct someone to do so on his or her behalf, the time for bringing the claim can be extended by up to 3 years.[32]

WITHDRAWAL OR AMENDMENT OF CLAIMS

13.12 Under article 50 of the AFCS 2011, a claim can be amended or withdrawn by written notice to Veterans UK at any time before the decision on the claim is issued. A claim which has been withdrawn cannot be reinstated, but a new claim can be made, subject however to the normal time limits.

FAILURE TO PROVIDE INFORMATION OR TO ATTEND MEDICAL EXAMINATION

13.13 Article 63 of the AFCS 2011 provides that a claim is to be treated 'as never having been made' if:

- (i) having been requested in writing to provide further information which is reasonably required for the determination of the claim, the claimant fails to do so within 3 months of the date on which the request is made and does not give a satisfactory explanation for the failure;
- (ii) having been given 10 or more days' notice to attend a medical examination at a specified time and place, the claimant fails to attend and fails to provide a satisfactory explanation for the failure within 3 months of the date of the examination.

This provision applies where a claim is made on the claimant's behalf.[33] It does not prevent a new claim from being made.[34]

---

32 AFCS 2011, art 49.

33 AFCS 2011, art 63(3).

34 AFCS 2011, art 63(4).

Chapter 14

Entitlement to Armed Forces Compensation – General Principles

14.1 The Armed Forces Compensation Scheme is a 'no fault' scheme which mirrors the War Pensions Scheme in that benefit is payable for injury caused by service, injury made worse by service, and death caused by service. However, a key difference between the two Schemes is that under the Armed Forces Compensation Scheme, in cases where there is more than one cause of injury or death, a claimant is only entitled to benefit if service is the predominant cause. Article 2 of the AFCS 2011 defines 'service' as meaning 'service in the armed forces' and 'predominant' as meaning 'more than 50%'.

CAUSATION IN THE ARMED FORCES COMPENSATION SCHEME

Injury 'caused by service' and 'predominant cause'

14.2 Article 8 of the AFCS 2011 provides:

> (1) Subject to articles 11 and 12, benefit is payable to or in respect of a member or former member by reason of an injury which is caused (wholly or partly) by service where the cause of injury occurred on or after 6th April 2005.
>
> (2) Where injury is partly caused by service, benefit is only payable if service is the predominant cause of the injury.

Article 2 of the AFCS 2011 defines 'service' as meaning 'service as a member of the forces' and 'injury' as including illness.

14.3 The meaning of 'caused by service' and 'predominant cause' in the context of the AFCS 2005 was considered by Judge Mesher in *EW v Secretary of*

State (AFCS).[1] The claimant in that case was a member of the British element of a multinational Rapid Reaction Corps stationed at the Citadelle in Lille who was not allowed to park at the Unit's headquarters. He was injured on a pedestrian crossing by a hit and run driver while on his way to work, wearing uniform and a high visibility Bergen. Judge Mesher held that the tribunal had erred in law in holding that the claimant could succeed only if he fell within the inclusionary 'travel to work' provisions of the 2005 Scheme. The judge held that the test was not whether a claimant was in service or on duty at the time of the incident in question, but whether the injury was caused, and predominantly caused, by service. The judge held (at [27]) that service was not a cause of the claimant's injury because:

> The injury on the journey to work being a manifestation of a risk run by the general public using the streets of Lille, that injury could not properly be regarded as caused by his service, let alone being predominantly caused by service. Nor was the nature of that risk in any way restricted to Lille as compared with any other place, including within the United Kingdom, where he might have been posted and had to live in non-service accommodation.

In *SV v Secretary of State for Defence (AFCS)*,[2] a case in which the claimant was very seriously injured in an off-duty diving accident, Judge Mesher emphasised that each case must be considered on its own merits. The fact that an injury is a manifestation of risk run by members of the general public does not necessarily mean that the injury has not been caused by service.

14.4 The principles of causation underlying the Armed Forces Compensation Scheme were considered in detail by a three-judge panel of the Upper Tribunal (Charles J, Judge Rowland and Judge Lane) in *JM v Secretary of State for Defence (AFCS)*.[3] The appellant made claims under the AFCS 2005, including a claim in respect of depression which he alleged was the result of a campaign of bullying and verbal abuse. The First-tier Tribunal dismissed the claimant's appeal against the rejection of his claim, holding that his depression was 'due to multiple factors and in particular personal, domestic and marital stress'. The Upper Tribunal allowed the claimant's appeal against that decision on the grounds of inadequacy of reasoning and procedural unfairness, and also gave detailed guidance on the steps to be taken in applying the Armed Forces Compensation Scheme causation test.

14.5 Although the Armed Forces Compensation Scheme requires the identification of 'service' as the cause, or predominant cause, of injury or death,

1 [2012] UKUT 186 (AAC), [2012] AACR 3.

2 [2013] UKUT 541 (AAC).

3 [2015] UKUT 332 (AAC).

the Upper Tribunal observed that 'service' is an abstract concept and (at [81] and [82]) that it is therefore necessary, as a matter of language and concept, to identify the events or processes – the 'process' cause or causes of the injury – and then to ask whether it is, or they are, sufficiently linked to service[4] to satisfy the test that the injury due to each process cause is caused by service (or, using a shorthand, that the process cause is a service cause).

14.6 By article 6(2) of the AFCS 2005 (and article 7(2) of the AFCS 2011), 'the rules of [the Armed Forces Compensation Scheme] are to be construed without reference to any other scheme applicable to the armed forces', but the Upper Tribunal nevertheless held (at [74]) that the war pensions instruments and the cases decided under them provide part of the background that assist in the identification of the underlying purposes of the Armed Forces Compensation Scheme Orders and thus their construction and application. The Service Pensions Order case law relating to 'attributable to service' therefore remains relevant because the cases give guidance on the link that is required between the 'process' cause and service to make it a service cause and so to satisfy the test that injury be caused wholly or partly by service. However, the Upper Tribunal stressed that its guidance on the relevance of cases decided under the War Pensions Scheme did not address the new Armed Forces Compensation Scheme 'predominancy test' (at [88] and [90]). The Upper Tribunal held that, as with the War Pensions Scheme,[5] while it is permissible to derive assistance from general principles of causation in areas of law such as employment law, social security law or the law of tort, there is no justification for importing into the field of war pensions principles of liability from other areas of law (at [95]).

14.7 Applying that analysis, the Upper Tribunal held (at [118]) that the correct approach to the issues of cause and predominant cause under the Armed Forces Compensation Scheme is:

- (i) first, identify the potential process cause or causes (i.e. the events or processes operating on the body or mind that have caused the injury);
- (ii) secondly, discount potential process causes that are too remote or uncertain to be regarded as a relevant process cause;
- (iii) thirdly, categorise the relevant process cause or causes by deciding whether the circumstances in which process causes operated were service or non-service causes. It is at this stage that a consideration of those circumstances comes into play, and the old cases on the

4 Often referred to as a 'factor of service'.

5 See para **3.8**.

identification of a service cause applying the old attributability test provide guidance;

(iv) fourthly, if all the relevant process causes are not categorised as service causes, apply the predominancy test.

On that basis, the Upper Tribunal held (at [123]) that in *EW v Secretary of State for Defence*[6] and *SV v Secretary of State for Defence (AFCS)*,[7] it had been unnecessary to consider whether service was the predominant cause of injury because the only question in each case was whether the 'process' cause – being struck by a car in one case and diving onto a sandbank in the other – was a service cause.

14.8 The Upper Tribunal considered that its approach would not prevent a successful claim under the Armed Forces Compensation Scheme in cases such as *Marshall v Minister of Pensions*,[8] where a claimant has a constitutional vulnerability to the injury giving rise to the claim. It held:

> 130. It is noteworthy that in all the cases to which Denning J referred there was a constitutional cause or predisposition to injury (and we refer to them as constitutional weaknesses of the claimant) as well as the crime or the stress or strain of employment.
>
> 131. We do not consider that Denning J's discussion of 'predominant cause' in *Marshall* provides persuasive guidance on how to apply the 'predominancy test' under the AFCS because he was dealing with a war pensions instrument in which the predominance of a cause was immaterial. Indeed, the main reason he referred to 'predominant cause' was to put paid to an error in construing the instrument into which the Minister and his medical advisers had fallen and for which there was no justification in its wording. Further, he gives no indication of the basis for his classification of predominant and lesser causes.
>
> 132. In this context we do not see any sign that the intention behind the AFCS is to deprive those with constitutional weaknesses from the protection usually regarded as appropriate in other compensation schemes, that is to say the 'thin skull' approach.
>
> 133. We acknowledge that, in exercising the judgment between process causes that have been categorised into service and non-service causes of the injury, a literal approach to the language of the test in the 2005 and 2011 Orders could, in an equivalent case to *Marshall*, found the view expressed by Denning J with the result that the claimant would not get an award because the predominant cause of the injury was the constitutional weakness and the cough was a lesser cause.
>
> 134. But in our view the width of the language permits a more sophisticated approach to deciding whether, as the Secretary of State put it, conceptually the service cause contributes more than one half of the causative stimulus for the injury

6 [2011] UKUT 186, [2012] AACR 3.

7 [2013] UKUT 541 (AAC).

8 See para **3.9**.

claimed, and thus whether service is the predominant cause in a case where (after the categorisation process) the only competing causes are service and constitutional or other pre-existing weaknesses. In such a case the decision-maker generally should firstly consider whether, without the 'service cause', the injury would:

a) have occurred at all, or

b) have been less than half as serious.

135. If the answer to the first question is that the injury would not have occurred at all in the absence of the service cause, we consider that this can and generally should found a conclusion that the service cause is the predominant cause of the relevant injury. It seems likely that a claimant in Mr Marshall's position would succeed on this basis.

136. If however that is not the answer to the first question, the second question will generally found the answer to whether the service cause is the predominant cause of the relevant injury. Thus the second question is likely to be determinative in the present case if it is found that the claimant's depression was caused both by service and by pre-existing domestic factors.

137. We consider that this approach fits with and promotes the underlying intention of the AFCS to pay compensation for an injury that has more than one process cause that under the categorisation exercise we have described fall to be taken into account as respectively service and non-service causes.

138. We repeat that this is not intended to be prescriptive guidance and that it may need to be modified or abandoned in some cases. For example, we acknowledge that timing issues could cause complications that warrant a departure from it.

INJURY MADE WORSE BY SERVICE

14.9 The circumstances in which a claimant can recover compensation under the Armed Forces Compensation Scheme for injury made worse by service are very limited. If an injury was caused by service after 6 April 2005 and has got worse before a final decision on the claim has been made, or is expected to get worse in the future, that worsening can be taken into account in making an award, or in some circumstances on a review of the award. Article 9 of the AFCS 2011 deals with cases where the original injury was *not* caused by service after 6 April 2005, either because it pre-dated service, or because it occurred during service but was not predominantly caused by service. In such cases, benefit is payable to *former* members of the forces who have been downgraded if the pre-existing injury has been worsened by service, but only if the predominant cause of the worsening of the injury was service after 6 April 2005.[9] Benefit is also payable to claimants who have been downgraded if an injury arose during service but was not caused by service, but again only if service after 6 April 2005 was the predominant cause of the worsening of the injury. Since benefit is only payable

9 AFCS 2011, art 9(1).

for the worsening of an injury if a person remains continually downgraded until service ends, a claim for worsening cannot be made prior to the termination of service. However, if a claim is made after that date in respect of an injury that is alleged to have been caused by service and the claim is rejected, Veterans UK will automatically consider whether the injury has been worsened by service.[10]

Qualifying injury

14.10 Under article 9(1) of the AFCS 2011, benefit is payable to a person in respect of an injury made worse by service if the injury:

(a) was sustained before the person entered service and was recorded in the person's entry medical,
(b) was sustained before the person entered service but without the person's knowledge and the injury was not found at the entry medical, or
(c) arose during service but was not caused by service.

Accordingly, benefit is not payable for the worsening of an injury if a person was aware of the injury and did not disclose it and the injury was not found at the person's entry medical.

14.11 In *JN v Secretary of State for Defence (AFCS)*,[11] which was decided under the corresponding provisions of the AFCS 2005, Judge Mesher held that:

(i) the term 'sustained' in (a) and (b), above, must cover the existence of some pre-service degenerative or other condition (such as arthritis), but not a mere susceptibility to injury (at [32]);
(ii) in order to succeed under (c), above, a claimant must show[12] that the injury which is alleged to have been worsened arose during service, whether before or after 6 April 2005, but was not caused by service, whether before or after that date;
(iii) service is only a cause of the injury if it was the predominant cause, so that a claimant does not have to show that service played no part in causing the injury which is alleged to have worsened since 6 April 2005 (at [27] and [28]).

10 Ministry of Defence, *Armed Forces Compensation Scheme Statement of Policy*, JSP 765 (December 2015), para 2.20.

11 [2013] UKUT 479 (AAC).

12 Because the burden of proof is on the claimant (see para **16.1**).

Worsening

14.12 In cases of the worsening of an injury which existed prior to service,[13] benefit is not payable if the injury is worsened less than 6 months or more than 5 years from the day on which service commenced.[14]

Downgrading

14.13 In cases where a pre-existing injury has been worsened,[15] article 9(3) of the AFCS 2011 specifies the circumstances in which downgrading[16] confers entitlement to benefit. In such cases, benefit is only payable if:

(a) the person was downgraded within the period of 5 years starting on the day on which the person entered service;
(b) the downgrading lasted for a period of at least 6 months (except where the member was discharged on medical grounds within that period);
(c) the person remained continually downgraded until service ends; and
(d) the worsening was the predominant cause of the downgrading.

14.14 For cases where injury arose during service but the injury was not caused by service,[17] article 9(5) of the AFCS 2011 provides that benefit is only payable if:

(a) the person was downgraded within the period of 5 years starting on the day on which the person sustained the injury and remains continually downgraded until service ends; and
(b) the worsening was the predominant cause of the downgrading.[18]

DEATH CAUSED BY SERVICE

14.15 Subject to the exceptions considered in Chapter 15, article 10(1) of the AFCS 2011 provides that benefit is payable in respect of the death of a member or former member of the forces by reason of the member's death if the death was caused wholly or partly by service and the cause of death occurred on or after

13 I.e. cases under AFCS 2011, art 9(1)(a) or 9(1)(b).

14 AFCS 2011, art 9(4).

15 I.e. cases under AFCS 2011, art 9(1)(a) or 9(1)(b).

16 AFCS 2011, art 2 defines 'downgraded' as meaning 'downgraded for medical reasons as a result of which the person downgraded undertakes a reduced range of duties but retains rank and pay'.

17 I.e. cases under AFCS 2011, art 9(1)(c).

18 See *JN v Secretary of State for Defence (AFCS)* [2012] UKUT 479 (AAC), [38] for an analysis of how this provision should be applied in cases of successive periods of downgrading.

6 April 2005 if one of the conditions in article 10(3) is satisfied. If death was caused partly by service, benefit is payable only if service was the predominant cause.[19]

14.16 Under article 10(3) of the AFCS 2011, death benefits are payable in respect of deaths which satisfy the above conditions if death occurs while a claimant is in service. If death occurs within 7 years of the termination of service, benefit is payable if death was caused by an injury which was caused by service, or by the worsening by service of an injury which existed before or arose during service and which was not caused by service. This latter condition is not linked to the conditions of entitlement to a benefit for an injury made worse by service. If death occurs more than 7 years after the end of service, death benefits are payable only if death is caused by a late onset illness,[20] or the predominant cause of death is an injury for which an award of injury benefit has been made which gave rise to an entitlement within tariff levels 1 to 9 (inclusive).[21]

---

19 See *JN v Secretary of State for Defence (AFCS)* [2012] UKUT 479 (AAC), [130]–[138].

20 'Late onset illness' is defined in AFCS 2011, art 3.

21 See Chapter 18.

Chapter 15

Exclusions from Entitlement

SCOPE OF EXCLUSIONS FROM ENTITLEMENT TO BENEFIT

15.1 Article 11 of the AFCS 2011 specifies exclusions from entitlement to benefit relating to travel between home and work, slipping and tripping, and sports and social events. The AFCS 2005 specified circumstances in which benefit *was* payable under that Order,[1] but article 11 of the AFCS 2011 specifies the circumstances in which benefit is *not* payable. Applying the usual principles of statutory interpretation, the exclusions in article 11 would therefore only apply if a claimant would otherwise be entitled to benefit under articles 8, 9 or 10 because service was the cause, or predominant cause, of the injury, worsening of injury, or death. However, that would very seldom be the case in the situations covered by article 11. Moreover, if service is in fact the cause, or predominant cause, of injury, worsening of an injury or death, it is difficult to justify disqualification from benefit, even in the circumstances provided for by article 11.

15.2 In *CAF/2150* and *2151/2007*,[2] Judge Jacobs held that the exclusionary provisions in article 11 of the AFCS 2005 (the equivalent of article 12 of the AFCS 2011) were merely declaratory because they dealt with situations in which injury, worsening of an injury or death would not normally be regarded as having been caused by service. Since this is also true of the situations covered by article 11 of the AFCS 2011, it seems that the article is intended to operate in the same way, i.e. to specify particular instances in which injury, worsening of an injury or death are not to be regarded as having been caused by service under articles 8, 9 or 10 of the AFCS 2011.

---

1 For an analysis of the earlier provisions, see *EW v Secretary of State for Defence* [2011] UKUT 186. (AAC), [2012] AACR 3.

2 Unreported.

15.3 As Judge Rowland observed in *JG v Secretary of State for Defence (AFCS)*,[3] the drafting of article 11 of the AFCS 2011 is very unsatisfactory. The exclusions in article 11 are subject to exceptions, but the fact that a situation falls within one of the exceptions to an exclusion does not mean that a claimant is necessarily entitled to benefit. In such cases the exclusion will not apply, but it will still be necessary to decide in the normal way whether any of the conditions of entitlement in articles 8, 9 or 10 have been satisfied.

TRAVEL BETWEEN HOME AND WORK

15.4 Subject to the exceptions considered below, article 11(1) of the AFCS 2011 provides:

> (1) … benefit is not payable to or in respect of a person by reason of an injury sustained by a member, the worsening of an injury, or death which is caused (wholly or partly) by travel from home to place of work or during travel back again.

'By travel'

15.5 The AFCS 2005 referred to an injury, worsening of an injury or death of a person occurring 'while travelling',[4] but article 11 of the AFCS 2011 applies to injury, worsening of an injury or death caused wholly or partly 'by travel' from home to place of work. Since 'travel' by itself cannot be a cause of injury, worsening of an injury or death, it is suggested that when applying this provision a similar approach should be taken as when considering whether something is a 'service' cause (see para **14.7**). Where injury, worsening of an injury or death has been caused in the course of travel, it will be necessary to identify the 'process' cause of the harm (e.g. being struck by a car) and then to decide whether that cause has a sufficiently close connection with travel between a person's home and work in order to decide whether the exclusion applies. Article 11(1) refers to injury, worsening of an injury or death caused wholly or partly 'by' travel from home to place of work, but 'during' travel back again. However, it seems inconceivable that the test of whether the exclusion applies depends on whether a person is on the outward or return journey between home to work, and it is suggested that the 'by travel' test applies in both cases.

---

3 [2014] UKUT 0194 (AAC).

4 AFCS 2005, art 10(4) and (5).

Home

15.6 'Home' is defined in article 11(10)(a) of the AFCS 2011 as 'accommodation, including service accommodation, in which a member has lived or is expected to live for 3 or more months, and a member may have more than one home'. This definition is broad enough to cover accommodation in which a person lives separately from the rest of his or her family whilst working, including accommodation in an overseas country to which a person has been posted. It also covers one of two or more homes occupied by a person who lives singly.

Place of work

15.7 'Place of work' is defined in article 11(10)(b) of the AFCS 2011 as 'the place of work to which a member is assigned or temporarily attached'. While the definition of 'home' requires a degree of permanence, the definition of 'place of work' covers any place of work to which a person has been assigned or temporarily attached, although not a place to which a person is merely directed to go in the course of his or her work. An operational theatre is not regarded by Veterans UK as a place of work.[5]

Exceptions to travel exclusion

Change of place of work

15.8 Under article 11(2)(b) of the AFCS 2011, the exclusion in respect of travel between home and work does not apply 'where a member is changing a place of work in the United Kingdom to a place outside the United Kingdom or during travel back again'. This exception clearly covers travel from home to a new place of work outside the United Kingdom, but apparently not where the old and the new place of work are both abroad. The position with regard to the return journey is also unclear: presumably, the exception is intended to apply where a person is posted back to the United Kingdom following a posting abroad.

Travel to and from approved sporting activities

15.9 By article 11(2)(a) of the AFCS 2011, the disqualification in article 11(1) does not apply to outward or return journeys between a person's home or place of work and a place where a sporting activity approved by the Defence Council

---

5 Ministry of Defence, *Armed Forces Compensation Scheme Statement of Policy*, JSP 765 (December 2015), para 2.25.

is taking place. Article 11(6) specifies what activities can be approved[6] and requires that prior to a sporting event the relevant Service has recognised the event and the organisation and training for it. By article 11(10)(c), 'sporting activity' includes an adventurous expedition approved by the Defence Council, and article 11(7) provides that the Defence Council may approve a single sport or sporting activity or a class of activities and may approve such activities unconditionally or subject to any specified condition.

Acts of terrorism and travelling to or from emergencies

15.10 Article 11(1) of the AFCS 2011 does not disqualify a claimant from benefit in the situations covered by article 11(9), that is:

> (9) where the injury, the worsening of the injury or death was caused (wholly or partly) by reason of—
>
> (a) acts of terrorism or other warlike activities in each case directed towards the person as a member of the forces as such; or
>
> (b) the member being called out to and travelling to an emergency.

In *CAF/2150* and *2151/2007*,[7] Judge Jacobs held that under the AFCS 2005 a claimant who was a chef and who was killed in a road accident whilst driving to work early, because the chefs under him had not reported for work and the civilian kitchen staff were under suspicion of theft, was not 'called out to or travelling to an emergency'. However, on appeal to the Court of Appeal the decision was set aside by consent and it is therefore not binding authority.[8] It is arguable that the word 'emergency' in this statutory context does not require any element of danger or requirement for military involvement, but only something in the nature of a pressing necessity to undertake the travel in the course of which an accident has occurred.

SLIPPING, TRIPPING AND FALLING

15.11 Subject to the exceptions considered below, article 11(3) of the AFCS 2011 provides that benefit is not payable 'to or in respect of a person by reason

---

6 The approved sporting activities are set out in Ministry of Defence, *Sport in the UK Armed Forces*, JSP 660.

7 Unreported.

8 See the observations of Judge Mesher in *EW v Secretary of State for Defence (AFCS)* [2011] UKUT 186 (AAC), [2012] AACR 3, [23].

of an injury sustained by a member, the worsening of an injury, or death which is caused (wholly or partly) by that member slipping, tripping or falling'.

Exceptions to slipping, tripping and falling exclusion

Hazardous activities and training

15.12 Article 11(3) of the AFCS 2011 does not disqualify a claimant from benefit where the member was participating in one of the activities specified in article 11(4) in pursuance of a service obligation, that is:

(a) activity of a hazardous nature;
(b) activity in a hazardous environment; or[9]
(c) training to improve or maintain the effectiveness of the forces.

These activities do not have to be approved sporting activities for the exception to apply.

Acts of terrorism and emergencies

15.13 The exclusion from entitlement to benefit in respect of slipping, tripping and falling is subject to the exceptions with regard to acts of terrorism or warlike activities and attendance at emergencies considered at para **15.10**.

DISQUALIFICATION RELATING TO SPORT

15.14 Unless a person is taking part in an approved sporting activity (see para **15.9**), benefit is not payable in respect of an injury, the worsening of an injury, or death which is caused (wholly or partly) by participation in sporting activity as a player, referee, or organiser or representative of a particular sport or sporting organisation. The exclusion does not apply in cases of acts of terrorism or warlike activities or attending an emergency considered at para **15.10**.

SOCIAL EVENTS

15.15 Subject to the exception in respect of acts of terrorism and warlike activities and attendance at emergencies considered at para **15.10**, article 11(8)(a) of the AFCS 2011 provides that benefit is not payable to or in respect of a person

---

9 A ship is regarded by Veterans UK as a hazardous environment, Ministry of Defence, *Armed Forces Compensation Scheme Statement of Policy*, JSP 765 (December 2015), para 2.29.

by reason of an injury sustained by a member, the worsening of an injury, or death which is caused (wholly or partly) by reason of attendance at a social event unless attendance was required by an order.[10] Article 11(8)(b) extends the disqualification to 'free time or a social event' associated with the sporting activities set out in article 11(5) (see para **15.9**).

OTHER EXCLUSIONS

15.16 Under article 12(1) of the AFCS 2011, benefit is not payable to, or in respect of, a person by reason of an injury sustained by a member, the worsening of an injury, or death which is caused (wholly or partly) by:

- (a) the use or effect of tobacco;
- (b) the consumption of alcohol;
- (c) the non-therapeutic use of drugs;
- (d) consensual sexual activity;
- (e) except where article 9 applies [i.e. injury made worse by service], events, experiences, exposures and activities occurring before the member or former member entered service;
- (f) an illness which is—
  - (i) caused by a single gene defect or is predominantly hereditary in origin;
  - (ii) a personality disorder;
  - (iii) an endogenous infection; or
  - (iv) an exogenous infection except where the infection is acquired in a non-temperate region and the person infected has been exposed to the infection in the course of service or where, in a temperate region, there has been an outbreak of the infection in service accommodation or a workplace; or
- (g) a self-inflicted injury whether or not causing death except where the self-inflicting of injury is a result of a mental illness caused by service.

---

10 See the observations of Judge Rowland with regard to the obscurity of this provision in *JG v Secretary of State for Defence (AFCS)* [2014] UKUT 0194 (AAC).

Chapter 16

Adjudication

BURDEN AND STANDARD OF PROOF

Burden of proof

16.1 Unlike the War Pensions Scheme, which puts the onus on the Secretary of State to disprove entitlement to benefit,[1] the Armed Forces Compensation Scheme places the burden of proving any issue on the claimant. In a memorandum to the Defence Select Committee submitted in 2002, the Ministry of Defence explained the reason for the change as follows:

> The burden of proof which operates for the war pension scheme was devised at a time when there was no developed social welfare system on which soldiers returning from the First World War could depend on for medical or financial support. In addition, the medical understanding of the causes and course of illness or injuries was much more limited than now. Hence the burden of 'disproof' was placed on the Government rather than the individual. In introducing a new scheme it seems right to adopt modern practice and require a burden of proof based on 'a balance of probabilities'.[2]

16.2 In accordance with the recommendations of the Boyce Review,[3] the Armed Forces Compensation Scheme places the burden of proving any issue on the claimant, but this principle is subject to an exception in cases where a contemporary official record relating to a material fact is missing. In such cases, there is a presumption in favour of the claimant where there is other reliable evidence of the fact in question, although this does not prevent the fact from being disproved by the Secretary of State. A 'material fact' need not be decisive, and a

---

1 See, generally, Chapters 3, 4 and 5.

2 *Memorandum from the Ministry of Defence* (1 March 2002), cited in Defence Select Committee, Third Report of Session 2001–02, HC 666 (1 May 2002), Ev 42.

3 Boyce Review, para 2.123.

record is treated as missing if it cannot be found after a diligent search or has been destroyed. Article 60 of the AFCS 2011 provides:

> (1) Subject to the provisions of this article, the burden of proving any issue is on the claimant.
>
> (2) Where paragraph (3) applies there is a presumption in favour of the claimant unless the Secretary of State proves to the contrary.
>
> (3) This paragraph applies where—
>
> (a) a contemporary official record relating to a material fact which is relevant to deciding a condition for payment of benefit under Part 2 is missing; and
>
> (b) there is other reliable evidence[4] to determine the material fact.
>
> (4) For the purpose of paragraph (3)—
>
> (a) 'a contemporary official record' means a record, including an electronic record, held by the Secretary of State for Defence or the Defence Council;
>
> (b) 'a material fact' need not be a decisive fact for the purpose of determining a claim under Part 2;
>
> (c) a record is missing where it has been—
>
> (i) lost and cannot be found after a diligent search; or
>
> (ii) destroyed.

16.3 Article 60 of the AFCS 2011 should be read in the light of the observations of Baroness Hale of Richmond in *Kerr v Department for Social Development*,[5] in which it was held that a failure by either party to play their proper part in an investigative system of adjudication might result in a finding against that party.[6] After referring to *R v Medical Appeal Tribunal (North Midland Region) ex parte Hubble*,[7] Baroness Hale said:

> [62] What emerges from all this is a co-operative process of investigation in which both the claimant and the department play their part. The department is the one which knows what questions it needs to ask and what information it needs to have in order to determine whether the conditions of entitlement have been met. The claimant is the one who generally speaking can and must supply that information. But where the information is available to the department rather than the claimant, then the department must take the necessary steps to enable it to be traced.

---

4 See para **5.2** for the meaning of 'reliable evidence' in the context of the SPO 2006.

5 [2004] UKHL 23, [2004] 1 WLR 1372 (also included as an appendix to *R1/04(SF)*).

6 See the observations of the three-judge panel of the Upper Tribunal in *JM V Secretary of State for Defence* [2015] UKUT 332 (AAC), [32].

7 [1958] 2 QB 228.

> [63] If that sensible approach is taken, it will rarely be necessary to resort to concepts taken from adversarial litigation such as the burden of proof. The first question will be whether each partner in the process has played their part. If there is still ignorance about a relevant matter then generally speaking it should be determined against the one who has not done all they reasonably could to discover it. As Mr Commissioner Henty put it in decision *CIS/5321/1998*, 'a claimant must to the best of his or her ability give such information to the [adjudication officer] as he reasonably can, in default of which a contrary inference can always be drawn.' The same should apply to information which the department can reasonably be expected to discover for itself.

Missing official records

16.4 The Boyce Review concluded that the burden and standard of proof under the Armed Forces Compensation Scheme should be modified in cases where a claimant might be placed at a disadvantage because relevant records had been lost, and in cases where claimants were disadvantaged by the lack of a system of prescribed diseases in armed forces compensation cases equivalent to that in the social security industrial injuries disablement benefit scheme. So far as the first situation is concerned, the Review recommended[8] that, where records which bear on a material issue have genuinely been lost by the Ministry of Defence, the standard rules and guidance to decision-makers should be modified so as to assist the individual service person by affording the benefit of a presumption, transferring the burden of proof to the Ministry of Defence on the balance of probabilities. In an injury case, this would work in the following way (at para 2.215):

> If the individual through appropriate evidence demonstrates on the balance of probabilities that s/he has an injury which was suffered while undertaking an activity in the course of service, it will be presumed that it was due to service, unless the MoD through appropriate evidence proves on the balance of probabilities that it was not.

The Boyce Review considered that, in accordance with standard legal principles in courts and tribunals, 'appropriate evidence' would include, but not be limited to, the individual's own consistent and credible evidence and/or consistent and credible corroborative testimony from family members, service or other colleagues, and a commanding or superior officer.

16.5 At common law, an adverse inference can be drawn against a party in cases where documents have been destroyed deliberately to prevent their use as evidence.[9]

---

8 Boyce Review, para 2.14.

9 *The Ophelia* [1916] 2 AC 206. The principle does not apply in cases where documents have been routinely destroyed (see *R(IS) 11/92*).

Standard of proof

16.6 Article 61 of the AFCS 2011 provides:

> 61. The standard of proof applicable in any decision which is required to be made under this Order is the balance of probabilities.

The term 'standard of proof' is used to denote the degree of probability with which an issue must be established. Proof on the balance of probabilities is the normal standard of proof in civil proceedings and is satisfied if a tribunal can say on the evidence that something is more probable than not (*per* Denning J in *Miller v Minister of Pensions*[10]).

EVIDENCE

16.7 Article 62 of the AFCS 2011 provides:

> (1) For the purposes of determining any issue under this Order, the Secretary of State is to produce such medical or other records of a member or a former member (whether living or deceased), as are held by the Secretary of State for Defence or the Defence Council and are relevant to the issues to be decided.
>
> (2) The Secretary of State is to consider any evidence which appears to be relevant to the issues which are to be decided and is to determine those issues on that evidence.
>
> (3) Where any decision required to be made under this Order is, or includes, a decision involving a medical issue, that decision is to be made in accordance with generally accepted medical and scientific knowledge prevailing at the time the decision is made.

16.8 Article 62(1) of the AFCS 2011 requires the Secretary of State to produce all relevant medical and other records in coming to a decision on a claim, but it is clear from article 62(2) that the evidence on which a decision is to be based is not limited to service records. Article 62(2) requires the Secretary of State to consider all relevant evidence which, as the Boyce Review pointed out, may include evidence of claimants themselves and other supporting testimony. Such evidence can be accepted if there is no official record of a fact required to establish a claim, but there is also nothing in the Armed Forces Compensation Scheme to prevent it from being accepted in preference to evidence contained in service records if in all the circumstances it should be accorded greater weight.

---

10 [1947] 2 All ER 372.

Medical issues

16.9 Under the War Pensions Scheme, a medical or scientific view which is not generally accepted can nevertheless found sufficient doubt for a claimant to establish liability under article 40 or article 41 of the SPO 2006. However, article 62(3) of the AFCS 2011 requires the Secretary of State to decide medical issues in accordance with generally accepted medical and scientific knowledge at the time the decision is made. The term 'generally accepted medical and scientific knowledge' suggests a high degree of consensus of opinion on the issue in question and, if no such consensus exists, it will be necessary to resolve a conflict of views on a scientific or medical question on a balance of probabilities, in accordance with article 61 of the AFCS 2011.

16.10 The SPVA formerly compiled Medical Appendices, summarising scientific evidence on the aetiology of a large number of medical conditions. These have been replaced by Synopses of Causation, which are used by lay decision-makers when deciding medical questions arising under the Armed Forces Compensation Scheme.

DECISIONS

Lay decision making

16.11 Article 43 of the SPO 2006 requires decisions on medical questions under the War Pensions Scheme to be certified by medical officers or medical specialists, in accordance with article 43(b)(iii). The Armed Forces Compensation Scheme replaced the previous system of medical adjudication with a system of lay decision making, under which it is for the Secretary of State 'to determine any claim for benefit and any question arising out of the claim'.[11] However, lay decision-makers, who make decisions under the Armed Forces Compensation Scheme in the name of the Secretary of State, can obtain advice from medical advisers where necessary. Medical advice is usually sought in the following types of case:

- (i) very serious injuries likely to result in an award at tariff levels 1 to 8;
- (ii) cases involving mental health problems;
- (iii) cases where a supplementary award is likely;
- (iv) temporary awards;
- (v) reconsideration or appeal cases;

---

11 AFCS 2011, art 51(1).

(vi) cases undergoing an exceptional review;
(vii) 'zoning' cases;
(viii) other cases calling for a medical input for example hearing loss and interim awards;
(ix) service termination reviews.[12]

The Boyce Review noted that medical advice was sought in around 50% of cases.[13]

Form of decision

16.12 Under article 51 of the AFCS 2011, the Secretary of State must give reasons for a decision. The decision and reasons must be in writing and must be given or sent to the claimant. The notification must also advise the claimant of his right to apply for a reconsideration of the decision under article 53[14] and of the claimant's rights of appeal to a tribunal.

RECONSIDERATION

16.13 Article 53 of the AFCS 2011 gives claimants the right to apply for a decision to be reconsidered. Reconsideration is separate from the power of review, which can only be exercised on specified grounds.[15] However, if a claimant applies for a review before an application for reconsideration of a decision has been determined, the review application supersedes the application for reconsideration.[16]

Exceptions

16.14 There is no right to apply[17] for reconsideration of a decision to:

(i) make a temporary award under article 26(1) of the AFCS 2011;[18]

---

12 Ministry of Defence, *Armed Forces Compensation Scheme Statement of Policy*, JSP 765 (December 2015), para 2.12.

13 Boyce Review, para 2.95.

14 See paras **16.13–16.18**.

15 See Chapter 17.

16 AFCS 2011, art 53(11).

17 AFCS 2011, art 53(2).

18 See para **19.24**.

(ii) make a fast payment under article 27(1) of the AFCS 2011;[19]
(iii) make an interim award under article 52(1) of the AFCS 2011.[20]

Applying for a reconsideration

16.15 An application for a reconsideration of a decision must be made within 1 year, starting with the date on which notice of the decision was given or sent to the claimant. The application must be in writing and signed by or on behalf of the person making the application, and must specify the ground of the application.[21]

16.16 In cases of physical or mental incapacity, the same provisions for extending the time for making the application apply as for original claims.[22] Article 63 of the AFCS 2011, which provides for an application to be treated as never having been made in cases where a claimant fails to provide information, or to attend a medical examination, also applies to reconsideration applications.[23]

16.17 A decision must be reconsidered if a claimant appeals against the decision to a tribunal and no previous reconsideration has taken place.[24]

Powers on reconsideration

16.18 The Secretary of State's powers on a reconsideration are set out in article 53(3) of the AFCS 2011:

> (3) On a reconsideration of the original decision, the Secretary of State may—
>
> (a) make a new decision which maintains the original decision; or
> (b) revise that decision by—
>
> (i) awarding benefit where no award of benefit was made in the original decision;
> (ii) changing the descriptor applied so as to maintain or increase the amount awarded in the original decision;[25]

19 See para **19.30**.

20 See para **19.27**.

21 AFCS 2011, art 53(4).

22 AFCS 2011, art 53(10) (see para **13.10**).

23 AFCS 2011, art 63(5) (see para **13.13**).

24 AFCS 2011, art 53(5).

25 See Chapter 18 for an explanation of the system of descriptors.

(iii) increasing the amount awarded in the original decision;

(iv) changing the date on which an award of benefit becomes payable.

The form of a reconsideration decision must satisfy the same requirements as those for an original decision.[26]

Further reconsideration applications

16.19 A further reconsideration application can be made only if on reconsideration a decision is revised by the making of a temporary[27] or interim[28] award. In those cases a claimant can make a further reconsideration application when the temporary or interim award is made final.[29]

26 AFCS 2011, art 53(6) (see para **16.12**).

27 See para **19.24**.

28 See para **19.27**.

29 AFCS 2011, art 53(8).

Chapter 17

Review of Armed Forces Compensation Scheme Decisions

REVIEW UNDER THE ARMED FORCES COMPENSATION SCHEME 2011

17.1 The AFCS 2005 allowed for a review of an injury benefit decision if the injury giving rise to the decision worsened or if the injury caused a further injury and the worsening was unexpected and exceptional and occurred within 10 years of the decision which was the subject of the review.[1] The Boyce Review recommended the introduction of a further review power outside the 10-year period in cases where to maintain an award would be manifestly unjust,[2] and this recommendation has been implemented in the AFCS 2011.[3]

Finality of decisions

17.2 Except in cases where a power of review has been expressly provided for (see below), article 54 of the AFCS 2011 stipulates that there is to be no review of a final decision awarding benefit. This provision reflects the policy intention that awards under the Armed Forces Compensation Scheme should be full and final and take due account of the expected progress and prognosis of the injury, including expected deterioration in the future.[4]

17.3 A 'final decision' is defined by article 54(2) of the AFCS 2011 as a decision determining a claim under article 51, a final award made following the making of an interim award under article 52,[5] a decision revising or maintaining

1 AFCS 2005, art 48.

2 Boyce Review, para 2.136.

3 AFCS 2011, art 57.

4 Boyce Review, para 2.130.

5 See para **19.27**.

a decision following a review, and a new or maintained decision following a reconsideration. By article 54(4), decisions are final where there has been no application for reconsideration, or the time for applying for reconsideration has expired.[6]

17.4 Under article 54(2) of the AFCS 2011, a review of a decision which makes no award of benefit can only be reviewed under article 59 (ignorance or mistake).

SERVICE TERMINATION

17.5 Article 55 of the AFCS 2011 provides for a 'once only'[7] power of review in cases where a decision to award injury benefit has been made within 7 years of the day on which service ends and an application for a review of the award is made within 1 year of the termination of service. The provision may therefore apply where a person has been awarded injury benefit and is subsequently medically discharged as a result of the injury for which the benefit was awarded, but it is not limited to such cases.[8] For a decision to be reviewed under article 55, any worsening of an injury or further injury does not have to be unexpected or exceptional, as in the case of other powers of review in respect of deterioration in a claimant's condition.

17.6 Following a review under article 55 of the AFCS 2011, an award can only be revised if the injury in respect of which it has been made has become worse or has caused a further injury to develop, and the injury and/or further injury together is described by a descriptor at a higher tariff level than that previously awarded, or an additional descriptor.[9] In all other cases, a new decision must be made maintaining the original decision. If the revision conditions are not satisfied, a new decision is made maintaining the original decision.

Eligibility

17.7 A decision can be reviewed under article 55 of the AFCS 2011 if:

(i) a person has been awarded injury benefit;

---

6 Except where the decision follows a reconsideration.

7 AFCS 2011, art 55(9).

8 This situation was previously covered by the AFCS 2005, but the scope of this provision is considerably greater.

9 AFCS 2011, art 55(5).

(ii) an injury benefit decision[10] has been made within 7 years of the day of the day on which service ends;[11]
(iii) the person's service has ended.[12]

If a person has had more than one period of service, the time limits under this article apply to the period of service in which the injury giving rise to the award of injury benefit occurred.[13]

Applying for a service termination review

17.8 Article 55(6) of the AFCS 2011 provides that an application for a review under article 55 must be made within 1 year starting with the date on which service ends. The application must be in writing and signed by or on behalf of the person making the application, and must specify the ground of the application.

17.9 In cases of physical or mental incapacity, the same provisions for extending the time for making the review application apply as for original claims.[14] Article 63 of the AFCS 2011 which provides for an application to be treated as never having been made in cases where a claimant fails to provide information, or to attend a medical examination, also applies to review applications under this article.[15]

Form of decision

17.10 A decision on a review application under this article must be in the same form as a decision on a claim.[16]

EXCEPTIONAL CIRCUMSTANCES WITHIN 10 YEARS

17.11 Article 56 of the AFCS 2011 provides for a 'once only'[17] power of review under which an injury benefit decision can be revised if within 10 years starting on the date of the decision:

---

10 See AFCS 2011, art 55(10) for the definition of 'injury benefit decision'.

11 I.e. the period of 7 years before termination of the relevant period of service.

12 AFCS 2011, art 55(1).

13 AFCS 2011, art 55(3).

14 AFCS 2011, art 53(10) (see para **13.11**).

15 AFCS 2011, art 63(5).

16 AFCS 2011, art 55(7).

17 AFCS 2011, art 56(6).

(i) the injury in respect of which the decision relates has become worse or has caused a further injury to develop;
(ii) the worsening or the development of the further injury is unexpected and exceptional;
(iii) the injury and/or further injury together is described by a descriptor at a higher tariff level than that previously awarded, or an additional descriptor.

The terms 'unexpected' and 'exceptional' are not defined, but must clearly exclude deterioration which is a normal consequence of the injury in respect of which the original award was made. If the criteria for revising the decision are not satisfied, a new decision must be made maintaining the original award.[18]

Applying for an exceptional circumstances review

17.12 Article 56(4) of the AFCS 2011 provides that an application for a review under this article must be made within the period of 1 year starting on the day on which the worsening or development of a further injury began. This apparently means the day on which the deterioration actually began, rather than the day on which it reached the stage at which it satisfied the criteria for revision of the original award. It will frequently be difficult to identify a particular day as marking the beginning of the deterioration in a claimant's condition if the deterioration has been gradual.

17.13 The provisions in this article relating to the form of claims and failure to provide information or attend a medical examination are the same as for applications for a service termination review (see para **17.9**).

Form of decision

17.14 As with review decisions under article 55 of the AFCS 2011, review decisions under this article must also be in the same form as a decision on a claim.

REVIEW OF DECISIONS AFTER 10 YEARS

17.15 Article 57 of the AFCS 2011 implements the Boyce Review recommendation that there should be a further power of review after the expiry of 10 years.[19] Under article 57, a decision can be revised following an application

18 AFCS 2011, art 56(2).

19 See para **17.1**.

for a review made more than 10 years after an injury benefit decision was made if it would be manifestly unjust to maintain the effect of the decision under review because:

(i) the injury in respect of which benefit has been awarded has become worse or has caused a further injury to develop;
(ii) the worsening or the development of the further injury is substantial, unexpected and exceptional;
(iii) the injury and/or further injury together is described by a descriptor at a higher tariff level than that previously awarded, or an additional descriptor.

17.16 A claimant applying for a review in respect of deterioration more than 10 years after the original injury benefit decision was made must therefore surmount two additional hurdles. Under article 57(4)(c) of the AFCS 2011, the worsening must be not only 'unexpected and exceptional', but also 'substantial'. However, a worsening which merits a descriptor at a higher tariff level than that originally awarded, or a further descriptor, will necessarily be substantial, so that it is not clear what this requirement adds. The claimant must also show that it would be manifestly unjust to maintain the decision under review, but it is difficult to imagine circumstances in which it would be just to maintain an injury benefit decision if the deterioration in the claimant's condition was substantial, unexpected and exceptional, and merited a different or additional descriptor.

17.17 As with applications for a review within 10 years, there is a time limit under article 57 of the AFCS 2011 of 1 year starting with the day on which the worsening or development of a further injury began for making an application for a review (see the comments in para **17.12**). The provisions with regard to the form of applications and decisions and failure to provide information or attend a medical examination are the same as for service termination reviews (see paras **17.8** and **17.9**).

AWARDS OF DAMAGES

17.18 Article 58 of the AFCS 2011 confers on the Secretary of State a review power to decrease or cancel any award of benefit to take into account any damages which a claimant has recovered in respect of the injury or death for which the award of benefit is payable. This provision provides the machinery for implementing decisions under article 40 to adjust benefits to take account of awards of damages (see para **21.3**). The decision on the review must be in the same form as a decision on a claim.[20]

---

[20] AFCS 2011, art 58(3).

IGNORANCE OR MISTAKE

17.19 Article 59 of the AFCS 2011 provides for an 'any time' power of review at the instigation of the Secretary of State or on the application of a claimant if a decision was given 'in ignorance of, or was based on, a mistake as to a material fact or of a mistake as to the law'.[21] A decision can be reviewed under this provision only if the fact was knowable at the time the decision was made and was disclosed to the Secretary of State (i.e. Veterans UK) at that time, and if the ignorance or mistake was that of the Secretary of State. If the ignorance or mistake relates to the diagnosis of an injury, the decision can be reviewed only where the correct diagnosis was knowable on the basis of medical knowledge at the time when the original diagnosis was made.[22]

Review powers

17.20 On carrying out a review under article 59 of the AFCS 2011, the Secretary of State can make a new decision which maintains the decision under review or revise the decision by:

- (i) awarding benefit where no benefit was originally awarded;
- (ii) changing the descriptor originally awarded so as to maintain, increase or decrease the amount awarded in the original decision;
- (iii) increasing or decreasing the amount awarded in the original decision or cancelling an award of benefit;
- (iv) changing the date on which an award of benefit becomes payable.

Form of decision

17.21 As with review decisions under article 55 of the AFCS 2011, review decisions under this article must be in the same form as a decision on a claim.

---

21 See para **6.4** for a discussion of the meaning of the similar terms in the SPO 2006.

22 AFCS 2011, art 59(2)(c).

Chapter 18

Injury Benefits – The Tariff

THE STRUCTURE OF THE TARIFF

18.1 Unlike the War Pensions Scheme, compensation for injury under the Armed Forces Compensation Scheme is determined by the severity of an injury and its effects, and not by the degree of a claimant's disablement. The Scheme ranks injuries according to their seriousness using a 15-level tariff,[1] with the most serious injuries at level 1 and the least serious at level 15.

18.2 The tariff contains nine tables, each covering a different type of injury, for example Table 1 covers burns and Table 2 covers injury, wounds and scarring. Table 3 covers mental disorders and Table 4 covers physical disorders – illnesses and infectious diseases. Within each table, particular injuries and the effects of such injuries are described by means of descriptors, each of which is assigned a tariff level; for example Table 2, Item 5 is 'Complex injury to chest, with complications, causing permanent significant functional limitation or restriction', and is a level 6 descriptor.

18.3 The tables also contain notes; for example, Table 3 (Mental disorders), Note 1 defines functional limitation or restriction as 'severe' where the claimant is 'unable to undertake work appropriate to experience, qualifications and skills at the time of onset of the illness and over time able to work only in less demanding jobs'. In *Secretary of State for Defence v MJ (AFCS)*,[2] Judge Rowland set aside a tribunal's decision because it was not clear whether the tribunal had regard to the notes to the table, rather than relying solely on dictionary definitions.

---

1 AFCS 2011, Sch 3.

2 [2014] UKUT 0094 (AAC).

THE OVERALL APPROACH TO THE TARIFF

18.4 The Court of Appeal gave guidance on the overall approach to be taken in applying the tariff in the leading case of *Secretary of State for Defence v Duncan and McWilliams*[3] (decided under the 2005 Scheme).

18.5 Corporal Duncan sustained a high velocity gunshot wound as a result of a bullet entering his inner thigh, passing through the underlying muscle and tissue structures and fracturing the femur before being carried across and out of the leg, causing an exit wound. An intramedullary nail was inserted into the leg to stabilise the fracture, but Corporal Duncan needed 11 surgical procedures and there was calcification of the muscles with the result that 6 months after the injury he had reduced rotation of the left hip and his range of movements of both hip and knee was reduced. He needed crutches to help him when walking and his left leg was a little shorter than his right. At the time of the tribunal hearing, he was still experiencing significant pain and had suffered serious mental anguish.

18.6 Marine McWilliams sustained a supracondylar fracture of the right femur during training, which was also fixed with an intramedullary nail. He stated that scarring on his thigh caused him some embarrassment. The tribunal found that he had some trouble with his knee which could give way when he was walking, that running was limited and that he got pain in his left lower leg after 10 minutes walking, that he could not wear combat boots and used trainers only, that he had been told that a further operation was likely and that he would never recover his former level of fitness.

18.7 The Court of Appeal decided that the Upper Tribunal had been wrong in holding that injuries resulting from proper and appropriate medical treatment could be said to exacerbate an injury or involve the creation of a separate injury, and in holding that Table 4 (Physical disorders – illnesses and infectious diseases) could be applied to functional limitations or restrictions resulting from physical injury.

18.8 Elias LJ laid down the following general principles:

(i) The Upper Tribunal was correct in holding that the starting point for all descriptors was the claimant's condition at the date of the decision on the claim (and not the claimant's condition at the date when the injury was sustained) (at [47] to [55]).

(ii) The object of the exercise in choosing the relevant descriptor or descriptors is to find the appropriate descriptor or descriptors which

---

3 [2009] EWCA Civ 1043, [2009] All ER (D) 121 (Oct).

most fully and fairly reflect the various features of the injury or illness, as the case may be. This requires a careful analysis of the facts and then a consideration of which descriptor is most appropriate (at [58]).

(iii) If no descriptor fully reflects the scope of the injury, the remedy is to make a temporary award[4] (at [56]).

(iv) It may be legitimate to cross-refer to other parts of the Scheme in some situations, for example, to decide which of two possible competing descriptors is more appropriate (at [58]). However, it is not legitimate to distort the application of the Scheme by identifying an inappropriate comparator on the basis that, looking at the compensation paid for other injuries, the most appropriate descriptor results in inadequate compensation (at [59]).

(v) In some cases, there will be difficulty in deciding whether related injuries should be considered as a single complex injury or two distinct injuries. It is ultimately a question of fact to determine which most fairly captures the essence of the injury, but it would be perfectly proper to have regard to the potential levels of compensation which would result and to compare them with similar sums awarded for other injuries in the same or other tables, provided it would not involve undue distortion (at [60]).

INTERPRETING THE TARIFF

18.9 In *Secretary of State for Defence v Duncan and McWilliams*,[5] the Court of Appeal also considered the meaning of some specific terms used in the tariff. It held that:

(i) The definition of 'complex injury' in the notes to Table 2 of the 2005 Scheme[6] was a clear definition and that it was a question of fact whether or not the injury affected all or most of the identified structures. In the case of Corporal Duncan, the injury was clearly 'complex' in the terms of the definition (at [79]).

(ii) The question of whether or not a 'complex' injury is limited to the initiating injury will depend on whether the original injury and any subsequent injuries which are to be attributed to service can be treated as a single injury or as two distinct injuries. If they are

4 Under AFCS 2011, art 26 (see para **19.24**).

5 [2009] EWCA Civ 1043, [2009] All ER (D) 121 (Oct).

6 The corresponding definition in the note to AFCS 2011, Sch 3 is, 'when applied to a limb injury the expression "complex injury" means that the injury affects all or most of the following structures: skin, subcutaneous tissues, muscle, bone, blood vessels and nerves'.

treated as a single injury, there is no reason why the second injury could not in an appropriate case change the characterisation of an injury to a complex injury. However, this was likely to be very exceptional because appropriate surgery could not constitute a relevant subsequent injury (at [80]) (but see paras **18.12** and **18.13**).

(iii) The Upper Tribunal was correct in holding that in order to 'cover' the area of a limb, the injury must affect all or most of the limb between (and including) the joints specified in the descriptor in question, whether or not the injury was visible on the surface (at [81] to [89]).

(iv) The Upper Tribunal was correct to hold that the words 'permanent functional limitation or restriction' cover any degree of limitation or restriction which was more than trivial (at [90] to [93]) (but see para **18.14** for the position under the AFCS 2011).

18.10 Amendments to the 2005 Scheme introduced in September 2008[7] contained definitions of the terms 'covering' and 'permanent', but the Boyce Review considered that there was a need for further clarification of some aspects of the Scheme.[8] Article 5(1) of the AFCS 2011 contains further interpretative provisions, which apply to both directly and indirectly affected body structures.[9]

The scope of the descriptors

18.11 In *Secretary of State for Defence v Duncan and McWilliams*,[10] Elias LJ used the term 'trajectory of the injury' to denote the consequences of an injury which are encompassed by a descriptor. Article 5(1) of the AFCS 2011 identifies particular expected effects of an injury and its appropriate clinical management which a descriptor is to be construed as covering, but the list is not exhaustive and does not extend to a consequence of an injury which is a discrete diagnosable disorder, for example a discrete depressive illness caused by pain. The effects of an injury and its appropriate clinical management that are to be taken as encompassed by a descriptor are:

(i) pain and suffering due to the primary injury;
(ii) the effect of operative intervention, including pain, discomfort and suffering;
(iii) the effect of therapeutic drug treatment;

7 By the Armed Forces and Reserve Forces (Compensation Scheme) (Amendment No. 2) Order 2008 (SI 2008/2160).

8 Boyce Review, para 2.81.

9 AFCS 2011, art 5(2).

10 [2009] EWCA Civ 1043, [2009] All ER (D) 121 (Oct).

(iv) the use of appropriate aids and appliances;

(v) associated psychological effects short of a discrete diagnosable disorder.

Medical treatment

18.12 In *Secretary of State for Defence v Duncan and McWilliams*,[11] it was held that additional injury, or the exacerbation of an injury resulting from proper and appropriate treatment of the original injury, was encompassed within the descriptor for the original injury. The Court of Appeal held that the Upper Tribunal had therefore been wrong to hold that the insertion of an intramedullary nail, which was a perfectly proper and appropriate treatment for a broken femur, was capable of converting the initial injury in the case of either claimant into a more serious injury, solely on the ground that it extended the range of the initial injury (at [68]).

18.13 Article 5(1) of the AFCS 2011 is consistent with the approach in *Secretary of State for Defence v Duncan and McWilliams*,[12] in so far as the expected consequences of proper and appropriate medical treatment are concerned. However, article 5(1) deals only with the *expected* effects of medical treatment. If the effects of medical treatment are *unexpected*, the question of whether any additional injury, or exacerbation of the original injury, should be reflected in the descriptor for the injury, or merit the award of an additional descriptor, will depend on whether the new injury or exacerbation of the original injury retains the necessary causal connection with service. In *Duncan and McWilliams*, Elias LJ considered (at [9]) that if medical treatment was the sole or predominant cause of injury, it must follow that service was not the cause, or predominant cause, so that what is now article 8 of the AFCS 2011 would not apply.[13] In such a case, applying the approach in *JM v Secretary of State for Defence (AFCS)*[14] (see para **14.7**), the 'process cause' of the additional injury or exacerbation – i.e. the medical treatment – would not be service-related, so that the result would be the same. Elias LJ considered (at [64]) that additional injury or exacerbation resulting from negligent treatment would 'break the chain of causation' because in those circumstances recovery of benefit would be precluded by article 11(a)(iii) of the AFCS 2005. Although there is no equivalent provision in the AFCS 2011, it is suggested that the result would be the same under the AFCS 2011 because, in accordance with common law principles, negligent medical treatment would generally constitute a new intervening cause of the

11 [2009] EWCA Civ 1043, [2009] All ER (D) 121 (Oct).

12 [2009] EWCA Civ 1043, [2009] All ER (D) 121 (Oct).

13 The exception to the exclusion in AFCS 2005, art 11(a)(iii) relating to emergency operations during military operations abroad has not been included in the AFCS 2011.

14 [2015] UKUT 332 (AAC).

additional injury or exacerbation. A condition such as MRSA contracted while a claimant was being treated in hospital would also not be attributable to service. However, in cases where there has been a deterioration in a person's medical condition following proper and appropriate medical treatment, there would appear to be no reason not to choose a different or additional descriptor encompassing the effects of a new injury, or exacerbation of the original injury, if nothing has occurred to sever the necessary causal link between service and the additional or exacerbated injury.

Functional limitation or restriction

18.14 Article 5(1) and (6) of the AFCS 2011 defines 'functional limitation or restriction' and specifies how it is to be assessed. Article 5(3) provides:

> (3) The term 'functional limitation or restriction' in relation to a descriptor means that, as a result of an impairment arising from the primary injury or its effects, a person—
>
> (a) has difficulty in executing a task or action; or
> (b) is required to avoid a task or action because of the risk of delayed recovery, or injury to self or others.

The Table 8 and Table 9[15] descriptors (Fractures and dislocations, and Musculoskeletal disorders, respectively) frequently require 'significant' functional limitation or restriction. Article 5(7)(b) of the AFCS 2011 provides that functional limitation or restriction is 'significant' where the functional limitation or restriction has an extensive effect. The combined effect of article 5(6) and (7)(b) is therefore to require a much higher degree of functional impairment than limitation which is more than trivial. It therefore differs from the test approved in *Secretary of State for Defence v Duncan and McWilliams*[16] (see para **18.9**).

18.15 Article 5(6) of the AFCS 2011 provides:

> (6) Functional limitation or restriction is to be assessed by—
>
> (a) taking account of the primary injury and its effects; and
> (b) making a comparison between the limitation and restriction of the claimant and the capacity of a healthy person of the same age and sex who is not injured or suffering a health condition.

15 AFCS 2011, Sch 3, Tables 8 and 9.

16 [2009] EWCA Civ 1043, [2009] All ER (D) 121 (Oct).

The term 'primary injury' is not defined. However, if a 'primary' injury has caused another injury, for example, because restricted movement in one leg has led to injury in the other leg, functional limitation or restriction in the second leg can presumably be regarded as one of the effects of the primary injury.

18.16 Article 5(6)(b) of the AFCS 2011 requires a comparison to be made between the claimant's limitation or restriction and that of the capacity of a healthy person of the same age or sex. The process is similar to that used in the War Pensions Scheme to assess a person's degree of disablement, but in the Armed Forces Compensation Scheme it is used for the purpose of deciding whether limitation or restriction is 'significant' in terms of the Table 8 and Table 9[17] descriptors.

Duration of effects

18.17 The choice of a descriptor will often depend on how long significant functional limitation or restriction is expected to last; for example Table 8, Item 27 is 'Fractured tarsal bones on one foot which have caused, or are expected to cause, significant functional limitation or restriction beyond 26 weeks'.[18] Article 5(4) of the AFCS 2011 provides that the period of the duration of the effects of an injury begins on the date of the injury. Article 5(5) provides for an exception in the case of conditions in Tables 3 and 4[19] (Mental disorders, and Physical disorders – illnesses and infectious diseases, respectively), where the period begins on the date that the claimant first sought medical advice in respect of the mental or physical disorder.

18.18 In *Secretary of State for Defence v Duncan and McWilliams*,[20] it was held that a decision-maker should take into account all the information available at the time when the assessment of an injury is made (at [48]). In deciding the actual or likely duration of the effects of an injury, a decision-maker is therefore not confined to considering the evidence as it was at the time when the injury was incurred.

18.19 The duration of mental disorder was considered in *Secretary of State for Defence v PQ (WP)*.[21] Descriptors in Table 3,[22] Items 1 to 3 cover mental disorder causing functional limitation or restriction. A tribunal held that the claimant had

---

17 AFCS 2011, Sch 3, Tables 8 and 9.

18 AFCS 2011, Sch 3, Table 8.

19 AFCS 2011, Sch 3, Tables 3 and 4.

20 [2009] EWCA Civ 1043, [2009] All ER (D) 121 (Oct).

21 [2014] UKUT 0399 (AAC).

22 AFCS 2011, Sch 3, Table 3.

functional limitation or restriction during a period when he was in fact in remission before a recurrence of PTSD-like symptoms after a period of about 4 years. Judge Turnbull held that the length of time for which a mental disorder has continued is to be determined by the length of time for which it causes functional limitation, and not the length of time for which there are continuing symptoms. However, a mental disorder may still cause functional limitation or restriction if the known likelihood of its recurrence causes a claimant to avoid a task, or where it would be unwise for the claimant to undertake the task because he would be unable to perform it if he did suffer a recurrence or because attempting to perform it if he did suffer a recurrence might render the recurrence worse than it otherwise would have been. Judge Turnbull also held that there was no reason why a recurrence of a mental illness could not be regarded as a further 'injury', in respect of which a new claim could be made.

'Permanent'

18.20 Article 5(7)(a) of the AFCS 2011 defines the point at which functional limitation or restriction is to be regarded as permanent as:

> (a) … where following appropriate clinical management of adequate duration—
>
> (i) an injury has reached steady or stable state at maximum medical improvement; and
>
> (ii) no further improvement is expected.

'Persistent'

18.21 In *MG v Secretary of State for Defence (AFCS)*,[23] Judge Wright held that 'persistent' bears its ordinary meaning of constantly repeated, enduring, or continually recurring.

'Operative treatment'

18.22 In *RA v Secretary of State for Defence (WP)*,[24] Judge Levenson held that an arthroscopy carried out for both diagnostic and treatment purposes was 'operative treatment' for the purposes of the Table 9,[25] Item 27 descriptor, whether or not anything was done beyond a diagnostic investigation. With effect

---

23 [2015] UKUT 0372 (AAC).

24 [2015] UKUT 201 (AAC).

25 AFCS 2011, Sch 3, Table 9.

from 31 May 2016, article 5 of the AFCS 2011 has been amended by article 2 of the Armed Forces and Reserve Forces (Compensation Scheme) (Amendment) Order 2016[26] so as to define 'operative treatment' as meaning 'surgical intervention intended to investigate or treat but excludes insertion of sutures under local anaesthetic, acupuncture, facet or other joint injection or other dental procedure'.

26 SI 2016/557.

Chapter 19

Injury Benefits

TYPES OF INJURY BENEFIT

19.1 Article 15(1) of the AFCS 2011 provides for the following injury benefits:

(a) a lump sum;
(b) a supplementary award;
(c) a guaranteed income payment until death;
(ca) an armed forces independence payment;
(d) a fast payment; and
(e) medical expenses.

LUMP SUM

19.2 All Armed Forces Compensation Scheme injury awards include a lump sum. The amount of the lump sum is the amount specified in column (b) of Table 10 of Schedule 3 to the AFCS 2011 for the tariff level of the relevant descriptor, for example for an injury described by a level 7 descriptor the lump sum is £90,000. A lump sum must be paid as soon as possible after the award has been made.[1]

SUPPLEMENTARY AWARD

19.3 Article 16(5) of the AFCS 2011 provides for a supplementary award to be paid in addition to a lump sum in certain cases where an injury does not necessarily have an impact on a claimant's earning capacity, but which can

1 AFCS 2011, art 64(1).

nevertheless have a substantial effect on a person's functioning or self-confidence.[2] A supplementary award of £60,000 is payable in cases of traumatic physical injury which are covered by a tariff descriptor and which result in incontinence of the bowel or bladder or both, impotence, or infertility or physical disablement due to an injury to the external genitalia. A supplementary award can be paid for each of those conditions, but only once for each condition. A supplementary award of £40,000 is payable where an injury results in the loss of one kidney or if treatment for an injury requires a kidney to be removed, but without the development of chronic renal failure.

19.4 Paragraph 2 of Part 2 of Schedule 3 to the AFCS 2011 provides for smaller supplementary awards in the case of certain types of limb, ear and fracture injuries.

CALCULATING LUMP SUM BENEFIT

Single descriptor

19.5 If a claimant receives one or more injuries in or arising from a single incident, and the injuries are described by a single descriptor,[3] the claimant receives the lump sum for the descriptor plus any supplementary award to which the claimant is entitled (the 'relevant amount'), but the maximum amount that the claimant can receive is the lump sum for a tariff level 1 injury, i.e. currently £570,000.[4]

Multiple descriptors – 100% Guaranteed Income Payment

19.6 If the injury or injuries is/are described by more than one descriptor and the relevant percentage for the claimant's GIP is 100% (see para **19.16**), the claimant receives the total of the relevant amounts (i.e. lump sum plus any supplementary award) for each descriptor, subject however to the current £570,000 maximum.[5]

---

2 AFCS 2011, arts 15(1)(b) and 16(6)(b) and Sch 3, Pt 2.

3 AFCS 2011, art 16(1)(c) provides that more than one injury may be described by one descriptor.

4 AFCS 2011, art 17(2).

5 AFCS 2011, art 19.

Body zones

19.7 In order to provide greater compensation for claimants with serious injuries affecting different parts of the body, in some cases the Armed Forces Compensation Scheme allows for the aggregation of compensation by reference to the 'body zones' affected by the injuries. The 'body zone' method allows each descriptor affecting the same part of the body to be compensated for at the same level, instead of at reducing levels for each successive descriptor.

19.8 Article 20(6) of the AFCS 2011 allocates injuries described by separate descriptors to 'body zones', as follows:[6]

(i) 'head and neck' which includes injury to the brain, skull, face, jaw, organs of the mouth and nose, cervical bony and spinal structures and thyroid;
(ii) 'torso' which includes injury to the abdomen, including wall, peritoneum and structural contents, bony pelvis, pelvic floor and structural contents, perineum and external male and female genitalia, bony thorax, chest wall, pleura and structural contents, thoracic, lumbar, sacral and coccygeal bony and spinal structures;
(iii) 'upper and lower limbs', which includes injury to all structures from the shoulder, including scapula and clavicle, to the tips of hand digits (upper limbs), injury to the buttocks and groin, and from the head of the femur to the tips of toes (lower limbs);
(iv) 'senses' which means an injury which is described by a descriptor in Table 7[7] of the tariff;
(v) 'mental health' which means an injury which is described by a descriptor in Table 3[8] of the tariff.

Where a descriptor affects more than one body zone, it is allocated to the body zone predominantly affected by the injury.[9] In the case of burns for which there is a descriptor in Table 1, the descriptor is allocated to the body zone that has the highest percentage of affected surface area.[10]

19.9 The 'body zone' method of assessing compensation can be used if the following conditions are satisfied:[11]

---

6 Each body zone includes associated nerves, arteries, veins and lymphatic structures, AFCS 2011, art 20(7).

7 AFCS 2011, Sch 3, Table 7.

8 AFCS 2011, Sch 3, Table 3.

9 AFCS 2011, art 20(4).

10 AFCS 2011, art 20(5).

11 AFCS 2011, art 20(1).

(i) one or more injuries sustained in or arising from a single incident gives rise to more than one descriptor;
(ii) the descriptors relate to two or more body zones;
(iii) at least one descriptor gives rise to an entitlement within tariff levels 1 to 11 in each of two or more body zones;
(iv) the relevant percentage for the claimant's GIP is less than 100%.[12]

19.10 Using the 'body zone' method, the highest relevant amount for each body zone is calculated in accordance with article 18. The body zone with the highest relevant amount then becomes the 'first body zone'; the body zone with the next highest relevant amount becomes the 'second body zone', and so on.[13] Where the lump sum is the same for two body zones, one is treated as the higher and the other as the lower.[14] The amounts payable in respect of each descriptor are prescribed percentages of the relevant amount (lump sum plus supplementary award), depending on the ranking of the body zone of the descriptor, as follows:

(i) Descriptor in first body zone: 100% of the relevant amount.
(ii) Descriptor in the second body zone: 80% of the relevant amount.
(iii) Descriptor in the third body zone: 60% of the relevant amount.
(iv) Descriptor in the fourth body zone: 40% of the relevant amount.
(v) Descriptor in the fifth body zone: 20% of the relevant amount.[15]

The maximum total amount payable for all descriptors is the lump sum for a tariff level 1 injury.[16]

Multiple descriptors – other cases

19.11 Under article 22 of the AFCS 2011, if a claimant receives one or more injuries in or arising from a single incident giving rise to descriptors in different body zones, but the 'body zone' method of calculating compensation cannot be used because there are no level 1 to 11 descriptors, or because any level 1 to 11 descriptors are in the same body zone, the descriptors are ranked in a similar way to body zones, i.e. the first descriptor becomes the descriptor for which the highest relevant amount (lump sum plus supplementary award) is payable, the second

---

12 See para **19.16**. If the relevant percentage is 100%, the lump sum is calculated in accordance with AFCS 2011, art 19 (see para **19.6**).

13 AFCS 2011, art 21(3).

14 Presumably this is the intention of AFCS 2011, art 21(3)(b), although the provision as drafted would have the effect of promoting third and subsequent body zones to the position of first and second body zones if the amount payable for each body zone was the same.

15 AFCS 2011, art 21(2).

16 AFCS 2011, art 17(2).

descriptor is the descriptor for which the next highest relevant amount is payable, and so on. Where the lump sum is the same for two descriptors, one is treated as the higher and the other as the lower.[17] The percentage of the relevant amount which is payable for each descriptor is then determined as follows:

(i) First descriptor: 100% of the relevant amount.
(ii) Second descriptor: 80% of the relevant amount.
(iii) Third descriptor: 60% of the relevant amount.
(iv) Fourth descriptor: 40% of the relevant amount.
(v) Fifth and subsequent descriptors: 20% of the relevant amount.

GUARANTEED INCOME PAYMENT

19.12 A GIP is payable for descriptors between level 1 and level 11 (inclusive). GIP is a lifetime benefit that is intended to compensate for long-term loss of earning capacity and pension, and for loss of promotion prospects. GIP is inflation-linked to the Consumer Price Index[18] and is non-taxable. Payment of GIP does not commence until a claimant is medically discharged or the claimant's service ends, or on the date of claim in other cases.[19] GIP is paid monthly in arrears.[20] A claimant is entitled to only one GIP irrespective of the number of injuries that the person has sustained.[21] Where a claimant has sustained more than one injury in separate incidents, GIP is the highest amount that has been awarded.[22]

Amount of Guaranteed Income Payment

19.13 The amount of GIP is based on a claimant's age, salary and the tariff level of the relevant injury. It is calculated by multiplying the 'relevant salary' by the 'relevant factor' to obtain the 'base figure'.[23] The annual amount of the GIP is the 'relevant percentage' of the 'base figure'.[24]

---

17 Presumably, this is the intention of AFCS 2011, art 22(5)(b), although the provision as drafted would have the effect of promoting third and subsequent descriptors to the position of the first and second descriptors if the amount payable for each descriptor was the same.

18 AFCS 2011, art 72.

19 AFCS 2011, art 64(2).

20 AFCS 2011, art 65.

21 AFCS 2011, art 16(8).

22 AFCS 2011, art 16(9).

23 AFCS 2011, art 24(2).

24 AFCS 2011, art 24(1).

'Relevant salary'

19.14 'Relevant salary' is defined in article 24(6) of the AFCS 2011 as 'the salary of a member on the day on which the member's service ends or in the case of a former member, the salary on that day up-rated for inflation'.[25] If one or more of the injuries giving rise to GIP was sustained on a day when a member held acting rank, the relevant salary is the member's salary on that day if it was higher than on the day on which service ended, adjusted for inflation if the claim was made at a later date.[26]

'Relevant factor'

19.15 The 'relevant factor' is the figure specified by column (b) of the Table in Schedule 4 to the AFCS 2011 for the claimant's 'relevant age',[27] i.e. the claimant's age on the day on which service ends, or the date of claim if service has already ended.[28] For example, for a claimant who left service aged 29, the factor in column (b) of Schedule 4 is 1.107. The 'base figure' for that claimant will therefore be the claimant's relevant salary, multiplied by 1.107.

'Relevant percentage'

19.16 The tariff levels from levels 1 to 11 are divided into four bands for the purpose of determining the 'relevant percentage', which is applied to the base figure to give the amount of a claimant's GIP. For a single injury sustained in one incident, the bands and relevant percentage for each band are as follows:

- (i) Band A. Tariff levels 1, 2, 3 and 4. Relevant percentage: 100%.
- (ii) Band B. Tariff levels 5 and 6. Relevant percentage: 75%.
- (iii) Band C. Tariff levels 7 and 8. Relevant percentage: 50%.
- (iv) Band D. Tariff Levels 9, 10 and 11. Relevant percentage: 30%.

More than one descriptor from same incident

19.17 Under article 24(3) and (6)(a) of the AFCS 2011, where an award for an injury sustained in or arising from one incident is described by more than one descriptor, the 'relevant percentage' is determined as follows:

---

25 Up-rating is carried out in accordance with AFCS 2011, art 73.

26 AFCS 2011, art 24(7).

27 AFCS 2011, art 24(6)(c).

28 AFCS 2011, art 24(6)(d).

(i) if the two highest scoring descriptors are in the same band, the relevant percentage is the percentage for the next band above, for example if both descriptors are in Band C the relevant percentage is the percentage for Band B, i.e. 75%;
(ii) if the two highest scoring descriptors are in different bands, the relevant percentage is the percentage for the band which includes the higher of the two highest scoring descriptors;
(iii) if the two highest scoring descriptors are in Band A, the relevant percentage is 100%.

ADDITONAL INJURY FROM SAME INCIDENT

19.18 Article 23 of the AFCS 2011 allows a descriptor to be altered, or an additional descriptor to be awarded, or a supplementary award to be made if a claimant has already been awarded injury benefit and the claimant makes a further claim for another injury sustained in the same incident, or a claim for an injury consequential on such an injury. These powers can also be exercised when the decision on the first claim or the further claim is revised under article 53,[29] or the decision is reviewed under articles 55, 56, 57 or 59.[30] In such cases, only any additional benefit is paid and the total for all injuries sustained in the same incident must not exceed the maximum for an injury at tariff level 1.[31]

INJURY TO PAIRED BODY STRUCTURES

19.19 In cases where a person loses, or loses the function of, the second of a pair of body structures after losing the first, article 25 of the AFCS 2011 provides for compensation greater than twice the amount payable for the loss of only one of the structures. The parts of the body to which the provision applies are:

(i) arms or parts of an arm;
(ii) feet (but not toes);
(iii) hands (but not fingers);
(iv) kidneys;
(v) legs or parts of a leg;
(vi) total loss of sight in both eyes;
(vii) total loss of hearing in both ears.

---

29 See para **16.18**.

30 See Chapter 17.

31 AFCS 2011, art 23(4).

19.20 The provision applies if the following conditions are satisfied:

(i) the claimant has lost, or wholly lost the function of, one of a pair of the body structures listed above;
(ii) the claimant has been awarded injury benefit for that injury;
(iii) in another incident the claimant loses, or wholly loses the function of, the second of the pair of body structures affected by the first incident;
(iv) both injuries are caused by service.

19.21 Where the provision applies, the descriptor which is applied for the second injury is the descriptor for both of the paired structures, for example, if a claimant has lost one eye (Table 7, Item 14) and loses the second eye in a separate service-related incident, the descriptor which is applied on the second claim is Table 7, Item 2 (loss of both eyes).[32] Thus, instead of receiving a second level 8 award, for which the lump sum is £60,000, the claimant receives a level 2 award, for which the lump sum is £470,000. All previous sums paid in respect of the first injury are deducted from the new lump sum to give the lump sum amount payable on the second claim and the previous GIP is replaced by a new GIP based on the tariff level for the loss of both of the paired structures.

19.22 In accordance with the recommendations of a report by the Independent Medical Expert Group[33] published in January 2011, the same provisions are applied to upper-body paired structures where the second injury is not due to service, but is an acute loss due to trauma or infection.[34] The body structures to which this policy is applied are:

(i) arms;
(ii) hands;
(iii) total loss of sight in both eyes;
(iv) total loss of hearing in both ears.

19.23 These provisions are also applied in a modified form where loss of, or loss of use of, the second of an affected pair of body structures develops gradually, for example due to ageing or degenerative disease. In such cases, an additional payment is made of half the lump sum representing the difference between the

---

32 AFCS 2011, Sch 3, Table 7.

33 Independent Medical Expert Group, *The Boyce Review of the Armed Forces Compensation Scheme: The Independent Medical Expert Group report and recommendations on medical aspects* (Ministry of Defence, 19 January 2011) (see para **23.7**).

34 Ministry of Defence, *Armed Forces Compensation Scheme Statement of Policy*, JSP 765 (December 2015), para 3.27.

single and double injuries. The GIP is also increased by one band, except where the individual is already in receipt of a 100% GIP.[35]

TEMPORARY AWARDS

19.24 Article 26 of the AFCS 2011 allows a 'temporary award' to be made on a new claim or on a review application for an injury for which there is no descriptor, pending amendment of the tariff to include a descriptor which describes the injury. For a temporary award to be made, the following conditions must be satisfied:

- (i) there must be no descriptor matching the injury at the date of the claim or review application;
- (ii) the injury must be sufficiently serious to warrant an award of injury benefit.
- (iii) the injury must be listed in ICD10 or DSM4.[36]

The temporary award is at the tariff level which is considered appropriate for the injury and a lump sum and GIP are paid for an injury at that level.

19.25 If the tariff is amended within 1 year beginning on the day on which the claimant is sent notification of the temporary award, the award is made permanent and GIP continues in payment. The same procedure applies if the tariff is amended before the claim or review application has been determined. If the tariff is not amended within the 1-year period, a decision is made refusing to make a permanent award and payment of GIP ceases. However, no benefit has to be repaid.

19.26 There is no right to a reconsideration or a review of a decision to make a temporary award.[37]

INTERIM AWARDS

19.27 Under article 52 of the AFCS 2011, an interim award can be made where the prognosis for an injury is not certain and it is therefore not possible to determine the appropriate descriptor. The most appropriate descriptor is selected

---

35 Ministry of Defence, *Armed Forces Compensation Scheme Statement of Policy*, JSP 765 (December 2015), para 3.29.

36 See AFCS 2011, art 26(1)(c) for the full title of these publications.

37 AFCS 2011, art 26(4).

and an interim award is made for a maximum period of 2 years. The period of the award must be specified.[38]

19.28 If the specified period is less than 2 years, it can be extended on one or more occasions,[39] but a final award must be made within 2 years of the date on which the interim award was first made, unless the prognosis remains uncertain at the end of the initial 2-year period and it is just and equitable in all the circumstances to extend the period further. In that case, a final award must be made within 4 years of the date on which the interim award was first made.

19.29 If the final decision is to award a descriptor at a higher level than the descriptor awarded in the interim award, only the difference between the amounts payable under the two awards is paid. If the final decision is to make an award at a lower tariff level, no further benefit is payable,[40] although no benefit already paid under the interim award is recoverable.[41]

FAST PAYMENT

19.30 A claimant who has made a claim for an injury which occurred during service and which was caused by service[42] and which will give rise to entitlement to an award at tariff levels 1 to 8 is entitled to a fast payment of an amount equivalent to the lump sum entitlement for a level 8 injury, i.e. £60,000.[43] The amount of the fast payment is deducted from the award when the claim has been determined.[44] There is no right to a reconsideration of a decision not to make a fast payment.[45] A fast payment must be paid as soon as reasonably practicable after the award has been made.[46]

---

38 AFCS 2011, art 52(3).

39 AFCS 2011, art 52(5).

40 Although presumably the new amount of any GIP will be payable.

41 AFCS 2011, art 52(8).

42 This requirement is interpreted as meaning that it must be clear beyond doubt that the injury was caused by service, Ministry of Defence, *Armed Forces Compensation Scheme Statement of Policy*, JSP 765 (December 2015), para 3.55.

43 AFCS 2011, art 27.

44 AFCS 2011, art 27(2).

45 AFCS 2011, art 27(4).

46 AFCS 2011, art 64(1).

ARMED FORCES INDEPENDENCE PAYMENT

19.31 The Armed Forces Independence Payment was introduced with effect from 8 April 2013[47] following the introduction of PIP as a social security benefit replacing DLA. The intention of the benefit is that veterans who have been assessed under the Armed Forces Compensation Scheme as being seriously injured will be automatically entitled to receive benefit to cover the extra cost of care needs, without having to claim PIP, DLA or Attendance Allowance. The Armed Forces Independence Payment is paid at a rate of £138.05 per week,[48] equivalent to the enhanced rates of both the daily living and mobility components of PIP and the highest rates of both the care and mobility components of DLA. Payments are paid 4-weekly, in arrears.[49]

Eligibility for Armed Forces Independence Payment

19.32 An Armed Forces Compensation Scheme claimant is entitled to Armed Forces Independence Payment if the person becomes and remains entitled to GIP in respect of which the relevant percentage is 50% or more.[50] Article 24A(1)(c) of the AFCS 2011 makes it a condition of entitlement that 'at all times on or after the date of an award of guaranteed income payment, the person has no outstanding claim or appeal for, nor is in receipt of, an extra-costs disability benefit'.[51] The intention of this provision is probably that a claimant is ineligible for an armed forces payment at any time when the person is in receipt of PIP, DLA or Attendance Allowance or has an outstanding claim for any of those benefits, but read literally the provision appears to mean that, unless the claim has been refused, any claim for those benefits made after an award of GIP disqualifies a claimant from receiving Armed Forces Independence Payment. Under article 24B, entitlement to Armed Forces Independence Payment ceases when any of the conditions of entitlement cease to be satisfied, but a new claim can be made.

Claiming Armed Forces Independence Payment

19.33 Under article 24A(1)(a) of the AFCS 2011, it is a condition of entitlement to Armed Forces Independence Payment that a valid claim is made

---

47 By Armed Forces and Reserve Forces (Compensation Scheme) (Amendment) Order 2013 (SI 2013/436), arts 1(1) and 2(3).

48 The amount will be up-rated annually in line with the corresponding social security benefits.

49 AFCS 2011, art 65A.

50 AFCS 2011, art 24A(1)(b).

51 Defined in AFCS 2011, art 2 as PIP, DLA or Attendance Allowance in Great Britain and equivalent benefits in Northern Ireland.

satisfying the same requirements as for other Armed Forces Compensation Scheme benefits. However, although a claim for Armed Forces Independence Payment must be made to Veterans UK, the benefit is paid and administered by the Department for Work and Pensions.

19.34 Articles 24D to 24F of the AFCS 2011 allow up to £56.75 per week to be deducted from Armed Forces Independence Payments to meet the liability of a claimant for payments under the Motability scheme, and for such arrangements to be terminated.

MEDICAL EXPENSES

19.35 Article 28 of the AFCS 2011 gives the Secretary of State a discretion[52] to pay the whole or part of any necessary medical expenses incurred by a claimant who has been awarded injury benefit for one or more injuries giving rise to an award at tariff levels 1 to 8 and who is ordinarily resident[53] outside the United Kingdom at the time the expenses are incurred, provided that ordinary residence outside the United Kingdom commenced within 1 year starting with the day on which service ended. The period of 1 year can, however, be extended by a reasonable further period if the claimant was physically or mentally incapable of making arrangements to move outside the United Kingdom for part or all of the 1-year period.[54]

19.36 'Necessary expenses' include, but are not limited, to:

(i) medical, surgical or rehabilitative treatment;
(ii) professional nursing care;
(iii) appropriate medical aids and appliances;
(iv) reasonable expenses incidental to (i) to (iii).

19.37 Medical expenses must be paid as soon as practicable after the award has been made.[55]

---

52 Ministry of Defence, *Armed Forces Compensation Scheme Statement of Policy*, JSP 765 (December 2015), paras 3.67–3.71 set out how this power is exercised.

53 'Ordinarily resident' refers to a person's abode in a particular place or country which the person has adopted for settled purposes as part of the regular order of his or her life for the time being, whether of short or long duration (see *R v Barnet London Borough Council ex parte Nilish Shah* [1983] 2 AC 309). Ministry of Defence, *Armed Forces Compensation Scheme Statement of Policy*, JSP 765 (December 2015) states that an individual will be considered to be 'ordinarily resident' in a country where they live permanently, spending at least 10 months of the year there.

54 AFCS 2011, art 28(5).

55 AFCS 2011, art 64(1).

Chapter 20

Death Benefits

TYPES OF DEATH BENEFIT

20.1 Article 29 of the AFCS 2011 provides for the following death benefits where the death of a member or former member of the armed forces was caused by service:[1]

(i) a survivor's GIP;
(ii) a bereavement grant;
(iii) a child's payment.

20.2 There is a discretion under article 29(3) and (4) of the AFCS 2011 to withhold death benefits if the deceased and his or her partner married or entered into a civil partnership less than 6 months before the date of death, but the circumstances in which this power would be exercised are not clear.

SURVIVOR'S GUARANTEED INCOME PAYMENT

Eligibility

20.3 A survivor's GIP is a lifetime inflation-linked tax-free benefit which is payable to a member or former member's spouse, civil partner or surviving adult dependant.[2] Survivor's GIP is paid monthly in arrears.[3]

---

1 See para **14.15** for the conditions which have to be satisfied for death to be caused by service.

2 AFCS 2011, art 29(1)(a).

3 AFCS 2011, art 65.

Surviving adult dependant

20.4 For a person to be a 'surviving adult dependant' of a member or former member, the following conditions must have been satisfied at the date of death:[4]

(i) the parties were cohabiting as partners 'in a substantial and exclusive relationship';
(ii) the deceased left no surviving spouse or civil partner;
(iii) the parties were not prevented from marrying or forming a civil partnership (e.g. because the deceased's partner was still married);
(iv) the person was financially dependent on the deceased or they were financially interdependent.

'Substantial and exclusive relationship'

20.5 Part 1 of Schedule 1 to the AFCS 2011 sets out matters which are taken into account in deciding whether a relationship was 'substantial', and Part 2 specifies circumstances which prevent a relationship from being treated as 'exclusive'. Under paragraph 1 of Part 1, in considering whether the relationship between the parties was 'substantial', regard must be had to any evidence which the claimant considers demonstrates a substantial relationship and, in particular, examples of the types of evidence in paragraph 2 which could, either alone or together, demonstrate the existence of such a relationship. The types of evidence referred to in paragraph 2 are:

(i) evidence of regular financial support of the claimant by the deceased;
(ii) evidence of a valid will or life insurance policy, valid at the time of the deceased's death, in which the deceased nominated the claimant as principal beneficiary or co-beneficiary with children, or the claimant nominated the deceased as the principal beneficiary;
(iii) evidence indicating that the deceased and the claimant were purchasing accommodation as joint owners or evidence of joint ownership of other valuable property, such as a car or land;
(iv) evidence of a joint savings plan or joint investments of a substantial nature;
(v) evidence that the deceased and the claimant operated a joint account for which they were co-signatories;
(vi) evidence of joint financial arrangements such as joint repayment of a loan or payment of each other's debts;
(vii) evidence that the deceased or the claimant had given the other a power of attorney;

4 AFCS 2011, art 30.

(viii) evidence that the names of both the deceased and the claimant appeared on a lease or rental agreement, if they lived in rented accommodation;
(ix) evidence that the deceased and the claimant shared responsibility for children;
(x) evidence of the length of the relationship.

20.6 Under paragraph 3 of Part 2 of Schedule 1, a relationship is not exclusive if:

(i) one or both parties is married to, or is the civil partner of, someone other than the party to the relationship;
(ii) one or both of the parties is a party to another relationship which is, or could be considered to be, a substantial and exclusive relationship on the basis of the provisions set out above.

Amount of survivor's Guaranteed Income Payment

20.7 The amount of a survivor's GIP is 60% of the 'base figure', which is calculated by multiplying the 'relevant salary' by the 'relevant factor'.[5] 'Relevant salary' is 'the salary of a member at the date of death, or in the case of a former member, the salary on that day up-rated for inflation'.[6] The salary is up-rated for inflation in accordance with article 73 of the AFCS 2011. If death was due to an injury sustained in an incident which occurred on a day when a member held acting rank, the relevant salary is the member's salary on that day if it was higher.[7] The 'relevant factor' is the figure specified by column (b) of the Table in Schedule 4 for the claimant's age at the date of death.

20.8 If the deceased left more than one surviving spouse, each spouse gets an equal share of 60% of the base figure.[8]

BEREAVEMENT GRANT

Eligibility

20.9 Under article 29(1)(b) of the AFCS 2011, a bereavement grant is payable to:

---

5 AFCS 2011, art 34(1).
6 AFCS 2011, art 34(3)(a).
7 AFCS 2011, art 34(4).
8 AFCS 2011, art 34(6).

(i) a surviving spouse;
(ii) a civil partner;
(iii) a surviving adult dependant;[9]
(iv) since 17 November 2011, an eligible child if the deceased did not leave a surviving spouse, civil partner or surviving adult dependant.[10]

A bereavement grant is not payable if the deceased was a member of the Armed Forces Pensions Scheme 2005 and dies in service,[11] unless the person's salary was less than the amount of the bereavement grant,[12] in which case the amount of the bereavement grant is £25,000 less the deceased's salary.[13]

Eligible child

20.10 By article 31 of the AFCS 2011, an 'eligible child' is a child who was a child or adopted child of the deceased, or who was financially dependent on the deceased on the day of death, who:

(i) is aged under 18; or
(ii) is aged under 23 and in full-time education or vocational training; or
(iii) was dependent on the deceased at the date of death and is unable to engage in gainful employment because of physical or mental impairment.

A child born after the death of a member or former member can only be treated as an eligible child if the child is born before the first anniversary of the death.[14]

20.11 Article 32 of the AFCS 2011 contains detailed provisions for determining the day on which full-time education is deemed to end, and for ignoring breaks in full-time education or vocational training in certain circumstances.

---

9 See paras **20.4–20.6** for the meaning of this term.
10 AFCS 2011, art 29(6).
11 AFCS 2011, art 29(4).
12 AFCS 2011, art 29(5).
13 AFCS 2011, art 35(2).
14 AFCS 2011, art 33(1).

Amount of bereavement grant

20.12 The amount of bereavement grant is £25,000 if the deceased died in service or £37,500[15] if death occurred after service ended.[16] If the deceased had more than one surviving spouse or eligible child entitled to bereavement grant, each is entitled to an equal share. However, an eligible child is only entitled to bereavement grant if a claim for child's payment has been made for or on behalf of the child, or if Veterans UK is aware that a claim will be made on behalf of a child born after the death of the deceased.[17]

CHILD'S PAYMENTS

20.13 An eligible child[18] is entitled to a child's payment, normally payable monthly in arrears,[19] but no benefit is payable for any period prior to the birth of the child.[20]

Amount of child's payment

20.14 The amount of a child's payment is calculated by reference to the base figure,[21] which is determined in the same way as the base figure for survivor's GIP.[22] The member's salary is up-rated for inflation in accordance with article 73 of the AFCS 2011.[23] If the deceased left a surviving spouse, civil partner or surviving adult dependant, the percentages of the base figure payable for each child are as follows:[24]

- (i) 15% for each of the first two eligible children;
- (ii) 10% for the third eligible child;
- (iii) where there are more than three eligible children, 40% of the base figure, divided by the number of eligible children.

---

15 This reflects the entitlement to death benefits under occupational pension schemes for members who die in service.

16 AFCS 2011, art 35.

17 AFCS 2011, art 35(5).

18 See para **20.10** for the definition of 'eligible child'.

19 AFCS 2011, art 65.

20 AFCS 2011, art 33(2).

21 AFCS 2011, art 36(1).

22 See para **20.7**.

23 AFCS 2011, art 36(11).

24 AFCS 2011, art 36(3).

20.15 If the deceased left no surviving spouse, civil partner, or surviving adult dependant and no more than four eligible children, each child gets 25% of the base figure. If the deceased left more than four eligible children, each child gets an equal share of the base figure.[25]

Recalculation of child's payment

20.16 On the death of a surviving spouse, civil partner or surviving adult dependant who was in receipt of a survivor's GIP, the amount of a child's payment is recalculated on the basis that the member had died without leaving that partner,[26] provided that there is no other surviving spouse who is entitled to survivor's GIP.[27] The recalculated payment becomes payable on the day after the death.[28]

20.17 Where a child ceases to be a relevant child, there is no alteration in the benefit payable to the other children.[29]

Adjustment of child's payment

20.18 Article 37 of the AFCS 2011 confers a discretion to adjust a child's payment which is being paid on the basis that one or more children were eligible children at the date of a member's death and that there were no other eligible children. The discretion can be exercised if it later appears that:

(i) a person in respect of whom a child's payment has been paid was not an eligible child;
(ii) a further person was an eligible child; or
(iii) a child who was born after the member's death was an eligible child.

Three or more awards of child's payment

20.19 Under article 38 of the AFCS 2011, a child who would be entitled to child's payments in respect of the death of more than two members receives only the two highest paying awards.

---

25 AFCS 2011, art 36(4).

26 AFCS 2011, art 36(5) and (6).

27 I.e. in the case of a bigamous marriage legally contracted abroad.

28 AFCS 2011, art 36(7).

29 AFCS 2011, art 36(8).

Chapter 21

Adjustment and Cessation of Benefit

OTHER PENSION BENEFITS

21.1 In order to prevent duplication of benefits, article 39 of the AFCS 2011 provides for payments from other schemes to be deducted from Armed Forces Compensation Scheme benefits. The schemes to which this applies are:

(i) The Armed Forces Pensions Schemes 1975, 2005 and 2015;
(ii) The Gurkha Pension Scheme;
(iii) The Armed Forces Early Departure Payment Scheme.

21.2 The Armed Forces Compensation Scheme benefits which are subject to adjustment to take account of payments from these schemes are GIP, survivor's GIP and child's payment. If a claimant is entitled to GIP for any period during which the person is also entitled to an ill-health pension which is paid for the same injury as the injury for which GIP is paid, GIP is reduced by 100%[1] of the ill-health pension.[2] In the following cases, 75% of other scheme benefits are deducted[3] from Armed Forces Compensation Scheme benefits:

(i) if a claimant is entitled to GIP for any period during which the person is also entitled to a payment, or to a pension which is not an ill-health pension which is paid for the same injury as the injury for which GIP is paid;[4]

1 The amounts of the other benefits which are taken into account are the gross amounts, irrespective of any commutation, AFCS 2011, art 39(6).

2 AFCS 2011, art 39(3)(b).

3 The reason for the different levels of deductions when calculating the GIP is that Armed Forces Pensions Scheme ill-health pensions are tax-free, but other Armed Forces Pensions Scheme payments are taxable. The 75% deduction for taxable awards results in GIP being increased by 25% of the taxable income.

4 AFCS 2011, art 39(3)(a).

(ii) if a person is entitled to survivor's GIP or child's payment for any period during which the person is also entitled to a pension.[5]

If the amount of the non-Armed Forces Compensation Scheme benefit changes, the amount of GIP, survivor's GIP or child's payment can be altered to take account of the change.[6]

ABATEMENT FOR AWARDS OF DAMAGES

21.3 Article 40 of the AFCS 2011 provides for awards of damages to be set off against armed forces compensation benefits if the damages are for injury or death for which compensation is payable under the Scheme. It also applies to compensation under the Criminal Injuries Compensation Schemes in Great Britain and Northern Ireland, and to the Ministry of Defence compensation scheme for criminal injuries sustained abroad.[7] 'Damages' includes any payment received as a result of a claim within the scope of this provision, whether or not proceedings are issued, and whether or not the claim is settled.[8]

21.4 Unlike article 52 of the SPO 2006, this provision apparently places a claimant under no obligation to pursue a civil claim for damages and permits the Secretary of State to abate armed forces compensation benefits only by amounts of damages which have actually been recovered. In contrast to the discretionary powers of abatement conferred by article 52 of the SPO 2006, article 40(2) of the AFCS 2011 provides that the Secretary of State is to withhold or reduce benefit where damages have been or will be recovered for injury or death for which Armed Forces Compensation Scheme benefit is payable. However, there is no specific requirement for the total amount of damages awarded to be taken into account, and there would seem to be no justification for abating armed forces compensation benefits by elements of an award of damages for losses not covered by the Scheme, for example care costs.

21.5 Article 40 of the AFCS 2011 does not stipulate how Armed Forces Compensation Scheme benefits are to be abated, in particular, whether awards of damages should be set off against lump sum payments, or GIP, or both. One approach might be to set off damages for pain, suffering and loss of amenity against Armed Forces Compensation Scheme lump sum payments and to set off

---

5 AFCS 2011, art 39(4).

6 AFCS 2011, art 39(5).

7 AFCS 2011, art 40(8).

8 AFCS 2011, art 40(7).

damages for continuing losses, such as loss of earnings and pension losses, against GIP for the period in respect of which damages have been awarded.

Exclusions

21.6 Armed Forces Compensation Scheme benefits cannot be abated if they have been taken into account in the assessment of damages.[9] Armed Forces Compensation Scheme payments cannot be abated to take into account bereavement grant and Armed Forces Independence Payments, or if Armed Forces Compensation Scheme benefits have been taken into account in the assessment of damages.[10]

Duty to notify claim

21.7 Article 40(5) of the AFCS 2011 provides for a claimant to be required to provide details of any steps taken or planned to obtain damages in respect of the injury or death and to provide a written undertaking that if damages are recovered the claimant will notify the Secretary of State and repay any benefit.

NEGLIGENCE OR MISCONDUCT

21.8 Article 41 of the AFCS 2011 allows up to 40% of benefit to be withheld where the negligence or misconduct of a member or former member contributed to that person's injury or death. No deduction can be made under this head from Armed Forces Independence Payment.

CHELSEA PENSIONERS

21.9 Chelsea Pensioners are not entitled to GIP, Armed Forces Independence Payment or Survivor's GIP, but claimants' benefits may be restored if they leave the Royal Hospital Chelsea.[11]

---

9 AFCS 2011, art 40(3)(a).

10 AFCS 2001, art 40(3).

11 AFCS 2011, art 42.

SUSPENSION OF BENEFIT PENDING APPEALS BY THE SECRETARY OF STATE

Appeal against tribunal decision

21.10 Article 66 of the AFCS 2011 allows the Secretary of State to give a direction suspending payment of benefit in whole or in part if consideration is being given to making an application for leave[12] to appeal to the Upper Tribunal or to a Social Security Commissioner[13] against a tribunal decision.[14] The suspension will lapse if no application for permission to appeal is made within 6 weeks beginning on the date on which the tribunal's written decision and the reasons for the decision are received by the Secretary of State,[15] but it will continue in force until the appeal has been determined if permission to appeal is given, or until any review of the tribunal's decision has been completed. If the Upper Tribunal or Social Security Commissioner remits the case for rehearing, the appeal is not determined until the remitted case has been reheard. A direction suspending benefit must be in writing and must be given or sent within the 6-week period.[16]

21.11 If permission to appeal is refused, the suspension will remain in force for a further period of 1 month beginning on the date on which notification of the refusal of permission to appeal was received if within that time the application for permission to appeal is renewed to the Upper Tribunal or Social Security Commissioner.[17] The suspension will then continue in force until the application and, if permission to appeal is given, the appeal, have been determined.[18]

Further appeals

21.12 If the Secretary of State is considering appealing against the decision of the Upper Tribunal (or of a Pensions Appeal Commissioner in Northern Ireland), article 67 of the AFCS 2011 allows a direction to be given suspending payment of benefit in whole or in part.[19] The suspension will lapse if no application for leave to appeal is made within 3 months beginning with the date on which written

---

12 Permission to appeal in England and Wales.

13 Appeals lie to a Social Security Commissioner against certain type of decision in Northern Ireland (see para **24.9**).

14 AFCS 2011, art 66(1).

15 AFCS 2011, art 66(4).

16 AFCS 2011, art 66(3).

17 AFCS 2011, art 66(7)(c).

18 AFCS 2011, art 66(7).

19 AFCS 2011, art 67(1).

notice of the decision was received by the Secretary of State, but it will continue in force until the appeal has been determined if permission to appeal is given, or until any review of the decision has been completed.[20] If the Upper Tribunal or Social Security Commissioner remits the case for rehearing, the appeal is not determined until the remitted case has been reheard.[21] A direction suspending benefit must be in writing and must be given or sent within the 3-month period.

21.13 If permission to appeal is refused, the suspension will remain in force for a further period of 1 month beginning on the date on which notification of the refusal of permission to appeal was received if within that time the application for permission to appeal is renewed to the Court of Appeal, Court of Session or Northern Ireland Court of Appeal, as appropriate. The suspension will then continue in force until the application and, if permission to appeal is given, the appeal, have been determined.[22] If the appellate court remits the case for rehearing, the appeal is not determined until the remitted case has been reheard.[23]

21.14 This provision also applies to onward appeals from an appellate court to the Supreme Court.[24]

'Look-alike' appeals

21.15 Article 68 of the AFCS 2011 gives the Secretary of State power to suspend payment of benefit in whole or in part until the determination of an appeal in 'look-alike' cases where an award of benefit might have to be reviewed if the appeal was allowed.

---

20 AFCS 2011, art 67(5).

21 AFCS 2011, art 66(8).

22 AFCS 2011, art 67(5).

23 AFCS 2011, art 67(7).

24 AFCS 2011, art 67(9).

Chapter 22

Modifications for Reserve Forces

22.1 Article 13 of, and Schedule 2 to, the AFCS 2011 modify the Armed Forces Compensation Scheme in its application to members of the Reserve Forces. In summary, the principal modifications are as follows:

(i) paragraph 2 of Schedule 2 provides for the salary of a member of the Reserve Forces to be determined by reference to the salary of a regular member of the forces of equivalent substantive or temporary rank and seniority, together with any reservist's award[1] to which the claimant is entitled on the day on which the claimant leaves service, or would have been entitled if the claimant had been in relevant service[2] on the day on which service ended, and amounts which the Defence Council has determined should be treated as salary;

(ii) paragraph 3 of Schedule 2 extends the meaning of 'place of work' in article 11(1)(b) to cover a place of work to which a member is assigned or temporarily assigned for the purpose of service in the reserve forces;

(iii) paragraph 4 of Schedule 2 modifies the amount of bereavement grant provided for by article 35 to take into account membership of a reserve forces pension scheme;

(iv) paragraph 5 of Schedule 2 modifies the provisions of article 39 relating to the adjustment of GIP, survivor's GIP and child's payment to take into account payment from other service and civilian schemes.[3]

---

1 'Reservist's award' is an award under Reserve Forces Act 1996, ss 83 and 84, subject to the exclusions set out in AFCS 2011, Sch 2, para 1.

2 'Relevant service' is defined in the Reserve Forces (Call-out and Recall) (Financial Assistance) Regulations 2005 (SI 2005/859) and the Reserve Forces Act 1996 (Isle of Man) Regulations 2010 (SI 2010/2643).

3 See para **21.1**.

PART III

ADMINISTRATION AND ADJUDICATION

Chapter 23

Administration of Benefits

23.1 From 1916 until 1953, war pensions were administered by the Ministry of Pensions. In 1953, the Ministry of Pensions merged with the Ministry of National Insurance to become the Ministry of Pensions and National Insurance. In 1966, war pensions became the responsibility of the Ministry of Social Security, which merged with the Ministry of Health in 1968 to form the Department of Health and Social Security. Following the break-up of that department in 1998, war pensions were administered by the Department of Social Security until its abolition in 2001 when, for 6 months, they were administered by the Department for Work and Pensions. However, in December of that year responsibility for the administration of war pensions was transferred to the Ministry of Defence by the Transfer of Functions (War Pensions etc.) Order 2001.[1] The functions of the Ministry of Defence in relation to war pensions and, from 2005, armed forces compensation used to be carried out by an Executive Agency called the SPVA, but on 1 April 2014 the SPVA merged with the Ministry of Defence's Defence Business Services to become part of Veterans UK. Through all these changes, the administration of war pensions, and latterly armed forces compensation benefits, has been carried out at Norcross, near Blackpool, to where the Ministry of Pensions moved in 1940.

DECISION MAKING

23.2 War pensions and armed forces compensation decisions are made by Veterans UK officials in the name of the Secretary of State under the so-called *Carltona*[2] principle. War pensions claims may involve both factual and medical questions. Factual questions such as whether the claimant was a member of the

1 SI 2001/3506.

2 *Carltona v Commissioner of Works* [1943] 2 All ER 560.

armed forces are decided by departmental officials.[3] However, articles 40 and 41 of the SPO 2006 require fulfilment of the conditions of entitlement under those articles to be certified, and article 42(5) requires certification of the percentage degree of disablement. Under article 43(b)(i), unless there has been an appeal, any matter which requires to be certified must be determined in accordance with a certificate of a medical officer or board of medical officers appointed or recognised by the Secretary of State, or by a member of a panel of independent experts nominated by the President of one of the Royal Colleges if the medical question raises a serious doubt or difficulty. If there has been an appeal, article 43(a) requires a matter which is required to be certified to be determined in accordance with the tribunal's decision, or the decision on any further appeal.

23.3 In *AL v Secretary of State for Defence*,[4] Judge Knowles held that the role of the medical adviser is not confined to considering the claimed condition alone. The judge said:

> 37. Though the Secretary of State is the decision-maker, Article 43 gives a prominent role to the Medical Adviser since medical questions requiring certification are determined by the Secretary of State in accordance with the Medical Adviser's certificate. Certification is necessary to secure entitlement [see Articles 40 and 41] and to establish the degree of disablement [Article 42]. The basic condition for an award requires a connection between service and disablement or death. The mere fact that a condition develops in service does not signify that it is caused or worsened by service.
>
> 
>
> 38. Thus the Medical Adviser asked to consider a claim is not restricted to the claimed condition alone. Article 35(6) underscores this as set out in paragraph 27 above. All conditions that appear to the Adviser to be raised by the claimed disablement and evidence – whether or not these conditions have been expressly referred to in the claim form – should be considered. The Respondent made the valid point in this context, that Medical Advisers are well used to considering medical evidence against the context of claim forms which, for example, may refer to a condition which is not the correct diagnosis for the claimant's condition or which may omit to refer to a medically recognised condition altogether.
>
> 
>
> 39. The Respondent's position is that a Medical Adviser asked to review a claimant's case should – and in practice, does – always consider the totality of the medical evidence presented to him or her. If that evidence gives a reason to believe that there is a further condition relevant to the claimed disablement for which the claimant has not claimed but which should be investigated further, the Medical Adviser will not ignore that evidence. I find that this formulation accords with the manner in which claims are made under the Scheme and with good clinical practice.

---

3 *Gillan v Minister of Pensions* (1953) 5 WPAR 286.

4 [2016] UKUT 141 (AAC).

40. What is the practical effect of that duty? The Medical Adviser's responsibility is to consider the claim that has been made. In practice, where consent is given by a claimant to the Respondent for access to the claimant's medical records under the Data Protection Act 1998, that consent extends only to the medical records required to be reviewed to determine the condition as claimed.

41. Thus, where a claim is made for one condition alone and the Medical Adviser takes the view that a further closely related condition is also established on the evidence as existing and attributable to service, the claim is likely to be granted in respect of both those conditions. The Respondent submitted that, in such a scenario, it was easy to see how the original claim could be construed as impliedly including the closely related (but medically distinct) further condition and/or that the symptoms expressly complained of required the diagnostic label of that further condition.

42. However different considerations apply where a claim is made for one condition and the medical evidence indicates that there is a further condition likely to be attributable to service but which is completely unconnected to the claimed condition. The Respondent submitted that the Medical Adviser would not treat the claim as impliedly encompassing the second condition and would not consider the second condition as a matter of diagnostic labelling. Instead the certificate issued would relate to the claimed condition alone but the claimant would be separately informed that there was reason to believe s/he may have [a] claim in respect of the second condition and would be advised to make such a claim. In any event, the Respondent stated that any medical evidence and records relating to that second condition would be sought with a further Data Protection consent to cover that material being obtained from the claimant.

43. In summary, the Respondent emphasised that the Medical Adviser does not take a purely reactive role on the basis of the content of the claim form alone. S/he carries out a full review of the overall medical evidence and the existence of other conditions which may be attributable to service is not ignored. The Appellant agreed with that formulation.

44. I accept the above description of the Medical Adviser's role where certification is required by the SPO. The process of verifying a claim requires a claimant to submit him/herself to an examination by a doctor commissioned on behalf of the Respondent. This examination includes both a mental health and a physical health assessment. Its conclusions are written up and the examining doctor gives his/her opinion as to diagnosis and effect on function of all conditions identified. The Medical Adviser uses this examination together with the evidence (service records, medical records etc) in order to determine whether any claimed or closely related condition is attributable to service and if so, the degree of disablement. Where there are two separate conditions which may be attributable to service but records are available only in relation to one condition, the Medical Adviser sets in train the process described in paragraph 42 above.

23.4 The system of lay decision making for armed forces compensation claims does not require the certification of decisions on medical questions, but decision-makers can seek advice from medical advisers (see para **16.11**).

CENTRAL ADVISORY COMMITTEE ON PENSIONS AND COMPENSATION

23.5 This committee is the successor to the Central Advisory Committee on War Pensions, which was established under section 3 of the War Pensions Act 1921. The role of the committee is to provide advice on policy issues affecting the War Pensions and Armed Forces Compensation Schemes, including review of the control and governance arrangements, so as to maintain credible and visible consultative arrangements for the Schemes. Details of the membership of the committee can be found on its website.[5]

VETERANS ADVISORY PENSIONS COMMITTEES

23.6 These committees were formerly known as War Pensions Committees, which were established under the War Pensions Act 1921 and the Social Security Act 1989. The functions and procedures of the committees are set out in the War Pensions Committees Regulations.[6] There are 13 committees across the United Kingdom, which advise and liaise with veterans and their families and relevant organisations on the needs and concerns of veterans.[7]

INDEPENDENT MEDICAL EXPERT GROUP

23.7 The Independent Medical Expert Group was set up in response to the recommendations of the Boyce Review to advise the Minister for Defence on medical and scientific aspects of the Armed Forces Compensation Scheme.[8] It consists of a chairperson and seven members who are senior licensed medical consultants in relevant specialties, together with a member representing ex-service organisations, a service representative who sits on the Central Advisory Committee on Pensions and Compensation, an injured person who has claimed under the Armed Forces Compensation Scheme, and the Chief of Defence Personnel's Medical Adviser.

---

5 www.gov.uk/government/organisations/central-advisory-committee-on-pensions-and-compensation.

6 SIs 2000/3180, 2005/3032 and 2006/3152.

7 Further information on the work of the committees and contact details can be found by following the links at www.gov.uk.

8 Independent Medical Expert Group, *The Boyce Review of the Armed Forces Compensation Scheme: The Independent Medical Expert Group report and recommendations on medical aspects* (Ministry of Defence, 19 January 2011).

Chapter 24

Appeal Tribunals

THE DEVELOPMENT OF THE TRIBUNAL SYSTEM

24.1 The Pensions Appeal Tribunal was established in July 1917 and sat for the first time in August of that year. The tribunal consisted of a county court judge, an Admiral, a General, a surgeon, a physician and a trade union representative.[1] In July 1918, a smaller tribunal was set up, consisting of a chairman, who was usually a lawyer, and two service members. The tribunal was assisted by a medical assessor, who could conduct medical examinations and question witnesses, but who could not participate in the tribunal's decision-making process. In theory, the tribunal's role was advisory, although in practice the authorities regarded themselves as bound to accept the tribunal's decisions.

24.2 The Pensions Appeal Tribunals were placed on a statutory footing by the War Pensions (Administrative Provisions) Act 1919, which provided for the members of tribunals to be appointed by the Lord Chancellor and their equivalents in Scotland and Ireland (as it then was), and for the tribunal chairman to be a barrister or solicitor of not less than 7 years' standing. The other tribunal members were a qualified medical practitioner and a disabled ex-serviceman, who had to be an officer if the appeal was brought by a former officer or nurse. The tribunals constituted under the 1919 Act marked the start of a fully independent war pensions adjudication system.

24.3 The tribunals established by the 1919 Act dealt only with appeals against the rejection of claims and cases where a person's negligence or misconduct was in issue. In order to avoid the need for periodic re-assessment of claimants whose condition had stabilised, the War Pensions Act 1921 was passed to allow final assessments of disablement to be made. The 1921 Act created separate tribunals, known as Assessment Tribunals, to hear appeals against the making of final

---

1 The members of the first tribunal were HHJ Parry, Admiral Sir Wilmot Fawkes, Lieutenant-General Sir Alfred Codrington, Sir Norman Moore, Mr B Pollard and Mr A Bellamy.

assessments and against the percentage assessment of disablement when an assessment was made final. Assessment Tribunals included a service member and two doctors, one of whom acted as the tribunal chairman.

24.4 The Second World War resulted in a need to provide compensation for injury sustained by non-service personnel, for example Civil Defence Volunteers, merchant seamen and civilians injured as a result of enemy action. The Pensions Appeal Tribunals Act 1943 gave appeal rights to all classes of personnel entitled to claim compensation for injury or death, and remains the source of rights of appeal against both war pensions and armed forces compensation decisions. Section 6 of the 1943 Act provided for the creation of separate Pensions Appeals Tribunals in England and Wales, Scotland and Northern Ireland and authorised the making of rules of procedure in each jurisdiction.[2] Originally, assessment appeals continued to be heard by tribunals which included a service member and at least two medical practitioners of at least 7 years' standing. The 1943 Act also required the service member of the tribunal to be a former officer in cases relating to officers and to be a former non-commissioned member of the forces in other cases and to be of the same sex as the person to whom the claim related. However, these provisions relating to the composition of Pensions Appeal Tribunals were all repealed by section 60 of the Child Support, Pensions and Social Security Act 2000, after which the practice became simply for all tribunals to be comprised of a lawyer chairman, a medical practitioner and a service member.

24.5 In cases other than assessment appeals, the Pensions Appeal Tribunals Act 1943 also created a right of appeal against tribunal decisions on questions of law to a High Court judge nominated by the Lord Chancellor, called a 'nominated judge' in England and Wales, and equivalent rights of appeal to the Court of Session in Scotland and the Supreme Court in Northern Ireland. Provision was made for the appellant to recover any costs reasonably incurred in bringing or defending an appeal, irrespective of whether or not the appeal was successful. There was no right of appeal against a decision of the nominated judge, or the equivalent judges in Scotland and Northern Ireland.[3]

24.6 The jurisdiction of the nominated High Court judges in England and Wales and of their equivalents in Scotland and Northern Ireland was transferred to what were then the Social Security Commissioners by section 5 and paragraph 4 of Schedule 1 to the Armed Forces (Pensions and Compensation) Act

---

2 This remains the position in Scotland and Northern Ireland. In Scotland the rule-making authority is the Lord President of the Court of Session and the current rules of procedure are the Pensions Appeal Tribunals (Scotland) Rules 1981 (SI 1981/500), as amended. In Northern Ireland the rule-making authority is the Lord Chief Justice of Northern Ireland and the current rules of procedure are the Pensions Appeal Tribunals (Northern Ireland) Rules 1981 (SI 1981/231), as amended.

3 Pensions Appeal Tribunals Act 1943, s 6.

2004. The Social Security Commissioners constituted a single appellate body in Great Britain, and a separate appellate body in Northern Ireland. The transfer of appeals to the Social Security Commissioners resulted in a further right of appeal to the Court of Appeal in England and Wales and its equivalents in Scotland and Northern Ireland.[4] Social Security Commissioners were called Pensions Appeal Commissioners when hearing war pensions appeals.

24.7 Following the report of a review of tribunals under the chairmanship of Sir Andrew Leggatt,[5] the tribunal system in England and Wales was fundamentally reformed by the Tribunals, Courts and Enforcement Act 2007. Where existing tribunals had jurisdiction in more than one part of the United Kingdom, the reforms also extended to Scotland and Northern Ireland. With effect from 3 November 2008, section 3(1) of the 2007 Act combined a large number of separate tribunals into a single tribunal called the First-tier Tribunal. The First-tier Tribunal was divided into Chambers, each under its own President. The original intention was for the functions of the Pensions Appeals Tribunals in England and Wales to be transferred to the new Social Entitlement Chamber. However, that proposal was opposed in Parliament, and it was eventually decided to create a separate First-tier Chamber, called the War Pensions and Armed Forces Compensation Chamber, to take over the functions of the Pensions Appeal Tribunals in England and Wales. Tribunal rules of procedure in England and Wales are now made by a Tribunal Procedure Committee under the authority of the 2007 Act, but in Scotland and Northern Ireland they continue to be made under the authority of the Pensions Appeal Tribunals Act 1943. In the exercise of powers conferred by article 8 of the First-tier Tribunal and Upper Tribunal (Composition of Tribunals) Order 2008,[6] the Senior President of Tribunals issued a Practice Statement[7] providing for the composition of tribunals in the War Pensions and Armed Forces Compensation Chamber to be the same as previously in the great majority of cases, i.e. a judge,[8] a medical member and a service member.

24.8 An order[9] under the Tribunals, Courts and Enforcement Act 2007 also transferred the functions of the Social Security Commissioners in Great Britain

---

4 Pensions Appeal Tribunals Act 1943, s 6C, added by Armed Forces (Pensions and Compensation) Act 2004, s 5 and Sch 1, para 4.

5 Sir Andrew Leggatt, *Report of the Review of Tribunals: Tribunals for Users – One System, One Service* (16 August 2001).

6 SI 2008/2835.

7 Practice Statement: Composition of Tribunals in relation to matters that fall to be decided by the War Pensions and Armed Forces Chamber on or after 3 November 2008, Senior President of Tribunals (30 October 2008).

8 Legal members of tribunals were designated as tribunal judges under the Tribunals, Courts and Enforcement Act 2007.

9 The Transfer of Tribunal Functions Order 2008 (SI 2008/2833).

to a new appellate tribunal called the Upper Tribunal, established under section 3(2) of the Act. Section 11 of the Act created a right of appeal from the First-tier Tribunal to the Upper Tribunal on a point of law, resulting for the first time in a right of appeal on a point of law against assessment decisions in England and Wales. The order that transferred the functions of the Social Security Commissioners to the Upper Tribunal amended the Pensions Appeal Tribunals Act 1943 so as to provide for the right of appeal on a point of law from any decision of the Pensions Appeal Tribunal in Scotland to lie to the Upper Tribunal and for there to be a similar right of appeal in assessment cases from the Pensions Appeal Tribunal in Northern Ireland.[10] These appeals are all assigned to the Administrative Appeals Chamber of the Upper Tribunal by article 10(a) of the First-tier Tribunal and Upper Tribunal (Chambers) Order 2010.[11] However, entitlement appeals and appeals against specified decisions in Northern Ireland continue to be dealt with by the Northern Ireland Pensions Appeal Commissioners. Since the Pensions Appeal Commissioners are *ex officio* judges of the Upper Tribunal,[12] the same judge may sit in both capacities when a claimant brings proceedings in both an entitlement case and an assessment case.

24.9 In summary, the jurisdiction of each of the tribunals dealing with war pensions and armed forces compensation appeals in the United Kingdom is now as follows:

(i) *England and Wales*. Appeals against all war pensions and armed forces compensation decisions are dealt with by the War Pensions and Armed Forces Compensation Chamber of the First-tier Tribunal. There is a right of appeal with the permission of the First-tier Tribunal or Upper Tribunal to the Upper Tribunal on a question of law from decisions of the First-tier Tribunal, and further onward rights of appeal from the Upper Tribunal to the Court of Appeal (England and Wales), and then to the Supreme Court.

(ii) *Scotland*. For claimants living in Scotland, appeals against all war pensions and armed forces compensation decisions are dealt with by the Pensions Appeal Tribunal (Scotland) and are regulated by the Pensions Appeal Tribunals (Scotland) Rules 1981,[13] as amended. There is a right of appeal with the permission of the Pensions Appeal Tribunal (Scotland) or Upper Tribunal on a question of law from decisions of the Pensions Appeal Tribunal (Scotland) to the Upper Tribunal. The Upper Tribunal covers both

10 Transfer of Tribunal Functions Order 2008 (SI 2008/2833), arts 7–9 and Sch 3, paras 4 and 13(3). See now Pensions Appeal Tribunals Act 1943, s 6A(1) and (1A).

11 SI 2010/2655.

12 Tribunals, Courts and Enforcement Act 2007, s 5(1)(e) and (f).

13 SI 1981/500.

England and Wales and Scotland, but there is a separate office in Edinburgh which administers Scottish appeals. Appeals from the Upper Tribunal in Scottish cases are dealt with by the Court of Session, from which there is a further right of appeal to the Supreme Court.

(iii) *Northern Ireland.* Appeals against war pensions and armed forces compensation decisions are heard at first instance by the Pensions Appeal Tribunal (Northern Ireland) and are regulated by the Pensions Appeal Tribunals (Northern Ireland) Rules 1981,[14] as amended. There is a right of appeal with the leave of the Pensions Appeal Tribunal (Northern Ireland) or the Upper Tribunal to the Upper Tribunal on questions of law against decisions of the Pensions Appeal Tribunal (Northern Ireland) in assessment cases. (The Pensions Appeal Commissioners' office in Belfast is also the Northern Ireland office of the Upper Tribunal.) There is a right of appeal with the leave of the Pensions Appeal Tribunal (Northern Ireland) or the Pensions Appeal Commissioners to the Pensions Appeal Commissioners on questions of law against all other decisions of the Pensions Appeal Tribunal (Northern Ireland). There are onward rights of appeal from the Pensions Appeal Commissioners or Upper Tribunal to the Court of Appeal (Northern Ireland), and then to the Supreme Court.

The legislation in its present form refers to each of the first instance tribunals as 'the appropriate tribunal'.[15]

14 SI 1981/231.

15 Pensions Appeal Tribunals Act 1943, s 12.

Chapter 25

Rights of Appeal

THE PENSIONS APPEAL TRIBUNALS ACT 1943

25.1 Rights of appeal in respect of both war pensions and armed forces compensation decisions are conferred by the Pensions Appeal Tribunals Act 1943. In summary, the structure of the relevant provisions of the 1943 Act is as follows:

(i) Appeals against decisions on whether an injury was attributable to or aggravated by service, or whether death was due to service, are brought under section 1.

(ii) Appeals against the making of an interim assessment of disablement, or a final assessment of disablement, or against an assessment of the degree of disablement, are brought under section 5.

(iii) Appeals concerning additional war pensions benefits, known as supplementary allowances, are brought under section 5A of the 1943 Act, which was originally added by section 57 of the Child Support, Pensions and Social Security Act 2000.[1] Decisions which can be appealed under section 5A are called 'specified decisions'.

(iv) The Armed Forces (Pensions and Compensation) Act 2004 amended section 5A of the 1943 Act to allow Armed Forces Compensation Scheme decisions to be designated specified decisions. Appeals against decisions made under the AFCS 2011 are therefore 'specified decision' appeals.

---

1 Section 57(4) of the 2000 Act also conferred rights of appeal against decisions in respect of service between the two World Wars.

ENTITLEMENT APPEALS

25.2 Appeals under section 1 of the Pensions Appeal Tribunals Act 1943 are known as 'entitlement appeals'. Section 1(1) and (2) deals with injury claims and section 1(3) deals with claims in respect of death.

Injury claims

25.3 Section 1(1) and (2) of the Pensions Appeal Tribunals Act 1943, so far as relevant, provides:

> (1) Where any claim in respect of the disablement of any person … is rejected by the Minister on the ground that the injury on which the claim is based—
>
> (a) is not attributable to any relevant service; and
> (b) does not fulfil the following conditions, namely, that it existed before or arose during any relevant service and has been and remains aggravated thereby;
>
> the Minister shall notify the claimant of his decision, specifying that it is made on that ground, and thereupon an appeal shall lie to the appropriate tribunal[2] on the issue whether the claim was rightly rejected on that ground.
>
> (2) Where … the injury on which the claim is based is accepted by the Minister as fulfilling the conditions specified in paragraph (b) of the last foregoing subsection but not as attributable to any relevant service, the Minister shall notify the claimant of his decision, specifying that the injury is so accepted, and thereupon an appeal shall lie to the appropriate tribunal on the issue whether the injury was attributable to such service.

25.4 Section 1(1) requires the decision-maker to consider first whether the injury in respect of which the claim has been made is attributable to service. If the injury is considered not to have been attributable to service, the decision-maker must then decide whether it was aggravated by service. If neither condition is satisfied, the claimant must be notified of the rejection of the claim. Under section 1(2), if the injury is found to have been aggravated by service but not attributable to service, the claimant must be notified accordingly and then has a right of appeal on the question of whether the injury ought to have been found to be attributable to service.

---

2 I.e. the War Pensions and Armed Forces Compensation Chamber of the First-tier Tribunal in England and Wales and the Pensions Appeal Tribunals in Scotland and Northern Ireland (see Chapter 24, n 15).

'On that ground'

25.5 In *CAF/656/2006*,[3] Mr Commissioner Bano (as he then was) held that the 'ground' of a decision under section 1 is a finding that the statutory conditions of entitlement are not satisfied, and not the reasons for that conclusion. That view was approved by the three-judge panel of the Upper Tribunal in *JM v Secretary of State for Defence (AFCS)*[4] (at [25]), although the Upper Tribunal did not refer to *Secretary of State v Rusling*,[5] in which it was held that there is a right of appeal against the Secretary of State's choice of a diagnostic label which has been used in allowing a claim, or *SV v Secretary of State for Defence (AFCS)*[6] in which *Rusling* was followed on this point. On the basis of *JM*, the 'ground' for the rejection of a claim under section 1(1) of the Pensions Appeal Tribunals Act 1943 is a finding that an injury is neither attributable to nor aggravated by service, and on an appeal against the decision a claimant can advance any matter relevant to establishing that the statutory conditions of entitlement are satisfied. However, in the light of *Rusling* it would seem that there is a right of appeal against a determination that the statutory conditions of entitlement have not been satisfied, and/or any ground for that determination which has been notified to the claimant in the written notice of the decision. In an appeal to the Upper Tribunal solely on a ground which does not affect the actual outcome of the claim, the Upper Tribunal may use its discretion under section 12(2)(a) of the Tribunals, Courts and Enforcement Act 2007 not to set aside a tribunal's decision (see para **32.32**). In *MG v Secretary of State for Defence (WP)*,[7] Judge Rowland recorded that permission to appeal had been refused in a related entitlement appeal in which the only issue was the label used to describe the disablement.

Claims in respect of death

25.6 Section 1(3) of the Pensions Appeal Tribunals Act 1943 provides:

> (3) Where any claim in respect of the death of any person … is rejected by the Minister on the ground that neither of the following conditions is fulfilled, namely—
>
> (a) that the death of that person was due to or hastened by an injury which was attributable to any relevant service;

---

3 Unreported.

4 [2015] UKUT 332 (AAC).

5 [2003] EWHC 1539 (QB) (see para **3.7**).

6 [2013] UKUT 541 (AAC). An appeal to the Court of Appeal against the Upper Tribunal's decision in this case was allowed by consent.

7 [2013] UKUT 54 (AAC).

(b) that the death was due to or hastened by the aggravation by any relevant service of an injury which existed before or arose during any relevant service;

the Minister shall notify the claimant of his decision, specifying that it is made on that ground, and thereupon an appeal shall lie to the appropriate tribunal[8] on the issue whether the claim was rightly rejected on that ground.

(3A) The last foregoing subsection shall not apply to any claim … in respect of the death of a person who dies after the expiration of the period of seven years beginning with the end of any relevant service of that person, but where any such claim is rejected by the Minister on the ground that neither of the following conditions is fulfilled, namely—

(a) that the death of that person was due to or substantially hastened by an injury which was attributable to any relevant service;

(b) that the death was due to or substantially hastened by the aggravation by any relevant service of an injury which existed before or arose during any relevant service;

the Minister shall notify the claimant of his decision, specifying that it is made on that ground, and thereupon an appeal shall lie to the appropriate tribunal on the issue whether the claim was rightly rejected on that ground.

Section 1(3) of the Pensions Appeal Tribunals Act 1943 replicates the conditions of entitlement to benefit in article 40(1)(b) of the SPO 2006 in respect of a death occurring no later than 7 years after the termination of service.[9] Section 1(3A) of the 1943 Act applies to cases occurring after the end of the 7-year period and replicates the conditions of entitlement in article 41(1)(b) of the SPO 2006.[10] If a claim is rejected under either provision, the claimant must be notified and has a right of appeal against the rejection.

Relevant service

25.7 Section 1(4) of the Pensions Appeal Tribunals Act 1943 confers a specific right of appeal in relation to the question of whether a period of service is to be taken into account for the purpose of deciding the rank of a claimant, or for deciding whether an injury was aggravated by service before the claimant entered into one of the relationships specified by the provision.

---

8 See Chapter 24, n 15.

9 See para **3.2**.

10 See para **3.2**.

Appeals against entitlement review decisions

25.8 In *Secretary of State for Defence v RC (WP)*,[11] the majority of the three-judge panel of the Upper Tribunal (Judge Rowland and Judge Mesher) held that there was a right of appeal against a refusal to carry out a review. Although the case was specifically concerned with a refusal to carry out a review of an assessment decision, the reasoning of the majority applies equally to entitlement decisions. The majority held (at [60]):

> It then follows from our construction of article 44 that there is a right of appeal against any decision properly given on an application for review under article 44(1), since we have decided that any such application must always lead to a decision under article 44(6).

The majority went on to hold that that principle applies even where the decision is expressed in terms that there are no grounds for reviewing an earlier decision. It follows that the notification requirements of the Pensions Appeal Tribunals Act 1943 should be followed in every case where the Secretary of State refuses to review an earlier decision, however the decision is expressed, and that the claimant should be informed that he or she has a right of appeal against the decision (see *Secretary of State for Defence v RC (WP)* at [62]).

ASSESSMENT APPEALS

Interim assessments

25.9 Section 5(1) of the Pensions Appeal Tribunals Act 1943 provides:

> (1) Where … the Minister makes an interim assessment[12] of the degree of the disablement, he shall notify the claimant thereof and an appeal shall lie to the appropriate tribunal[13] from the interim assessment and from any subsequent interim assessment, and the appropriate tribunal on any such appeal may uphold the Minister's assessment or may alter the assessment in one or both of the following ways, namely—
>
> (a) by increasing or reducing the degree of disablement it specifies; and
>
> (b) by reducing the period for which the assessment is to be in force.

---

11 [2012] UKUT 229 (AAC). See para **6.10** for an analysis of this decision.

12 See paras **8.18** and **8.19** for the power to make interim assessments.

13 See Chapter 24, n 15.

In this section the expression 'interim assessment' means any assessment other than such a final assessment as is referred to in the next following subsection.

25.10 Section 5(1) of the Pensions Appeal Tribunals Act 1943 provides for a right of appeal against a first and any subsequent interim assessment, and section 5(1)(a) gives a tribunal power on an appeal to maintain, increase or decrease the percentage assessment of disablement. Section 5(1)(b) gives a tribunal power to reduce, but not to increase, the period of an interim assessment. Section 5(1) does not allow a final assessment to be substituted for an interim assessment of disablement. In *TL v Secretary of State for Defence (WP)*,[14] Judge Rowland held that a reason had to be given for replacing an open-ended with a fixed-term interim assessment.

Final assessments

25.11 Section 5(2) of the Pensions Appeal Tribunals Act 1943 provides:

> (2) Where it appears to the Minister that the circumstances of the case permit a final settlement of the question to what extent, if any, the said person is disabled, and accordingly—
>
> (a) he decides that there is no disablement or that the disablement has come to an end; or
>
> (b) he makes a final assessment of the degree or nature of the disablement;
>
> he shall notify the claimant of the decision or assessment, stating that it is a final one, and thereupon an appeal shall lie to the appropriate tribunal on the following issues, namely—
>
> (i) whether the circumstances of the case permit a final settlement of the question aforesaid;
>
> (ii) whether the Minister's decision referred to in paragraph (a) hereof or, as the case may be, the final assessment of the degree or nature of the disablement, was right;
>
> and the appropriate tribunal on any such appeal may set aside the said decision or assessment on the ground that the circumstances of the case do not permit of such a final settlement, or may uphold that decision or assessment, or may make such final assessment of the degree or nature of the disablement as they think proper, which may be either higher or lower than the Minister's assessment, if any and if the

14 [2013] UKUT 522 (AAC).

appropriate tribunal so set aside the Minister's decision or assessment they may, if they think fit, make such interim assessment of the degree or nature of the disablement, to be in force until such date not later than two years after the making of the appropriate tribunal's assessment, as they think proper.

25.12 Section 5(2) of the Pensions Appeal Tribunals Act 1943 therefore confers a right of appeal against the following types of decision made on a final assessment of disablement:

(i) a decision that a claimant does not have a disablement;
(ii) a decision that a claimant did have a disablement, but the disablement has come to an end;
(iii) a decision to make a final assessment of disablement;
(iv) the assessment of the degree of disablement on the making of a final assessment.

25.13 A decision that an injury was attributable to service, but that the claimant does not have any disablement, i.e. a nil assessment,[15] allows a decision to be made that a claimant should not receive any injury benefit on the basis of the claimant's current condition, but leaves it open for an award to be made at a later date if the injury subsequently gives rise to some functional limitation, for example loss of mobility. However, this provision enables a nil assessment to be challenged by way of an appeal if a person considers that his or her existing degree of disablement entitles him or her to an award.

25.14 The right of appeal against a decision that a disablement has come to an end enables a claimant to challenge a decision that war pension is no longer payable because an injury is no longer aggravated by service (see para **3.18**).

25.15 As noted in para **8.18**, the review powers now conferred by article 44 of the SPO 2006 make the distinction between interim and final assessments far less important than previously because a person can always apply for a review of a final assessment of disablement if their condition deteriorates. However, article 42(2)(d) provides that the degree of disablement must be assessed on an interim basis unless the member's condition permits a final assessment of the extent of the disablement, and section 5(2) of the Pensions Appeal Tribunals Act 1943 provides for a right of appeal against a decision to make a final assessment of disablement in cases where a person considers that their disablement has not reached a final and settled state.

15 See *Harris v Minister of Pensions* [1948] 1 KB 422.

25.16 A claimant can appeal against the percentage assessment of disablement in every case where a final assessment of disablement has been made. The powers of the tribunal in assessment cases are discussed in Chapter 29.

25.17 A tribunal hearing an appeal under section 5(2) of the Pensions Appeal Tribunals Act 1943 against a final assessment of disablement has power to increase or decrease the assessment of disablement. The tribunal can replace a final assessment with an interim assessment of the nature and degree of the claimant's disablement, but such an interim assessment cannot be for a period longer than 2 years from the date of the tribunal's decision.

Appeals against assessment decisions following a review

25.18 There is a right of appeal against refusals to review assessment decisions (including refusals to carry out a review), and against assessment decisions made as a result of a review (see para **25.8**).

SPECIFIED DECISIONS

25.19 Section 5A of the Pensions Appeal Tribunals Act 1943, which was added by section 57(1) of the Child Support, Pensions and Social Security Act 2000, requires that a claimant is notified of any 'specified decision' and the ground on which the decision has been made, and gives a right of appeal to a tribunal on the issue of whether the decision was rightly made on that ground.[16] A 'specified decision' is any decision which refuses or discontinues an award, or establishes or varies the amount of an award, or varies the date from which an award has effect,[17] under any of the following articles of the SPO 2006:

article 8	Constant attendance allowance
article 9	Exceptionally severe disablement allowance
article 10	Severe disablement occupational allowance
article 11	Clothing allowance
article 12	Unemployability allowances
article 13	Invalidity allowance
article 14	Comforts allowance
article 15	Allowance for lowered standard of occupation
article 16	Age allowance
article 17	Treatment allowance

---

16 See para **25.5**.

17 Pensions Appeal Tribunals (Additional Rights of Appeal) Regulations 2001 (SI 2001/1031), reg 3A, as substituted by Pensions Appeal Tribunals (Additional Rights of Appeal) (Amendment) Regulations 2006 (SI 2006/2893), reg 2 and Sch.

article 18	Abstention from work following treatment in a hospital or similar institution
article 19	Part-time treatment allowance
article 20	Mobility Supplement
article 23(2)	Supplementary pension to surviving spouses and surviving civil partners of members of the armed forces whose service terminated before 31st March 1973
article 24	Pensions to dependants who lived as spouses and dependants who lived as civil partners
article 25	Rent allowance to surviving spouses, surviving civil partners, dependants who lived as spouses and dependants who lived as civil partners, who have children
article 26	Elderly persons allowance
article 27	Temporary allowances
article 28	Allowances for children under the child's age limit
article 29	Pensions for orphans under the child's age limit
article 30	Award for children who have attained the child's age limit
article 31	Awards to or in respect of ineligible members of the families of unemployable pensioners
article 32	Funeral expenses
article 33	Relationships subsequent to the award of pension
article 46 and Schedule 3	Commencing dates of awards
article 53	Maintenance in a hospital or an institution
article 54	Chelsea pensioners
article 55	Children whose maintenance is otherwise provided for
article 57	Forfeiture of pensions etc.
article 58	Refusal of treatment
article 59	Serious negligence or misconduct
article 60	Failure to draw pension
article 66	Cancellation – failure to comply with request
article 71(2) and Schedule 4	Revocations, general and transitory provisions

Armed Forces Compensation Scheme decisions

25.20 Section 5 of, and Schedule 1 to, the Armed Forces (Pensions and Compensation) Act 2004 amended section 5A of the Pensions Appeal Tribunals Act 1943 to enable decisions made on armed forces compensation claims to be designated as specified decisions. Regulation 3 of the Pensions Appeal Tribunals Act 1943 (Armed Forces and Reserve Forces Compensation Scheme) (Rights of

Appeal) Regulations 2011[18] provides that a decision is a specified decision (and therefore appealable) if it:

(a) determines whether a benefit is payable;
(b) determines the amount payable under an award of benefit; and
(c) is issued under article 26(6) (refusal to make a temporary award permanent etc.) or 26(8) (addition of new descriptor) of the 2011 Order, relating to the making of a permanent award.

Regulation 3(2) provides that a decision is not a specified decision if it:

(a) makes or arises from the making of an interim award under article 52(1) of the 2011 Order;
(b) suspends the payment of an award of benefit;
(c) makes or arises from the making of a temporary award under article 26(2) of the 2011 Order;
(d) determines whether a fast payment is made under article 27(1) of the 2011 Order;
(e) relates to the payment, in whole or in part, of medical expenses under article 28(1) of the 2011 Order.

Appeals in respect of temporary awards

25.21 In *Secretary of State for Defence v FA (AFCS)*,[19] a tribunal of Pensions Appeal Commissioners in Northern Ireland held that a tribunal has power under the AFCS 2011 to decide whether the three conditions for the making of a temporary award are satisfied,[20] namely, whether the claimant has suffered an injury for which there is no tariff descriptor, whether the injury is sufficiently serious to warrant an award of injury benefit, and whether the injury is listed in ICD 10 or DSM4.[21] However, a tribunal has no power to decide the appropriate tariff level for the injury or to make a temporary award itself.

---

18 SI 2011/1240.

19 [2015] NICom 17.

20 A decision not to make a temporary award was not a specified decision under the AFCS 2005 as a result of the amendments to the Pensions Appeal Tribunals (Armed Forces and Reserve Forces Compensation Scheme) (Rights of Appeal) Regulations 2005 (SI 2005/1029) made by the Pensions Appeal Tribunals (Additional Rights of Appeal) (Amendment) Regulations 2006 (SI 2006/2893).

21 See paras **19.24–19.26**.

Revision and lapse of appeals

25.22 Rule 22 of the Tribunal Procedure (First-tier Tribunal) (War Pensions and Armed Forces Compensation Chamber) Rules 2008[22] (England and Wales Procedure Rules) provides that if the decision-maker revises the decision under appeal, the appeal is to proceed as an appeal against the revised decision. If the appellant wishes the appeal to proceed, the appellant must send the decision-maker, i.e. Veterans UK, within 42 days of being sent notice of the revised decision either representations in writing in relation to the revised decision, or a statement in writing that the appellant wishes the appeal to proceed but has no additional representations to make. Failure to take these steps will result in the appeal lapsing, but the notice of the revised decision must state what the appellant must do to prevent the lapse occurring. If the Statement of Case has already been submitted, the representations or statement must be sent to the tribunal.

25.23 The position with regard to the lapsing of appeals is different in each of the tribunals in Scotland and Northern Ireland. Rule 9 of the Pensions Appeal Tribunals (Scotland) Rules 1981[23] (Scotland Procedure Rules) provides that where the decision under appeal is revised, the appeal shall continue as if brought in relation to the revised decision, and that the appeal will lapse if the appellant does not wish to proceed with the appeal and notifies the tribunal accordingly. Rule 9(2) of the Pensions Appeal Tribunals (Northern Ireland) Rules 1981[24] (Northern Ireland Procedure Rules) provides that where, after a notice of appeal has been given, the Secretary of State decides the issue arising on the appeal in favour of the appellant, the Secretary of State shall give notice of his decision to the tribunal and to the appellant, and the appeal shall be struck out. Rule 9(3) provides that in an assessment appeal the making of a new increased assessment for the period under appeal (whether covering additional disabilities or not) shall be deemed to be a decision by the Secretary of State in favour of the appellant and, on notice given in accordance with rule 9(2), the appeal shall be struck out, without prejudice to any appeal against that decision. The practice in Northern Ireland is for every 'lapsing' case to be considered by the President of the Pensions Appeal Tribunal in order to ensure that the new decision is in fact more favourable to the appellant.

---

22 SI 2008/2686.

23 SI 1981/500.

24 SI 1981/231.

Chapter 26

Bringing an Appeal

PROCEDURE

26.1 The procedure for bringing an appeal under the Pensions Appeal Tribunals Act 1943 is governed by the separate rules of procedure in each of the three UK jurisdictions, although the Scotland and Northern Ireland Procedure Rules are broadly similar. Appeals brought by persons resident in England and Wales or abroad are dealt with by the War Pensions and Armed Forces Compensation Chamber of the First-tier Tribunal, and appeals brought by those resident in Scotland or Northern Ireland are dealt with by the Pensions Appeal Tribunals in those jurisdictions.[1] Proceedings can be transferred from one tribunal to another if the appellant changes address.[2] An appeal can also be transferred from England and Wales to Scotland or Northern Ireland if the appellant resided abroad when the proceedings were started and if the appellant has a closer connection with Scotland or Northern Ireland than with England and Wales, or if there is some other good reason for the appeal to be heard in Scotland or Northern Ireland. If the tribunal refuses such a request, it must send the appellant written reasons for the refusal.[3]

26.2 Rule 21(1) of the England and Wales Procedure Rules provides that an appellant must start proceedings by sending or delivering a notice of appeal to the decision-maker so that it is received within 12 months after the date on which written notice of the decision being challenged was sent to the appellant. In Scotland and Northern Ireland also the notice of appeal is sent to the decision-maker, i.e. Veterans UK. Rule 3 of the Scotland and Northern Ireland Procedure Rules allows for appeals to be brought by a person on behalf of persons under the age of 16 and claimants under a disability, without the need for the formal appointment of a representative.

---

1 Pensions Appeal Tribunals Act 1943, Sch 1, para 6.

2 Under powers conferred by Pensions Appeal Tribunals Act 1943, Sch 1, para 6B.

3 England and Wales Procedure Rules, r 19.

26.3 The procedure whereby a notice of appeal is sent to the body responsible for the decision under appeal, rather than to the tribunal, is unsatisfactory. As well as being inefficient, it results in the decision-maker having a significant measure of control over the initial stages of an appeal against one of its own decisions, and is therefore inconsistent with the principle underlying the Leggatt reforms in England and Wales[4] that tribunals should be seen to be independent of government. *The Armed Forces Covenant Annual Report 2014* commented:

> Members of the Armed Forces community are unique in the judicial process in that they have to lodge an appeal with the defendant organisation rather than appeal directly to the tribunal. While the implications of this process might only be with respect to the timing of the hearing of an appeal, they have an impact on perceptions.[5]

Form of notice of appeal

26.4 Rule 21(5) of the England and Wales Procedure Rules provides that the notice of appeal must be in English or Welsh and must be signed by the appellant. It must state:

(a) the name and address of the appellant;
(b) the name and address of the appellant's representative (if any);
(c) an address where documents for the appellant may be sent or delivered;
(d) details (including the full reference) of the decision being appealed;
(e) the grounds on which the appellant relies.

Although the rule provides that the notice of appeal must be signed by the appellant, in *CO v London Borough of Havering*,[6] Judge Wikeley held that the identical requirement in rule 23(6) of the Tribunal Procedure (First-tier Tribunal) (Social Entitlement Chamber) Rules 2008[7] was satisfied if the notice of appeal was signed on the appellant's behalf by the appellant's solicitor. Rule 7(2) of the England and Wales Procedure Rules allows the tribunal to waive any failure to comply with a requirement of the Rules, and in *Salisbury Independent Living v Wirral MBC (HB)*,[8] Judge Rowland stated that the requirement for a notice of appeal to be 'signed by the appellant' would generally be waived if the notice of appeal is signed by a representative, such as a welfare rights worker or Citizens Advice representative, who provides signed authority to bring the appeal. Rule 4

---

4 See Chapter 24, n 5.

5 Ministry of Defence, *The Armed Forces Covenant Annual Report 2014* (Ministry of Defence, 2014), p 16.

6 [2015] UKUT 28 (AAC).

7 SI 2008/2685.

8 [2011] UKUT 44 (AAC).

of the Scotland and Northern Ireland Procedure Rules expressly provides that the notice of appeal can be signed on behalf of the appellant, but require the date of signature to be stated and the document to be sent by post addressed to the Secretary of State for Defence. In England and Wales the form of notice of appeal is not prescribed, but does have to include the information prescribed by rule 21(5) of the England and Wales Procedure Rules. In Scotland and Northern Ireland, the notice of appeal must be in the approved form. However, the form used for making an appeal is the same throughout the United Kingdom.[9]

Time limits for appeals

26.5 Section 8 of the Pensions Appeal Tribunals Act 1943 originally provided for a time limit of 3 months for bringing appeals against interim assessment decisions and of 12 months for appealing against other decisions from the date of notification of the decision, with a discretion to extend time if there was a reasonable excuse for a delay in bringing the appeal. The 12-month time limit was reduced to 6 months in 2001 by section 58 of the Child Support, Pensions and Social Security Act 2000, but a 12-month time limit, applicable to all war pensions and armed forces compensation appeals, was introduced in 2011. In England and Wales, this is in rule 21(1) of the England and Wales Procedure Rules, as amended by the Tribunal Procedure (Amendment) Rules 2011.[10] The time limits for appealing in Scotland and Northern Ireland remain in section 8 of the 1943 Act, as amended by the Pensions Appeal Tribunals Act 1943 (Time Limit for Appeals) (Amendment) Regulations 2011.[11] In Scotland and Northern Ireland, rule 4 of the Scotland and Northern Ireland Procedure Rules allows an assessment appeal to be treated as in time if an appellant sends the Secretary of State a letter notifying him of his or her intention to appeal within the permitted appeal period and then submits an appeal form within 6 weeks, but otherwise the time limits for appealing in England and Wales are now the same as the time limits for appealing in Scotland and Northern Ireland.

26.6 However, the position with regard to extending time for appealing is different in England and Wales. The Pensions Appeal Tribunals (Late Appeals) Regulations 2001,[12] which continue to apply to appeals in Scotland and Northern Ireland, provide for the time limit for bringing an appeal to be extended by up to

---

9 War Pension and Armed Forces Compensation Scheme Notice of Appeal (appeal form), which can be obtained from Veterans UK, Ministry of Defence, Norcross, Thornton Cleveleys, Lancashire FY5 3WP; or downloaded from the website at www.gov.uk/government/organisations/veterans-uk, 'Making a claim: forms'.

10 SI 2011/651.

11 SI 2011/1239.

12 SI 2001/1032.

12 months if the appeal is brought as soon as reasonably practicable in the circumstances of the case and the main cause of non-compliance with the time limit was:

- (i) the death or serious illness of the claimant or a spouse or dependant of the claimant;
- (ii) the disruption of normal postal services;
- (iii) failure on the part of the Secretary of State to notify the claimant of the decision; or
- (iv) exceptional circumstances applying to the claimant which rendered it impracticable for the claimant to bring the appeal or to instruct another person to bring it.

In England and Wales, the power to admit a late appeal is governed by rule 5(3)(a) of the England and Wales Procedure Rules, which gives the tribunal power to 'extend or shorten the time for complying with any rule, practice direction or direction', but rule 21(4) stipulates that no appeal may be made more than 12 months after the expiry of the 12-month period for bringing an appeal provided for by rule 21(1). Rule 21(7) provides that the power to extend time or waive any failure to comply with the rules must not be exercised so as to allow an appeal to be brought after that date. Although the powers to admit late appeals are therefore different in England and Wales from those in Scotland and in Northern Ireland, there are unlikely to be many cases in which the differences are of practical significance.

26.7 There are also differences in England and Wales with regard to the procedure to be followed in the case of late appeals. Under rule 21(2) of the England and Wales Procedure Rules, the appellant must give reasons for a late appeal, and rule 21(6) requires a late appeal to be referred to the tribunal immediately if Veterans UK objects to it being treated as in time. Rule 21(3) provides that a late appeal is to be treated as having been made in time if Veterans UK does not object.

Appeals after the absolute time limit

26.8 In *R(AF) 1/09*, Judge Levenson followed the decision of Stanley Burnton J in *R (Secretary of State for Defence) v Pensions Appeal Tribunal (Lockyer-Evis and others, interested parties)*,[13] holding that a tribunal does not have power to hear an appeal brought after the expiry of the 24-month absolute time limit. However, in *PM v Secretary of State for Defence (AFCS)*,[14] the claimant had a

13 [2007 EWHC 1177 (Admin), [2008] 1 All ER 287.

14 [2015] UKUT 0647 (AAC).

mental illness. On 25 August 2009, the SPVA made an Armed Forces Compensation Scheme award following a review of an earlier decision, but there was no evidence that the claimant had received a letter notifying him of the review decision. The claimant appealed against the 2009 decision on 12 April 2014, but his appeal was struck out because it was brought after the expiry of the 2 year absolute time limit. Judge Rowland held that the tribunal had erred in law because it had failed to consider whether a failure to extend the time limit would result in a breach of the claimant's right to a fair trial under Article 6 of the European Convention on Human Rights. Judge Rowland referred to *Adesina v Nursing and Midwifery Council*,[15] in which, following the Supreme Court case of *Romiechowski v Poland*,[16] the Court of Appeal held that a discretion to extend a time limit in order to comply with Article 6 should only arise in 'exceptional circumstances', and where the appellant 'personally has done all he can to bring the appeal timeously.'

POSTHUMOUS APPEALS

26.9 The Pensions Appeal Tribunals Act 1943 was modified by the Pensions Appeal Tribunals (Posthumous Appeals) Order 1980[17] in order to allow an appeal to be made or continued on a claimant's death. Under article 3(1), if a claimant dies before being notified of the decision on a claim, the Secretary of State must, on becoming aware of the death, notify the 'designated person',[18] who can then appeal against the decision. If the claimant has been notified of the decision during his or her lifetime but has not appealed against it, article 3(2) allows the designated person to appeal as if the claimant had not died, but no award can be made in respect of any period after the claimant's death. Article 5 allows the designated person to continue an appeal on behalf of an appellant who has died before the decision on the appeal has been given. An appeal can be brought or continued in each case without the need for a grant of probate or letters of administration, subject to the directions of a tribunal President.[19]

26.10 In Scotland and Northern Ireland, if the tribunal is notified that the appellant has died before an appeal has been decided, the case is placed in the

---

15 [2013] EWCA Civ 818, [2013] 1 WLR 3156.

16 [2012] UKSC 20, [2012] 1 WLR 1604.

17 SI 1980/1082, as amended by the Pensions Appeal Tribunals (Posthumous Appeals) Amendment Order 2001 (SI 2001/408), the Pensions Appeal Tribunals (Posthumous Appeals) (Amendment) Order 2005 (SI 2005/245) and the Tribunals, Courts and Enforcement Act 2007 (Transitional and Consequential Provisions) Order 2008 (SI 2008/2683).

18 I.e. a relative of the deceased, or if there is no such person, the deceased's personal representatives. For the definition of 'designated person', see SPO 2006, art 68(5)(b).

19 Article 6.

'deferred list', which is a list of cases that are dormant for one reason or another and which can be put in the list for hearing only if a direction to that effect has been given by the tribunal President.[20] The President can give directions to ascertain the identity of the designated person and if the appeal was an entitlement appeal and the designated person proceeds with it on behalf of the appellant, the entitlement appeal and any appeal brought in respect of the appellant's death must be heard at the same time.[21]

WITHDRAWAL OF APPEALS

26.11 Rule 17 of the England and Wales Procedure Rules allows a party to withdraw an appeal by giving the tribunal written notice or orally at a hearing, but notice given at a hearing will take effect only if the tribunal consents to the withdrawal. Rule 9 of the Northern Ireland Procedure Rules allows an appeal to be withdrawn by written notice, but only before the hearing of the appeal. Rule 9 of the Scotland Procedure Rules provides for an appeal to lapse if the appellant notifies the tribunal that he or she does not wish to proceed with the appeal.

26.12 Rule 17(3) of the England and Wales Procedure Rules allows a party who has withdrawn an appeal to apply for the appeal to be reinstated if an application is made in writing and is received by the tribunal within 28 days after the date of receipt of notice of withdrawal, or within 28 days of the hearing if the application to withdraw was made orally, but those time limits can be extended under rule 5(3)(a).

26.13 In *WM v SSWP (DLA)*,[22] which was concerned with a rule similar to rule 17 in the Tribunal Procedure (First-tier Tribunal) Social Entitlement Chamber Rules 2008,[23] Judge Knowles held that a written notice of withdrawal given during the period while an appeal was adjourned part-heard was effective immediately and did not need the consent of the tribunal for the withdrawal to take effect. The tribunal therefore had no power to proceed with the adjourned hearing.

STATEMENT OF CASE

26.14 The rules of procedure which were largely common to all three UK jurisdictions prior to the 2008 tribunal reforms in England and Wales required the

20 Scotland and Northern Ireland Procedure Rules, rule 25.

21 Scotland and Northern Ireland Procedure Rules, rule 23.

22 [2015] UKUT 0642 (AAC).

23 SI 2008/2685.

decision-maker to prepare a response to the appeal called a Statement of Case. In order to harmonise the rules of procedure in the War Pensions and Armed Forces Compensation Chamber of the First-tier Tribunal with the rules of procedure in other Chambers, the England and Wales Procedure Rules require the decision-maker to provide a 'response' and impose requirements similar to those in other First-tier Tribunal Chambers.

26.15 Rule 23(1) of the England and Wales Procedure Rules requires the decision-maker to send or deliver to the tribunal as soon as practicable after receiving a notice of appeal a response giving details about the decision-maker, to state whether the appeal is opposed and, if so, the grounds for opposition. The response may also include a submission as to whether it would be appropriate for the case to be dealt with without a hearing.[24] The decision-maker must provide with the response:

(i) a copy of any written record of the decision under appeal, and any statement of reasons for that decision;
(ii) copies of all documents relevant to the case in the decision-maker's possession,[25] unless a practice direction or direction states otherwise;
(iii) a copy of the notice of appeal, any documents provided by the appellant with the notice of appeal and, unless stated in the notice of appeal, the name and address of the appellant's representative (if any).

Veterans UK must send a copy of the response and any accompanying documents to the appellant at the same time as it provides it to the tribunal. The appellant may make a written submission in reply to the response within 1 month after the date on which the response was sent.

26.16 In Northern Ireland (but not in Scotland or in England and Wales), Veterans UK must send a copy of the notice of appeal to the tribunal by first class post within 14 days of receipt,[26] although Veterans UK routinely inform the tribunals in the other jurisdictions of the existence of an appeal before a Statement of Case is prepared. The Scotland and Northern Ireland Procedure Rules require the Statement of Case to include the following information:

---

24 England and Wales Procedure Rules, r 23(3).

25 In tribunal proceedings there is no presumption that a party has correctly identified all relevant documents on disclosure (*Secretary of State for Defence v LA (AFCS)* [2011] UKUT 391 (AAC)).

26 Pension Appeal Tribunals (Northern Ireland) Rules 1981, r 4(3).

(i) the relevant facts relating to the appellant's case as known to Veterans UK, including the relevant medical history of the appellant;

(ii) in the case of an entitlement appeal, the reasons for making the decision against which the appeal is brought.[27]

In Scotland and Northern Ireland, Veterans UK must send the appellant two copies of the Statement of Case and inform the appellant of the right to submit an answer to the Statement of Case, indicating whether and in what respects the facts in the Statement of Case are disputed, any further facts which in the appellant's opinion are relevant to the appeal, and any reasons for challenging the Secretary of State's decision or assessment.[28] An appellant who submits an answer to the Statement of Case must attach to it such documentary evidence in support as he or she reasonably can.[29]

26.17 Despite the differences in the requirements with regard to the Statement of Case in the three UK jurisdictions, in practice Veterans UK prepares the Statement of Case in the same way irrespective of which tribunal is dealing with the appeal.[30] The Statement of Case generally consists of a paginated bundle containing copies of the appellant's service record and personal details, a record of the decision under appeal, the certificate issued by the medical authorities containing the reasons for the decision, copies of relevant medical appendices, reports of service medical examinations, the notice of appeal and any accompanying documents and medical information obtained in connection with the claim.

26.18 Because the information required by rules 23(2)(a) to (d) of the England and Wales Procedure Rules is the same in every case, the War Pensions and Armed Forces Compensation Chamber does not require it to be included in the response.

---

27 Scotland and Northern Ireland Procedure Rules, rule 5.

28 Pensions Appeal Tribunals (Scotland) Rules 1981, r 5(2), Pensions Appeal Tribunals (Northern Ireland) Rules 1981, r 5(2).

29 Pensions Appeal Tribunals (Scotland) Rules 1981, r 5(2); Pensions Appeal Tribunals (Northern Ireland) Rules 1981, r 5(3).

30 Although Statements of Case in their standard form probably comply with the Scotland and Northern Ireland Procedure Rules in giving reasons for the decision which is the subject of the appeal, they almost certainly do not comply with the England and Wales Procedure Rules requirement to state whether the appeal is opposed and, if so, the grounds of opposition.

Chapter 27

Case Management

CASE MANAGEMENT POWERS

27.1 The War Pensions and Armed Forces Compensation Chamber of the First-tier Tribunal in England and Wales and the Pensions Appeal Tribunals in Scotland and Northern Ireland have powers under their rules to control the conduct of proceedings before them in order to ensure that appeals are dealt with fairly, efficiently and with the minimum of delay. In England and Wales, those powers are mostly conferred by rule 5 of the England and Wales Procedure Rules and the powers under that rule are called case management powers. Following amendments to the Pensions Appeal Tribunals Rules in 1998 in Scotland and Northern Ireland,[1] tribunal Presidents, or tribunal members nominated by the President, were given powers to review the documents in the Statement of Case, specifically in order to consider whether further information or evidence needed to be obtained on any point, or whether it was necessary to obtain a specialist medical or technical expert's report.[2] In England and Wales, appeals are routinely referred to tribunal judges for case management following receipt of the Statement of Case.

27.2 Rule 2(3) of the England and Wales Procedure Rules requires the tribunal to give effect to the 'overriding objective' of the Rules when it exercises any power under the Rules or interprets any rule or practice direction. Rule 2(1) defines the overriding objective as 'to enable the Tribunal to deal with cases fairly and justly', and by rule 2(2) 'dealing with a case justly and fairly' includes:

(a) dealing with the case in ways which are proportionate to the importance of the case, the complexity of the issues, the anticipated costs and the resources of the parties;

---

1 By the Pensions Appeal Tribunals (Scotland) (Amendment) Rules 1998 (1998/1225) and the Pensions Appeal Tribunals (Northern Ireland) Amendment Rules 1998 (SR 1998/265).

2 Scotland and Northern Ireland Procedure Rules, rule 5A.

(b) avoiding unnecessary formality and seeking flexibility in the proceedings;
(c) ensuring, so far as practicable, that the parties are able to participate fully in the proceedings;
(d) using any special expertise of the Tribunal effectively; and
(e) avoiding delay, so far as compatible with proper consideration of the issues.

Rule 2(4) requires the parties to help the tribunal to further the overriding objective and to co-operate with the tribunal generally.

27.3 Rule 5(1) and (2) of the England and Wales Procedure Rules gives the tribunal broad power to regulate its own procedure and issue directions, including the power to extend or shorten the time for complying with any rule, practice direction or direction (rule 5(3)(a)), to consolidate or hear together part or all of two or more cases (rule 5(3)(b)), to permit or require a party or another person to provide documents, information, evidence or submissions (rule 5(3)(d)), to deal with an issue as a preliminary issue (rule 5(3)(e)), and to adjourn or postpone a hearing (rule 5(3)(h)). Rule 18 allows one of a number of cases raising common issues of law or fact to be treated as a lead case, and provides for the procedure to be followed in such cases. In Scotland and Northern Ireland, a tribunal President has power under rule 31 of the Scotland and Northern Ireland Procedure Rules in each jurisdiction to extend the time for complying with any time limit imposed by the rules of procedure. Examples given in the Scotland and Northern Ireland Procedure Rules of where justice may require the power to be exercised are if the appellant or partner or a dependant of the appellant has died or suffered a serious illness, if the appellant is not resident in the United Kingdom, or if postal services have been disrupted. The Scotland and Northern Ireland Procedure Rules do not confer other specific case management powers, but following a review of the appeal documents under rule 5A the tribunal President can 'give such directions as he thinks fit on any matter arising in connection with the appeal'.[3] Either party may also apply to the tribunal President at any time 'for directions on any matter arising in connection with the appeal, or in connection with an application to the tribunal for leave to appeal to the Upper Tribunal'.[4]

Applying for directions

27.4 The procedure for applying for directions in England and Wales is laid down by rule 6 of the England and Wales Procedure Rules, which provides that a direction can be given on the application of any of the parties, or by the tribunal

---

3 Pensions Appeal Tribunals (Scotland) Rules 1981, r 5A(1); Pensions Appeal Tribunal (Northern Ireland) Rules 1981, r 5A(1)(c).

4 Scotland and Northern Ireland Procedure Rules, rule 30.

on its own initiative.[5] An application for a direction by one of the parties may be made by means of a written application, or orally during the course of a hearing.[6] The application must include the reason for making the application[7] and, unless the tribunal considers that there is a good reason not to do so, the tribunal must send written notice of any direction to the parties and to any other party affected by the direction. If a party or other person wishes to challenge a direction, they may do so by applying for another direction which amends, suspends, or sets aside the direction.[8]

27.5 In Scotland and Northern Ireland, rule 30 of the Scotland and Northern Ireland Procedure Rules requires an application for directions to 'state the matter on which directions are required'. The President must communicate the nature of the application to the other party, together with a statement informing the party of the right to make written comments on the application, which must be taken into consideration before any directions are given.

Non-compliance with directions

27.6 Rule 7(1) of the England and Wales Procedure Rules provides that an irregularity resulting from a failure to comply with a requirement of the Rules or of any practice direction or direction does not of itself render void the proceedings or any step taken in the proceedings. Under rule 7(2), if a party does not comply with such a requirement, the tribunal may take such action as it considers just, which may include:

- (i) waiving the requirement;
- (ii) requiring the failure to be remedied;
- (iii) striking out the party's case;[9]
- (iv) referring the breach to the Upper Tribunal.

The power to refer the breach to the Upper Tribunal is restricted to failure to comply with certain types of direction relating to the provision of evidence.[10] On such a reference, the Upper Tribunal has power under section 25 of the Tribunals, Courts and Enforcement Act 2007 to impose the same sanctions as the High Court,[11] i.e. a penalty for contempt of court including a fine or imprisonment for

5 England and Wales Procedure Rules, r 6(1).

6 England and Wales Procedure Rules, r 6(2).

7 England and Wales Procedure Rules, r 6(3).

8 England and Wales Procedure Rules, r 6(5).

9 See para **27.7**.

10 England and Wales Procedure Rules, r 7(3).

11 See Tribunal Procedure (Upper Tribunal) Rules 2008 (SI 2008/2698) (Upper Tribunal Procedure Rules), r 7(3) and (4).

a period of up to 2 years. Under rule 30(5) of the Scotland and Northern Ireland Procedure Rules, the sanction for non-compliance with a direction is for the case to be placed in the deferred list.[12]

Striking out

27.7 Rule 8 of the England and Wales Procedure Rules gives the tribunal power to strike out part or all of an appellant's case. Any part of the case in respect of which the tribunal has no jurisdiction must be struck out.[13] The tribunal may strike out the whole or any part of the proceedings if:

- (i) the appellant has failed to comply with a direction which stated that failure by the appellant to comply with the direction could lead to the striking out of the proceedings or part of them;
- (ii) the appellant has failed to co-operate with the tribunal to such an extent that the tribunal cannot deal with the proceedings fairly and justly; or
- (iii) the tribunal considers there is no reasonable prospect of the appellant's case, or part of it, succeeding.[14]

The tribunal can only strike out the proceedings under (ii) or (iii) if the appellant has been given the opportunity of making representations in relation to the proposed striking out,[15] and the appellant may apply in writing within 42 days of receiving notification of the striking out for the proceedings to be reinstated.[16] Since the effect of striking-out an appeal may be to deprive the appellant of a hearing, these powers are exercised cautiously. The powers to strike out are also available against a respondent.[17]

27.8 In Northern Ireland, a case may be struck out under rule 10 of the Northern Ireland Procedure Rules if the appellant fails to prosecute the appeal and does not satisfy the President that he had sufficient reason for his failure to do so. Alternatively, the President may direct the case to be placed in the deferred list.[18] Under rule 25 of both the Scotland and Northern Ireland Procedure Rules, a case can be struck out if it has been placed in the deferred list and no application has been made within 12 months for it to be placed in the list of cases for hearing, or

---

12 See para **26.12**.

13 England and Wales Procedure Rules, r 8(2).

14 England and Wales Procedure Rules, r 8(3).

15 England and Wales Procedure Rules, r 8(4).

16 England and Wales Procedure Rules, r 8(5).

17 England and Wales Procedure Rules, r 8(7).

18 See para **26.10**.

if such an application is refused. The case must also be struck out if a designated person does not apply for the case to be placed in the list for hearing within 12 months of being notified that the case has been placed in the deferred list.

Obtaining and using documents and other information

27.9 Rule 5(3)(d) of the England and Wales Procedure Rules gives the tribunal power to 'permit or require a party or another person to provide documents, information, evidence or submissions to the Tribunal or a party'. This power can be used to compel the production of documents which have not been included in the Statement of Case and documents which are in the possession of third parties. Although the power is very wide-ranging, it should not be used to compel the production of documents which are legally privileged (see *LM v London Borough of Lewisham*[19]). Under rule 16, the tribunal can also order any person to answer any questions or produce any documents in that person's possession or control which relate to any issue in the proceedings.

27.10 Rule 6 of the Scotland and Northern Ireland Procedure Rules allows an appellant to apply for an order for disclosure of documents in the possession of a government department. The application must be made within 6 weeks of the appellant's receipt of the Statement of Case and cannot be used to compel the disclosure of documents in the nature of government minutes of reports, or the name of any government medical officer who has provided a medical report or certificate relating to the appellant or any person in respect of whose death the appeal has been brought. If a minister certifies that it would be contrary to the public interest for the whole or part of the document to which the direction relates to be disclosed publicly, the President must give directions prohibiting or restricting the disclosure in public of the whole or part of the document. If a minister certifies that the whole or part of the document ought not to be disclosed for reasons of security, the President must issue a direction to the tribunal to consider whether the appellant's case would be prejudiced if the appeal were to proceed without the disclosure. If the tribunal takes that view, the appeal must be adjourned until such time as the necessity for non-disclosure no longer exists. There is provision for an appellant to make an application under this rule at the hearing if the appellant has a reasonable excuse for not having made the application earlier.

27.11 Rule 14 of the England and Wales Procedure Rules gives the tribunal power to make an order prohibiting the disclosure or publication of specified documents or information relating to the proceedings, or any matter likely to lead

[19] [2009] UKUT 204 (AAC), [2010] AACR 12.

members of the public to identify any person whom the tribunal considers should not be identified, if:

(i) the tribunal is satisfied that such disclosure would be likely to cause that person or some other person serious harm; and
(ii) the tribunal is satisfied, having regard to the interests of justice, that it is proportionate to give such a direction.

Under rule 14(3) of the England and Wales Procedure Rules, the documents or information are omitted from the Statement of Case if Veterans UK considers that a direction should be given under this provision, but the documents or information are sent to the tribunal for it to decide the issue. If a person has appointed a representative, the tribunal may direct that the documents or information can be disclosed to the representative if the tribunal is satisfied that the disclosure is in the interests of the person and that the representative will not disclose the information directly or indirectly to a third party without the tribunal's consent.[20]

27.12 Non-disclosure orders are used in cases where Veterans UK is in possession of medical information of which an appellant is unaware and which would be likely to cause serious harm if it were disclosed. The powers can also be used to prevent the identification of a person such as a child or vulnerable adult, and also enable the tribunal to make an order in the nature of a reporting restriction. In *Secretary of State for Defence v LA (AFCS)*,[21] Judge Jacobs observed that rule 14 had not been drafted with the prohibition of disclosure in the interests of national security in mind, since in such cases it might be difficult to show that an appellant would misuse any information, although national security considerations may be relevant in relation to the powers under rule 5 with regard to disclosure of documents.

27.13 Rule 22 of the Scotland and Northern Ireland Procedure Rules deals specifically with the disclosure of potentially harmful medical information, i.e. cases 'where the medical history of the appellant or of the person in respect of whose death an appeal is brought comprises material which in the opinion of the Secretary of State, it would be undesirable in the interests of the appellant to disclose to him'. Under rule 22(2), the Statement of Case in such cases is sent to the appellant's representative instead of to the appellant. If the appellant does not have a representative, the potentially harmful information is omitted in the copy of the Statement of Case sent to the appellant, but is included in the copy sent to the tribunal, with a notice stating that material has been omitted and the reasons for the omission.[22] The President must then use best endeavours to help the

20 England and Wales Procedure Rules, r 14(5).

21 [2011] UKUT 391 (AAC).

22 Scotland and Northern Ireland Procedure Rules, rule 22(3).

appellant find a suitable person or organisation to represent him or her at the hearing of the appeal, and if a representative is found Veterans UK must send the representative two copies of the omitted portion of the Statement of Case with a notice stating that the omissions were made under rule 22.[23] The President must indicate to the tribunal which portions of the Statement of Case have not been disclosed to the appellant, and the tribunal must then decide whether the omitted portions should be disclosed to the appellant in the appellant's interests. The tribunal must take the omitted portions of the Statement of Case into consideration when deciding the appeal.

Commissioning of medical or other expert evidence

27.14 Rule 24(3) of the England and Wales Procedure Rules and rule 15 of the Scotland and Northern Ireland Procedure Rules allow the tribunal to commission a medical or expert's report on a technical question. Under rule 5A of the Scotland and Northern Ireland Procedure Rules, a report can be directed when the Statement of Case is reviewed, but if a report is directed at the hearing of the appeal, the appellant must be given an opportunity of commenting on it and requesting a further hearing. The report can be sent to the appellant's doctor and to the appellant's representative if it would not be in the appellant's best interests for it to be communicated to the appellant personally.

---

[23] Scotland and Northern Ireland Procedure Rules, rule 22(4).

Chapter 28

The Hearing

COMPOSITION OF THE TRIBUNAL

England and Wales

28.1 Under the terms of a Practice Statement issued by the Senior President of Tribunals on 30 October 2008,[1] a decision that disposes of proceedings (i.e. a final decision) or a decision that determines a preliminary issue[2] made at or following a hearing must be made by a tribunal consisting of a tribunal judge, a service member[3] and a medical member.[4] There is provision for a tribunal to include two medical members if the Chamber President thinks it appropriate.

Scotland and Northern Ireland

28.2 In Scotland and Northern Ireland, paragraph 2A of the Schedule to the Pensions Appeal Tribunals Act 1943 requires that tribunal members include members who are legally qualified to hold judicial office, persons who are medically qualified, and persons with knowledge or experience of service in the armed forces. There is also a requirement to have regard to the desirability for tribunals to include persons with knowledge or experience of disability issues.

---

1 Practice Statement: Composition of Tribunals in relation to matters that fall to be decided by the War Pensions and Armed Forces Compensation Chamber on or after 3 November 2008, Senior President of Tribunals (30 October 2008).

2 With the exception of decisions under the England and Wales Procedure Rules, Pt 4.

3 Defined as a 'member who has substantial experience of service in Her Majesty's naval, military or air forces or who is a transferred-in other member from the Pensions Appeal Tribunal who is not a registered medical practitioner'.

4 A registered medical practitioner.

NOTICE OF HEARING

28.3 Rule 25 of the England and Wales Procedure Rules allows an appeal to be decided without a hearing if the parties do not object and if the tribunal considers that it is able to decide the appeal without a hearing. 'Paper hearings' are uncommon in war pensions and armed forces compensation appeals, but may become more frequent. If a case is dealt with in this way, the tribunal's reasons should show why the tribunal considers that it is able to decide the appeal without a hearing.

28.4 Hearings are held wherever possible in a venue which is convenient for the appellant. Rule 27 requires the parties to be given reasonable notice of the time and place of the hearing (including any adjourned or postponed hearing) and of any changes. The period of notice must be at least 14 days unless the parties consent to a shorter period of notice or there are urgent or exceptional circumstances. The period of notice of the hearing required by rule 8 of the Scotland and Northern Ireland Procedure Rules is not less than 10 clear days.

ADJOURNING OR POSTPONING A HEARING

28.5 In England and Wales, the power to adjourn or postpone a hearing is conferred by rule 5(3)(h) of the England and Wales Procedure Rules. It is usual to refer to a hearing being 'adjourned' if it has already begun, and being 'postponed' if it has not yet taken place. In Scotland and Northern Ireland, there is no express power to postpone a hearing that has not started, but by analogy with the position in courts, tribunals must have an implied power to postpone a hearing[5] if it is necessary to do so in the interests of justice.

28.6 The power under rule 5 to postpone or adjourn a hearing is discretionary, but the discretion must be exercised judicially[6] and in accordance with the overriding objective.[7] The overriding objective includes 'avoiding delay so far as compatible with proper consideration of the issues',[8] but also requires the tribunal to ensure 'so far as practicable, that the parties are able to participate fully in the proceedings'.[9] The purpose of an adjournment is always to ensure a fair hearing (see *R v Medical Appeal Tribunal (Midland Region) ex parte Carrarini*[10]).

---

5 See *Hinckley and South Leicestershire Building Society v Freeman* [1941] Ch 32.

6 See *Jacobs v Norsalta Limited* [1977] ICR 189.

7 See para **27.2**.

8 England and Wales Procedure Rules, r 2(2)(e).

9 England and Wales Procedure Rules, r 2(2)(c).

10 [1966] 1 WLR 883.

Accordingly, a postponement request should generally be granted if an appellant is prevented from attending a hearing because of illness or an emergency. In *CIS/2292/2000*,[11] it was held that a tribunal had erred in law in not granting an adjournment request made on behalf of a claimant who was in prison and whose oral evidence was important.

28.7 In *MHA v Secretary of State for Work and Pensions*,[12] the appellant sought an adjournment to obtain medical evidence. Judge Jacobs considered that the questions which were likely to arise in such a case were: What would be the benefit of an adjournment? Why was the party not ready to proceed? What impact will an adjournment have on the other party and the operation of the tribunal system? So far as the first question was concerned, it was relevant to take into account: (i) the evidence that was already before the tribunal; (ii) the evidence that was likely to be obtained if the proceedings were adjourned; (iii) how long it would take to obtain it; and (iv) whether the tribunal could use its expertise to compensate for the lack of additional evidence. Judge Jacobs considered that the impact of an adjournment on the tribunal system as a whole was unlikely to be of great significance in most cases.

28.8 In *JG v Secretary of State for Defence (AFCS)*,[13] the claimant was a trainee who was injured in a road accident on a public road while on his way back to base from a social event. At the hearing of his appeal against the refusal of his claim under the Armed Forces Compensation Scheme, the claimant's representative applied for a postponement of the hearing in order to obtain statements from other trainees who had attended the event, with a view to showing that they were under some compulsion to attend the event, and that attendance at the event was therefore 'required by an order' for the purposes of article 11(8)(a) of the AFCS 2011. The tribunal refused the postponement request on a number of grounds, including the absence of evidence of any element of compulsion to attend the social event and the possibility that the other trainees might not wish to give evidence. Judge Rowland allowed the claimant's appeal against the tribunal's decision, on the basis that it was irrational to refuse an adjournment for the purpose of obtaining statements from witnesses to support a case on the ground that, in the absence of such statements, there was no evidence supporting the case. Judge Rowland also considered that it was arguably wrong to refuse an adjournment on the ground that a witness might not wish to give evidence, without ascertaining whether that was in fact so, or considering whether it might be appropriate to issue a witness summons.

---

11 Unreported.

12 [2009] UKUT 211 (AAC).

13 [2014] UKUT 0194 (AAC).

28.9 Rule 14 of the Scotland and Northern Ireland Procedure Rules confers on the tribunal a specific power to adjourn a hearing if 'it appears to the tribunal that it is necessary to obtain further information on any point, or that the appellant or the Secretary of State should be allowed or required to procure or produce further evidence'. The appellant must be given an opportunity to comment in writing on any further information which is obtained, and either party can request a further hearing. If neither party requests a further oral hearing, the tribunal can come to a decision taking into account any written comments on the new information. If the appellant has been required to obtain or provide further evidence and does not do so due to wilful default, the case is placed on the deferred list.[14]

'IN ABSENCE' HEARINGS

28.10 Rule 29 of the England and Wales Procedure Rules allows a tribunal to proceed with a hearing in the appellant's absence if:

(i) it is satisfied that the appellant has been notified of the hearing or that reasonable steps have been taken to notify the appellant of the hearing; and
(ii) it considers that it is in the interests of justice to proceed with the hearing.

28.11 Rule 20 of the Scotland and Northern Ireland Procedure Rules allows an appeal to be heard in the absence of the parties and provides that if a party fails to attend or be represented at a hearing of which the appellant has been duly notified, the tribunal may:

(i) unless it is not satisfied that there is sufficient reason for such absence and does not think that the appellant's presence is necessary, hear and determine the appeal in the party's absence; or
(ii) adjourn the hearing, giving written reasons for the adjournment.

In Northern Ireland, an appeal may be heard in the absence of the appellant if the appellant or the appellant's representative has requested it, but the tribunal may, if it thinks that the presence of the appellant is necessary for the due determination of the appeal, give directions that the appeal shall not be heard in his absence. In both jurisdictions an appellant whose appeal has been determined in his or her absence can apply for the decision to be set aside, but the application must be made without undue delay. If the application is granted, the appeal must be

---

14 See para **26.10**.

re-heard before a differently constituted tribunal and such further order with regard to expenses may be made as the President thinks fit.

28.12 There are also specific provisions in Scotland and Northern Ireland with regard to appeals brought by appellants who are resident abroad. Rule 20A of the Scotland and Northern Ireland Procedure Rules provides that in such cases the appeal shall be heard in the appellant's absence and that when the appeal is ready for hearing the appellant must be notified of a period within which he or she can request that the appeal is not heard before a certain date because the appellant will be available to attend the appeal. If the appeal is an entitlement appeal, the President may make arrangements for the appellant to be medically examined in the country in which he is resident and must do so if the appeal is an assessment appeal, unless the President certifies that it is not practicable to do so. Where an appellant is medically examined abroad, the appeal must not proceed until a report on the examination has been received by the tribunal and a copy has been sent to the appellant or his representative, and to the Secretary of State.

28.13 'In absence' hearings are a particular feature of war pensions and armed forces compensation appeals because of the number of ex-service appellants who live abroad. In such cases, there may be no practicable alternative to an 'in absence' hearing, but rule 29 of the England and Wales Procedure Rules requires consideration in every case of whether it is in the interests of justice to proceed with a hearing in an appellant's absence. As envisaged by the Scotland and Northern Ireland Procedure Rules, it may be possible to postpone the hearing of an appeal for a reasonable period if the appellant intends to visit the United Kingdom.

28.14 Rule 1(3) of the England and Wales Procedure Rules defines 'hearing' as including 'a hearing conducted in whole or in part by video link, telephone or other means of instantaneous two-way electronic communication', and there have been a number of social security cases in which the Upper Tribunal has drawn attention to the need for tribunals to consider the various ways in which appellants can participate in proceedings.[15] In *MG v Secretary of State for Defence (WP)*,[16] Judge Wright held that a tribunal had erred in law by failing to consider whether an appellant could participate in a hearing using electronic means of communication. Many court and tribunal venues are now equipped with video-conferencing facilities and it may also be possible for an appellant to participate in a hearing by means of telephone conferencing. Technologies such as Skype

15 See e.g. *LC v Secretary of State for Work and Pensions (DLA)* [2015] UKUT 100 (AAC), *DT v Secretary of State for Work and Pensions (DLA)* [2015] UKUT 390 (AAC), and *SW v Secretary of State for Work and Pensions (DLA)* [2015] UKUT 319 (AAC).

16 [2015] UKUT 704 (AAC).

offer increasing possibilities for appellants who cannot be physically present at a tribunal hearing to play an effective part in the proceedings.

28.15 In the case of appellants resident in the United Kingdom, it may be necessary for a tribunal not to take at face value an indication by an appellant that he or she wishes the appeal to be heard in his or her absence.[17] The appellant may be unaware that hearings generally take place as near as possible to an appellant's home, that the proceedings are relatively informal, that the appellant's expenses of attending the hearing are reimbursed, and of the representation provided by service charities and others. In exceptional cases, it may also be possible to arrange a hearing at a claimant's home or a venue such as a doctor's surgery.

28.16 If a tribunal decides to proceed with the hearing of an appeal in the appellant's absence, it will be necessary for the reasons for the decision to show why the tribunal considers that that course of action is in the interests of justice. In *AM v Secretary of State for Work and Pensions (ESA)*,[18] Judge Wikeley set aside a tribunal's decision because the tribunal failed to explain why it had decided to continue with a hearing, rather than adjourning, after the appellant was forced to leave the tribunal room because of vomiting. In *MG v Secretary of State for Defence (WP)*,[19] Judge Wright held that a tribunal had erred in law because the Statement of Reasons did not show that the tribunal had addressed adequately whether it was in the interests of justice and consistent with the overriding objective for it to decide the appeal in the appellant's absence. In that case, the appellant had expressed a wish to attend the hearing and may have been misled by correspondence from the tribunal into thinking that he would be unable to do so, but even where an appellant who lives abroad has asked for an appeal to be heard in his or her absence, it will be necessary for the tribunal's statement of reasons to make it clear why the tribunal considers that it is in the interests of justice and consistent with the overriding objective for the hearing to take place without the appellant attending. The issue needs to be kept under review until a decision is made. Deciding a case on one basis in the claimant's absence may be fair, but deciding it on another basis may not.[20]

---

17 An example is the social security case of *CS v Secretary of State for Work and Pensions (ESA)* [2013] UKUT 0508 (AAC), in which Judge Ward set aside the decision of a tribunal which proceeded in the absence of a claimant whose letter of appeal raised a number of issues about his mental state, including a reference to voices in his head telling him not to attend the hearing.

18 [2013] UKUT 0563 (AAC).

19 [2015] UKUT 704 (AAC).

20 See *KO v Secretary of State for Work and Pensions (ESA)* [2013] UKUT 544 (AAC).

ATTENDANCE AND REPRESENTATION

28.17 Rule 26 of the England and Wales Procedure Rules gives each party to proceedings the right to attend the hearing. Rule 11(1) allows a party to appoint a representative (whether a legal representative or not) to represent the party in the proceedings. Rule 11(2) requires that notice of the appointment of a representative is given to the tribunal and to the other party. Following the appointment of a representative, rule 11(3) permits documents to be sent to the representative instead of to the appellant personally, and rule 11(4) allows the representative to do anything that a party is allowed or required to do, except sign a witness statement. Rule 11(6) provides that a person who accompanies a party to a hearing may act as the claimant's representative or assist in presenting the party's case with the permission of the tribunal if notice of the appointment of a representative has not been given previously, but in practice a person accompanying an appellant to a hearing is invariably allowed to assist the appellant even if notification of the appointment of the representative has not been given in advance.

28.18 Rule 11 of the Scotland and Northern Ireland Procedure Rules provides that appellants may conduct their case themselves or may be represented by any person appointed by the claimant to assist them for that purpose.

28.19 Appellants are frequently represented at hearings by representatives of the Royal British Legion and other service charities, who are sent a copy of the Statement of Case if appellants have stated on the appeal form that they intend to be represented. Non-legal representatives advise appellants and speak for them at appeal hearings, but they are not generally expected to have detailed legal knowledge. Representation may be available through intermediaries from bodies such as the Free Representation Unit and the Bar Pro Bono Unit. Free representation can also sometimes be provided via service charities by firms of solicitors which provide *pro bono* assistance to service charities.

28.20 The Procedure Rules allow Veterans UK to be represented at hearings and it is usual for a presenting officer to attend appeals. Presenting officers are expected to assist tribunals in reaching a fair and just conclusion and, although they are allowed to question appellants, they are not expected to be partisan or hostile. Presenting officers generally bring an appellant's complete case files to a hearing, so that any queries about the documentation in the Statement of Case can be resolved.

PUBLIC AND PRIVATE HEARINGS

28.21 Under rule 28 of the England and Wales Procedure Rules, all hearings must be held in public, but a tribunal may give a direction directing that part or all of a hearing is held in private. If it does so, the tribunal may decide who is permitted to attend the hearing or any part of it. A tribunal may also exclude from part or all of a hearing:

- (i) any person whose conduct the tribunal considers is disrupting or is likely to disrupt the hearing;
- (ii) any person whose presence the tribunal considers is likely to prevent another person from giving evidence or making submissions freely;
- (iii) any person who the tribunal considers should be excluded in order to give effect to a direction under rule 14(2) (withholding information likely to cause harm);
- (iv) any person where the purpose of the hearing would be defeated by the attendance of that person.

EVIDENCE

28.22 Rule 15 of the England and Wales Procedure Rules gives a tribunal extensive powers to control the evidence which is placed before it and to decide how the evidence is to be presented. The tribunal also has power to limit the number of witnesses called to give evidence, either generally or in relation to a particular issue. Rule 15(2) provides that evidence may be admitted even if it would not be admissible in civil proceedings in the courts, and may be excluded if a direction relating to the evidence was not complied with. Rule 15(3) allows the tribunal to consent to a witness giving evidence on oath. In practice, these powers are rarely exercised. Rule 16 allows a tribunal to compel the attendance of a witness and for a person who has been ordered to attend a hearing to apply for the order to be discharged, but again such orders are rare.

28.23 Rule 12 of the Scotland and Northern Ireland Procedure Rules expressly allows the appellant to give evidence in support of the appeal. Either the appellant or the Secretary of State may call a doctor or any other person as a witness, but a party intending to call a doctor to give evidence must notify the tribunal not later than 7 days before the hearing. The other party can then call a doctor to give evidence without giving notice. Rule 12(5) prevents the tribunal from excluding evidence on the sole ground that the evidence would not be admissible in a court of law.

MEDICAL EXAMINATIONS

28.24 Rule 24(1) of the England and Wales Procedure Rules and rule 17 of the Scotland and Northern Ireland Procedure Rules allows the medical member of a tribunal to carry out a medical examination of the appellant at the hearing with the appellant's consent if the appeal relates to the appellant's disablement or incapacity for work, but in England and Wales a Practice Statement[21] has been issued discontinuing such examinations. Tribunal venues may not have suitable facilities for conducting medical examinations, and rule 24(3) allows for the tribunal to arrange for a medical examination and report in cases where a medical question arises. By exercising its case management powers, the tribunal ought to be able to identify cases in which a medical examination is required in advance of the hearing. Furthermore, section 5B(b) of the Pensions Appeal Tribunals Act 1943 prevents a tribunal from taking into account any circumstances not obtaining at the time when the decision under appeal was made,[22] so that the claimant's condition at the time of the appeal hearing is not necessarily the condition on the basis of which the tribunal is required to reach its decision.

PROCEDURE AT THE HEARING

28.25 The 2001 Leggatt Report,[23] which led to the passing of the Tribunals, Courts and Enforcement Act 2007, concluded (at paras 7.4 and 7.5) that:

> All the members of a tribunal must do all they can to understand the point of view, as well as the case, of the citizen. They must be alert for factual or legal elements of the case which appellants may not bring out, adequately or at all, but which have a bearing on the possible outcomes.
> … the tribunal approach should be an enabling one: supporting parties in ways which give them confidence in their own abilities to participate in the process, and in the tribunal's capacity to compensate for the appellant's lack of skills or knowledge.

Rule 11(3) of the Scotland and Northern Ireland Procedure Rules provides that 'it shall be the duty of the tribunal to assist any appellant who appears to be unable to make the best of their case'.

28.26 In order to achieve these aims, tribunals adapt their procedures to meet the needs of particular appellants, especially if they are unrepresented. Typically however, the tribunal chairman will begin proceedings by introducing those present in the tribunal room, explaining the procedure at the hearing and clarifying the issues. The appellant will then answer questions from his or her representative or give evidence, and the appellant and any witnesses may then be

---

21 Practice Statement No 4.

22 See para **29.5**.

23 Sir Andrew Leggatt, *Report of the Review of Tribunals: Tribunals for Users – One System, One Service* (16 August 2001).

questioned by the presenting officer and by members of the tribunal. After hearing brief closing statements by each representative, the appellant and the representatives leave the room while the tribunal reaches a decision. In most cases, the tribunal announces its decision at the end of the hearing.

28.27 Rule 13 of the Scotland and Northern Ireland Procedure Rules provides that at the hearing the tribunal shall give an opportunity to the appellant or the appellant's representative to address the tribunal and call witnesses and, if the appellant is not represented, the examination of the appellant's witnesses may, if the appellant wishes, be conducted by the chairman of the tribunal on behalf of the appellant. Each party's representative may question the other party's witnesses and the Secretary of State's representative must be allowed to call witnesses and to address the tribunal. Under rule 16, if an appeal is adjourned or has been remitted for rehearing, the President may direct another tribunal to conduct the new hearing if it is not practicable for the same tribunal to do so without undue delay.

Record of proceedings

28.28 The England and Wales Procedure Rules no longer require a record of proceedings to be made, but a judge is under a judicial obligation to make a note of the evidence[24] and the other members of a tribunal invariably do so. The record may take the form of an electronic recording. Rule 19 of the Scotland and Northern Ireland Procedure Rules requires the chairman of the tribunal to make a written record of the proceedings in a form approved by the President as soon as practicable after an appeal has been decided, sufficient to indicate:

(i) any question of law raised at the hearing;
(ii) the evidence which was adduced at the hearing;
(iii) in Scotland, any determination of the tribunal on such questions of law or evidence.

The record of proceedings must be preserved until the expiry of the maximum period for bringing a late appeal against the tribunal's decision[25] and during that period either party may apply for a copy of the record.

---

24 See e.g. *R(I) 81/51* and *R(I) 42/59*.

25 See para **32.14**.

Use of specialist knowledge and tribunal's observations

28.29 An appellant must be given a chance of commenting on possible conclusions based on the specialist knowledge of one of the tribunal members. In *Butterfield and Creasy v Secretary of State for Defence*,[26] Park J held:

> There is a potential problem if a medical member of a tribunal is the only person present with specialist medical knowledge, and he perceives a possible medical objection to the appellant's case, particularly an objection which has not been taken in advance by the Secretary of State and of which the appellant has not had prior notice. If the medical member believes that there is such an objection, plainly he must say so. He is a member of the Tribunal because of his medical expertise, and if he thinks that his medical expertise is relevant in some specific way which has not otherwise been pointed out, he must draw on it in the course of the hearing and the tribunal's deliberations. I do not for a moment suggest that the medical member of the tribunal should in some way suppress his personal expertise and reactions to medical issues which arise. However, if the point which concerns him is a new one and might in itself be decisive, it does seem to me that fairness requires that it be explained to the appellant or to the appellant's representative, and that the appellant should be given a realistic opportunity to consider it. In some cases, though I hope not many, this may require the offer of an adjournment, however inconvenient and irksome that may be.

28.30 Fairness may also require the tribunal to give the appellant an opportunity to comment on an issue raised in the minds of the tribunal by their observations of the appellant at the hearing (see *CSDLA/288/2005*[27] and *R(DLA) 8/06*).

EXPENSES AND ALLOWANCES

28.31 Under rule 26 of the England and Wales Procedure Rules and rule 26 of the Scotland and Northern Ireland Procedure Rules, the tribunal must pay a subsistence allowance and the expenses reasonably and actually incurred in travelling to the hearing of the following persons:

- (i) the appellant;
- (ii) where an appellant is unable to attend a hearing for health reasons, a relative or friend attending the hearing on the appellant's behalf;
- (iii) an attendant if required by the appellant for reasons of health.

---

26 [2002] EWHC 2247 (Admin).

27 Unreported.

An allowance for loss of time is also payable where an appeal is successful or where there were reasonable grounds for the appeal.

28.32 Travel expenses of appellants and, if necessary, attendants are also paid for the expenses of attending a medical examination ordered by the tribunal. In Scotland and Northern Ireland the travel expenses of a witness other than a medical witness can be paid if the President or tribunal chairman certifies that in the exceptional circumstances of the case the attendance of the witness was necessary.

28.33 In Scotland, the tribunal is required to send an appellant a rail warrant in respect of the cost of rail travel. Claim forms for other expenses are given to appellants at the hearing by the tribunal clerk.

28.34 Rule 20(3) of the England and Wales Procedure Rules requires the tribunal to pay a reasonable allowance up to a prescribed maximum in respect of the expenses incurred in securing the attendance of a medical witness or of obtaining a medical report or certificate if the tribunal considers that the attendance of the witness or the provision of the document was reasonably necessary. The Scotland and Northern Ireland Procedure Rules provide for the costs of obtaining reports and certificates from certain types of medical institutions to be reimbursed.

28.35 In Scotland and Northern Ireland, there is power to pay the fees of an expert or other witness who has been summonsed by the tribunal.

Chapter 29

Powers of the Tribunal on an Appeal

THE ROLE OF THE TRIBUNAL

29.1 Sections 1 and 5A of the Pensions Appeal Tribunals Act 1943 confer rights of appeal to a tribunal against entitlement decisions and against specified decisions (including armed forces compensation decisions) on the question of whether a decision was rightly made on the ground notified to the claimant. Section 5 gives rights of appeal against assessment decisions. However, as noted in para **25.5**, the 'ground' of a decision is a finding that the statutory conditions of entitlement are not satisfied, rather than the reasons for that conclusion.

29.2 In the leading social security case *R(IB) 2/05*, a tribunal of Social Security Commissioners held (at [24]) that, within the limits of the relevant legislation, a tribunal can make any decision which the decision-maker could have made on the legal questions properly before that officer, including dealing with new questions, so as to reach the right result on an appeal. The Social Security Commissioners held (at [25]) that 'the tribunal in effect stands in the shoes of the decision-maker for the purpose of making a decision on the claim'. It follows that the tribunal is not concerned with whether the decision under appeal was one which was properly open to the decision-maker on the basis of the evidence which was taken into account when the decision was made, but rather with the question of what is the correct decision on the claim (or review application) on the basis of the evidence before the tribunal. If the appeal is against a review decision, the tribunal can exercise the powers exercisable by the Secretary of State on a review,[1] but the tribunal can only revise a decision or assessment to a claimant's detriment if it finds that one or more of the conditions in article 44(4) of the SPO 2006 has been satisfied.[2]

1 See para **6.17**.

2 See *JM v Secretary of State for Defence* [2014] UKUT358 (AAC), [2015] AACR 7.

LIMITATIONS ON THE TRIBUNAL'S POWERS

29.3 The Child Support, Pensions and Social Security Act 2000 amended the Pensions Appeal Tribunals Act 1943 (and the corresponding social security and child support legislation) so as to introduce limitations on a tribunal's powers when determining an appeal. Section 59 of the 2000 Act added a new section 5B to the 1943 Act, as follows:

> **5B Matters relevant on appeal**
>
> In deciding any appeal under any provision of this Act, the appropriate tribunal—
>
> (a) need not consider any issue that is not raised by the appellant or the Minister in relation to the appeal; and
>
> (b) shall not take into account any circumstances not obtaining at the time when the decision under appeal was made.

Issues raised by the appeal

29.4 Section 5B(a) gives the tribunal a discretion whether to consider an issue in an appeal which has not been raised by one of the parties, but does not oblige it to do so. In *CDLA/1000/2001*,[3] it was held that the question of whether an issue is raised by an appellant is to be determined by reference to the substance of the appeal, rather than merely by reference to the wording of the grounds of appeal. Since the Pensions Appeal Tribunals Act 1943, unlike the corresponding social security legislation, provides for separate rights of appeal in relation to different kinds of issue, the issues which the tribunal can consider will be defined by the type of appeal which the tribunal is considering. The question of how a tribunal's discretion should be exercised to consider issues not raised by the parties is therefore less likely to arise in war pensions and armed forces compensation appeals than in social security and child support cases. For example, on an appeal against an entitlement decision, the tribunal will be concerned with the question of whether the disablement asserted by the claimant was attributable to, or aggravated by, service. The scope of the tribunal's jurisdiction will be confined to considering the decision which is the actual subject of the appeal, so that the tribunal will not be permitted to consider, for example, whether some other disablement was due to service, or the correct percentage assessment of disablement for the claimed condition if the tribunal allows the entitlement appeal. On the other hand, on the basis of *R(IB) 2/05*, the tribunal will be entitled (and indeed obliged) to consider all matters relevant to the decision which is under appeal. Since section 1 of the 1943 Act requires the decision-maker to make a decision on both attributability and aggravation by service, the tribunal will have

---

3 Unreported.

to consider aggravation by service if it upholds the decision in respect of attributability.

'Down to the date of decision'

29.5 Section 5B(b) of the Pensions Appeal Tribunals Act 1943 is more problematical. Although it prohibits the tribunal from taking into account circumstances which did not obtain at the time when the decision under appeal was made, it does not prevent the tribunal from taking into account *evidence* which has come into existence between the date of the decision and the date of the tribunal hearing, and which was therefore not available to the decision-maker. The tribunal can have regard to such evidence for the purpose of drawing inferences about the circumstances which obtained at or before the date of the decision under appeal, in particular, with regard to the nature and severity of a claimant's injury or illness at the date of the decision.

29.6 In armed forces compensation cases, descriptors frequently require a prognosis to be made of the length of time for which specified effects of an injury are expected to last, for example Table 3,[4] Item 5, 'Mental disorder, which has caused, or is expected to cause functional limitation or restriction at 26 weeks, from which the claimant has made, or is expected to make, a substantial recovery within 5 years'. In *Secretary of State for Defence v Duncan and McWilliams*,[5] it was held that the starting point for all descriptors is the claimant's condition at the date of the decision on the claim, rather than the claimant's condition at the date when the injury was sustained,[6] but a decision about a claimant's expected condition at some future time will necessarily involve a greater or lesser degree of prediction with regard to future events.

29.7 In the social security case *R(DLA) 3/01* (cited by Judge Rowland in *Secretary of State for Defence v CM (AFCS)*[7]), the claimant was entitled to DLA only if she was likely to satisfy the qualifying conditions of the benefit for a period of 6 months. Applying the very similar provision to section 5B(b) of the Pensions Appeal Tribunals Act 1943 in section 12(8)(b) of the Social Security Act 1998, Mr Commissioner Jacobs (as he then was) held that a tribunal was entitled to take into account evidence of a claimant's actual rate of recovery between the date of the decision under appeal and the tribunal hearing, provided that the fact that a claimant had not recovered as quickly as expected merely reflected the natural vagaries of an uncertain recovery process. However, other circumstances

4 AFCS 2011, Sch 3, Table 3.

5 [2009] EWCA Civ 1043, [2009] All ER (D) 121 (Oct).

6 See para **18.8**.

7 [2014] UKUT 0018.

occurring after the date of the decision under appeal would have to be ignored, whether that was to the claimant's advantage or disadvantage. Mr Commissioner Jacobs held:

> 59. In the case of a benefit in which a prediction has to be made of future disablement, it is always relevant to know whether the claimant's disablement at the date of decision was static or changing. The classification of the disablement is a circumstance obtaining at that time. It will be relevant both to the six months qualifying period and to the period of an award. I give directions on changing disablement in the context of a claimant who is in a period of post-operative recovery, as that is the position in this case, but the principles are applicable to all cases of changing disablement.
>
> 60. An appeal tribunal is entitled, and required, to take account of the fact that at the time of the decision a claimant is in a period of post-operative recovery. That is a circumstance obtaining at that time. If a rule requires a prediction of future events but the actual events are known by the time of a hearing, a court would take account of what had actually occurred rather than undertake an artificial exercise of prediction: see for a recent discussion of this principle the decision of the Court of Appeal in *Charles v. Hugh James Jones and Jenkins (a firm)* [2000] 1 All England Law Reports 289 at pages 299 to 301. However, section 12(8)(b) prevents appeal tribunals from applying this principle.
>
> 61. In some cases, a claimant who is recovering may suffer a set back, slowing down the rate of recovery. Take the example given in paragraph 44 of a claimant recovering from heart surgery who develops pneumonia after the date of decision. That is clearly a fresh circumstance, which an appeal tribunal would have to leave out of account. In that case section 12(8)(b) would operate to the claimant's disadvantage. However, it can also work to the claimant's advantage on an appeal. If the period of a claimant's recovery is dramatically reduced by the use of a new drug, this would also be a fresh circumstance which the appeal tribunal would have to leave out of account.
>
> 62. In other cases, the fact that a claimant's recovery has not progressed as quickly as expected does not necessarily indicate that a fresh circumstance has occurred. This may do no more than reflect the natural vagaries of an uncertain recovery process that cannot be predicted accurately or with confidence. In this case, the actual rate of recovery is not a fresh circumstance that the appeal tribunal must ignore.
>
> 63. There is no clear test that will allow appeal tribunals to distinguish between cases in which there has been a set back to recovery and those where the evidence only shows that the rate of recovery is inherently uncertain. An appeal tribunal must use common sense to draw the distinction between these cases.
>
> 64. It must ask: how long was the claimant likely to satisfy the conditions of entitlement for a disability living allowance, disregarding fresh circumstances? The answer will depend on the tribunal's assessment of the admissible evidence. The appeal tribunal may, and must, take account of any evidence about the claimant's likely disablement beyond the date of decision that can sensibly be related to the circumstances obtaining at that date. The conclusion will be a

finding of fact on probability which the appeal tribunal may substitute for the finding of fact on that issue made by the officer acting on behalf of the Secretary of State.

65. The claimant's own evidence is admissible, but however credible it may be, it is likely to be of limited value. It will be based on the claimant's personal feelings and the claimant will not have a yardstick against which to judge the rate of recovery.

66. If there is in evidence a prognosis of the likely rate of recovery, the tribunal must weigh that evidence in the light of these considerations, among others. (i) A prognosis is no more than an opinion. (ii) The factors that affect the rate of recovery from an operation are so many, so variable and so dependent on the individual patient that it is impossible for a prognosis to take into account all the variables in an individual case, let alone to reach a firm conclusion. (iii) Some of the variables will be specific to the claimant. Others will be general. It is unlikely that the prognosis will record those that were taken into consideration. This lack of transparency prevents the reasoning behind the prognosis from being examined and, therefore, reduces the weight that can be given to it.

67. It will always be relevant to consider whether there is an identifiable occurrence that has caused a change in the rate of recovery. That occurrence may be, and perhaps is likely to be, a fresh circumstance. However, some occurrences may be sufficiently predictable as a feature of the recovery process to be regarded as but a part of it.

68. The length of the recovery may be so abnormal as itself to indicate that some unidentified fresh circumstance must have occurred. However, if the actual recovery period is not abnormal, there is no reason why the tribunal should not have regard to that, so long as the tribunal asks itself the correct question (see para. 64) and bases its answer on admissible evidence.

69. I trust that this is a sensible approach that makes sections 8(2) and 12(8)(b) workable by appeal tribunals and, while faithful to the proper interpretation of the legislation, does not impose unattainable restrictions on claimants who want to challenge a decision on appeal.

DISADVANTAGEOUS DECISIONS

29.8 A tribunal may have power to make a decision which is more disadvantageous to a claimant than the decision which is under appeal. For example, on an appeal against an assessment of disablement made on a claim, the tribunal has power under section 5(1)(a) of the Pensions Appeal Tribunals Act 1943 to reduce the percentage assessment of disablement. The power was enacted at a time when assessment tribunals included two doctors and when claimants were routinely examined at the hearing of an assessment appeal. The tribunal was therefore usually in at least as good a position to assess the appellant's medical condition as the doctor who carried out the medical examination on which the decision under appeal was based.

29.9 Although it was confirmed in *R(IB) 2/04* that a tribunal has power in social security cases to make a supersession decision which is less favourable to an appellant than the decision which is under appeal, in the interests of fairness claimants will need to be informed of the right to withdraw their appeal in order to protect their existing award. In order for claimants to make an informed and considered decision about their best course of action, it may be necessary to offer an unrepresented claimant an adjournment in order to obtain advice.

29.10 The undesirability of tribunals expressing a view about the merits of an appeal has been referred to in a number of social security cases. In *CDLA/884/2008*,[8] Judge Rowland observed (at [10]):

> A tribunal is in a difficult position. If it gives the claimant too robust a warning at the beginning of a hearing, it runs the risk of giving the impression of having prejudged the case. If it does not give such a robust warning, the warning may not adequately convey to the claimant the case he or she needs to consider resisting with the consequence that a decision not to withdraw the appeal, or not to ask for an adjournment, is not fully informed. This is a powerful reason for tribunals refraining from making decisions less favourable to claimants than the decisions being challenged, except in the most obvious cases (e.g., where the evidence is overwhelming or the facts are not in dispute and no element of judgment is involved or where the law has been misapplied by the Secretary of State) or after an appropriate adjournment.

29.11 The difficulties of acting fairly in a case where a tribunal is minded to make an award which is less favourable than the decision under appeal are even greater if the appellant is not present at the hearing, since in those circumstances it will generally be impossible to warn the appellant of the possible consequences of not withdrawing the appeal. In *JM v Secretary of State for Defence (WP)*,[9] the appellant had been arrested and was in prison at the time of the hearing. He had arranged to be represented, but his representative told the tribunal that she had no instructions. The tribunal reduced the appellant's assessment of disablement from 60% to 30%, but, in setting aside the tribunal's decision, Judge Rowland held that the tribunal had failed to explain how it understood that the claimant could properly be represented in those circumstances, or alternatively, on what basis it was just to hear the case without the appellant being properly represented.

29.12 As Judge Rowland pointed out in *CDLA/884/2008*,[10] a tribunal which considers that an existing award is over-generous can draw the attention of the Secretary of State to its view in the decision, although once a tribunal has made

---

8 Unreported.

9 [2014] UKUT 358 (AAC), [2015] AACR 7.

10 Unreported.

an assessment decision it will only be possible to review it on the ground of a change of circumstances.[11] However, the tribunal can reduce the period of an interim assessment or substitute an interim assessment of no longer than 2 years for a final assessment, thereby enabling the claimant's condition to be re-assessed at the end of the period of the new award.

---

11 See para **6.7**.

Chapter 30

The Decision

ENGLAND AND WALES

30.1 Rule 31(1) of the England and Wales Procedure Rules allows a tribunal to give a decision orally at a hearing, and this practice is generally followed unless a tribunal needs more time to reach a conclusion, or there is some other reason not to announce the decision at the end of the hearing.

30.2 Rule 31(2) of the England and Wales Procedure Rules provides that as soon as reasonably practicable after making a final decision or a decision on a preliminary issue, the tribunal must issue a decision notice giving the following information:

(i) the tribunal's decision;
(ii) the right to apply for a written statement of reasons if the decision is given without reasons;
(iii) any right of appeal against the decision and the time within which, and the manner in which, the right must be exercised.

The tribunal need not give any information which has been withheld under rule 14(2) (harmful information).[1]

Reasons

30.3 Rule 32(1) of the England and Wales Procedure Rules allows reasons for a tribunal's decision to be given either orally at a hearing or in a written statement of reasons, but in England and Wales a tribunal is required to provide *written* reasons for its decision only if a written application for a statement is made by one of the parties. Following the making of a final decision or a decision on a

1 See para **27.11**.

preliminary issue, an application for a written statement of reasons must be made within 42 days of the date on which the decision notice was sent or provided to the party making the application.[2] Decision notices are often given to appellants at the end of a hearing, and in such cases the time for applying for a statement of reasons will run from the date on which the hearing took place. Although there is power under rule 5(3)(a) to extend the 42-day period, a failure to apply in time for a statement of reasons may result in the loss of a right of appeal.[3]

30.4 Rule 32(4) of the England and Wales Procedure Rules provides that a written statement of reasons must be provided within 28 days of the date on which the request is received, or a soon as reasonably practicable after the end of that period.

30.5 Tribunals in England and Wales are encouraged to give 'summary reasons', setting out the essence of the tribunal's reasons for its decision, if full written reasons for a decision are not given at the end of a hearing.[4]

SCOTLAND AND NORTHERN IRELAND

30.6 Under rule 18 of the Scotland and Northern Ireland Procedure Rules, the chairman must draw up a decision notice recording a summary of the tribunal's decision, and also a written statement of reasons for the decision. The decision notice must be sent to the parties as soon as reasonably practicable after the appeal has been decided and the statement of reasons may be sent to the parties at the same time. If a statement of reasons is not sent or given to the parties, either party may apply for a copy within 6 weeks of the date on which the decision notice was sent or given. The decision notice must inform the parties of the conditions governing appeals to the Upper Tribunal (or Pensions Appeal Commissioners in Northern Ireland in all cases except assessment appeals) and of the right to apply for a copy of the statement of reasons if it has not already been provided.

MAJORITY DECISIONS

30.7 In *Brain v Minister of Pensions*[5] and *Minister of Pensions v Horsey*,[6] it was held that a claim could not be accepted or rejected by a majority decision of

---

2 England and Wales Procedure Rules, rule 32(3).

3 See para **32.9**.

4 Practice Statement No. 6.

5 [1947] KB 625.

6 [1949] 2 KB 526.

a Pensions Appeal Tribunal. However, the correctness of those decisions has been doubted[7] and in Scotland they were not followed by the Inner House of the Court of Session in *Secretary of State for Social Security v KM*.[8] *KM* was followed by a Social Security Commissioner in Northern Ireland on an appeal from a Pensions Appeal Tribunal in *C1/09-10(AF)*.[9]

30.8 So far as England and Wales is concerned, article 8 of the First-tier Tribunal and Upper Tribunal (Composition of Tribunal) Order 2008[10] now provides:

> 8. If the decision of the tribunal is not unanimous, the decision of the majority is the decision of the tribunal; and the presiding member has a casting vote if the votes are equally divided.

(The issue of a casting vote can only arise if the parties have agreed to a matter being decided without a member under paragraph 15(6) of Schedule 4 to the Tribunals, Courts and Enforcement Act 2007.) Although there is no obligation under the England and Wales Procedure Rules for a decision notice to state whether a decision is unanimous or by a majority, reasons for any dissent must be given if the decision notice states that the decision is that of a majority.[11]

CONSENT ORDERS

30.9 Rule 30 of the England and Wales Procedure Rules allows the tribunal to make an order by consent without a hearing and without giving reasons if it considers it appropriate to do so.

---

7 See HWR Wade and CE Forsyth, *Administrative Law*, 11th edn (Oxford University Press, 2014), p 784.

8 [1998] ScotCS 67.

9 Unreported.

10 SI 2008/2835.

11 See *Secretary of State for Work and Pensions v SS (DLA)* [2010] UKUT 384 (AAC), [2011] AACR 24, considered in *JD v Secretary of State for Defence (WP)* [2014] UKUT 379 (AAC).

Chapter 31

Correcting, Setting Aside and Reviewing Decisions

CORRECTING ACCIDENTAL ERRORS

31.1 Rule 34 of the England and Wales Procedure Rules gives a tribunal power to correct 'any clerical mistake or other accidental slip or omission in a decision, direction or any document' by sending notification of the amendment to the parties and by amending any information which has been published in relation to the amended document. The power cannot be used to alter a decision or to correct an error which is fundamental to an appeal, but 'deals with matters that were in a judge's mind when writing but for some reason did not find their way onto the page', such as typing errors and mistakenly writing a wrong date (see *AS v Secretary of State for Work and Pensions (ESA)*[1]). The power does not cover matters that the judge had meant to mention but forgot to include in a decision.

SETTING ASIDE

31.2 Rule 35 of the England and Wales Procedure Rules allows a tribunal to set aside a final decision or part of such a decision and to re-make the decision if it is in the interests of justice to do so and one or more of the following conditions is satisfied:

(i) a document relating to the proceedings was not sent to, or was not received at an appropriate time by, a party or a party's representative;

(ii) a document relating to the proceedings was not sent to the tribunal at an appropriate time;

---

1 [2011] UKUT 159 (AAC).

(iii) a party or a party's representative was not present at a hearing related to the proceedings;
(iv) there has been some other procedural irregularity in the proceedings.

A party applying for a decision or part of a decision to be set aside must do so within 1 month after the date on which notice of the decision was sent, subject to the power to extend time under rule 5(3)(a).

31.3 This power provides a remedy in cases where a party has been deprived of the right to a hearing as a result of a procedural mishap, even though there has been no breach of the rules, for example, where a notice of hearing was properly sent but did not reach the appellant (see *R(SB) 19/83*). It can also be used where a party or a party's representative did not attend a hearing in time because of travel delays, or where a document did not reach the tribunal. In such cases, it will be permissible to have regard to the strength of a party's case in deciding whether it is in the interests of justice to set a decision aside (see *Akram v Adam*[2]).

REVIEW

31.4 Section 9 of the Tribunals, Courts and Enforcement Act 2007 confers on the First-tier Tribunal wide powers to review a decision, subject however to any limitations imposed by rules of procedure. Under rule 38, the tribunal can only undertake a review if there has been an application for permission to appeal (see Chapter 32) and if the tribunal is satisfied that there was an error of law in the decision. If the tribunal carries out a review, it may:

(i) correct accidental errors in the decision;
(ii) amend the reasons for the decision;
(iii) set the decision aside.[3]

If the tribunal sets the decision aside, it may:

(i) re-decide the matter concerned; or
(ii) refer that matter to the Upper Tribunal.[4]

Rule 38(2) provides that the tribunal must notify the parties in writing of the outcome of a review and of the rights of appeal against the review decision. Under

---

2 [2004] EWCA Civ 1601, [2005] 1 WLR 2762.

3 Tribunals, Courts and Enforcement Act 2007, s 9(4).

4 Tribunals, Courts and Enforcement Act 2007, s 9(5).

rule 38(3), if the tribunal takes any action in relation to a decision following a review without first giving every party an opportunity to make representations, the notification of the outcome must state that any party that did not have the opportunity to make representations may apply for the action taken on the review to be set aside and for the decision to be reviewed again.

Chapter 32

Appeals to the Upper Tribunal

RIGHT OF APPEAL TO THE UPPER TRIBUNAL

32.1 As explained in Chapter 24, appeals lie to the Upper Tribunal on a point of law from the First-tier Tribunal in England and Wales, from the Pensions Appeal Tribunal (Scotland) and, in assessment cases only, the Pensions Appeal Tribunal (Northern Ireland). Appeals from the Pensions Appeal Tribunal (Northern Ireland) in other cases lie to the Pensions Appeal Commissioners in Northern Ireland and are considered in Chapter 33. Appeals to the Upper Tribunal are usually dealt with by a single judge, but paragraph 3 of the Senior President's Practice Statement on the composition of tribunals in the Administrative Appeals Chamber[1] provides for a case to be decided by a panel of two or more judges if the Senior President or the Chamber President considers that it involves a question of law of special difficulty or an important point of principle or practice, or that it is otherwise appropriate.

32.2 In *LS v London Borough of Lambeth (HB)*,[2] a three-judge panel of the Upper Tribunal held that there is a right of appeal against any decision of the First-tier Tribunal, except for an excluded decision, so that an appeal can be brought against a decision made by a First-tier Tribunal judge in the exercise of the case management powers in rule 5 of the England and Wales Procedure Rules. It may often be appropriate to wait until a case has been finally decided before bringing an appeal against such decisions because an unfair interlocutory decision may render the subsequent substantive decision wrong in law, so that the substantive decision can be challenged when it is made,[3] but there is now power

---

1 Practice Statement: Composition of Tribunals in relation to matters that fall to be decided by the Administrative Appeals Chamber of the Upper Tribunal on or after 26th March 2014, Sir Jeremy Sullivan, 26 March 2014.

2 [2010] UKUT 461 (AAC).

3 *R v Medical Appeal Tribunal (Midland Region) ex parte Carrarini* [1966] 1 WLR 883.

to extend the time for bringing an appeal against an interlocutory decision until the substantive hearing has taken place.[4]

POINT OF LAW

32.3 In *R (Iran) v Secretary of State for the Home Department*,[5] the Court of Appeal summarised (at [9]) the points of law which are most likely to arise in practice as follows:

> i) Making perverse or irrational findings on a matter or matters that were material to the outcome ('material matters');
> ii) Failing to give reasons or any adequate reasons for findings on material matters;
> iii) Failing to take into account and/or resolve conflicts of fact or opinion on material matters;
> iv) Giving weight to immaterial matters;
> v) Making a material misdirection of law on any material matter;
> vi) Committing or permitting a procedural or other irregularity capable of making a material difference to the outcome or the fairness of the proceedings;
> vii) Making a mistake as to a material fact which could be established by objective and uncontentious evidence, where the appellant and/or his advisers were not responsible for the mistake, and where unfairness resulted from the fact that a mistake was made.

32.4 The most common reason for allowing appeals against tribunal decisions is inadequacy of reasons. Statements of reasons in war pensions and armed forces cases are often brief because they are usually given in the presence of the parties at the end of a hearing, but the adequacy of reasons depends on the context and complexity of a case, rather than on the length of the statement.[6] The requirements for an adequate statement of reasons were summarised (in a planning context) by Lord Brown of Eaton-under-Heywood in *South Bucks District Council v Porter (No 2)*[7] as follows (at [36]):

> The reasons for a decision must be intelligible and they must be adequate. They must enable the reader to understand why the matter was decided as it was and what conclusions were reached on the 'principal important controversial issues', disclosing how any issue of law or fact was resolved. Reasons can be briefly stated,

---

4 See n 10.

5 [2005] EWCA Civ 982, [2005] INLR 633.

6 See e.g. CAF/5182/ 2014, unreported, in which Judge Levenson upheld the decision of a tribunal consisting of four sentences.

7 [2004] UKHL 33, [2004] 1 WLR 1953.

the degree of particularity required depending entirely on the nature of the issues falling for decision. The reasoning must not give rise to a substantial doubt as to whether the decision-maker erred in law, for example by misunderstanding some relevant policy or some other important matter or by failing to reach a rational decision on relevant grounds. But such adverse inference will not readily be drawn. The reasons need refer only to the main issues in the dispute, not to every material consideration. They should enable disappointed developers to assess their prospects of obtaining some alternative development permission, or, as the case may be, their unsuccessful opponents to understand how the policy or approach underlying the grant of permission may impact upon future such applications. Decision letters must be read in a straightforward manner, recognising that they are addressed to parties well aware of the issues involved and the arguments advanced.

APPLYING TO THE FIRST-TIER OR PENSIONS APPEAL TRIBUNAL FOR PERMISSION TO APPEAL

32.5 An application for permission to appeal[8] to the Upper Tribunal is made in the first instance to the First-tier Tribunal (in England and Wales) or to the Pensions Appeal Tribunal (in Scotland and Northern Ireland). If permission is refused or the application is not admitted, a new application can be made to the Upper Tribunal but an application for permission must always be made first to the Pensions Appeal Tribunal in Scotland or Northern Ireland or to the First-tier Tribunal in England and Wales.[9]

England and Wales

32.6 Under rule 36 of the England and Wales Procedure Rules, an application for permission to appeal must be in writing and must be made no later than 42 days after the latest of the following dates:

(i) the sending of the decision notice;[10]

(ii) the sending of written reasons for the decision in the case of a decision which disposes of all issues in the proceedings (a final decision) or a decision on a preliminary issue in a case where the

---

8 'Permission to appeal' is called 'leave to appeal' in Scotland and Northern Ireland, but is referred to throughout this chapter as 'permission to appeal'.

9 Upper Tribunal Procedure Rules, r 21(2).

10 Applicable if permission to appeal is sought against a decision which does not require the giving of reasons, e.g. a case management decision. In such cases the tribunal has power under England and Wales Procedure Rules, r 36(2A) to direct that the time for applying for permission to appeal should run from the date of the final decision.

tribunal has directed an issue to be dealt with as a preliminary issue under rule 5(3)(e);

(iii) notification of amended reasons for, or correction of, the decision following a review;

(iv) notification that an application for a decision to be set aside has been unsuccessful, provided that the set-aside application was made within the 1-month time limit.[11]

32.7 Under rule 36(5) of the England and Wales Procedure Rules, the application must:

(i) identify the tribunal decision which is being challenged;
(ii) identify the alleged error or errors of law;
(iii) state the result the party making the application is seeking.[12]

32.8 Under rule 36(4) of the England and Wales Procedure Rules, if the application has been made late and the time for making the application has not been extended under rule 5(3)(a), the application must include an application for an extension of time and give the reason why the application was not made in time. If the tribunal does not extend the time for making a late application, it must refuse to admit it.

32.9 If no application for a written statement of reasons has been made previously, rule 36(6) of the England and Wales Procedure Rules requires the application for permission to appeal to be treated as such an application. Unless the tribunal decides to give permission to appeal at that stage, the application must not be treated as an application for permission to appeal. If an application for a written statement of reasons is refused because of delay in making the application, the tribunal must only admit the application if it is in the interests of justice to do so.

32.10 Under rule 39 of the England and Wales Procedure Rules, an application for a decision to be corrected, set aside, or reviewed, or for permission to appeal, can be treated as an application for any other of those things.

Consideration of the application

32.11 Applications for permission to appeal in the War Pensions and Armed Forces Compensation Chamber are generally dealt with by the Chamber President, or by a judge nominated by the President. On receiving an application

---

11 See para **32.2**.

12 In practice, this requirement is generally dispensed with.

for permission to appeal, the tribunal is required by rule 37 of the England and Wales Procedure Rules to consider whether, taking into account the overriding objective in rule 2, the decision should be reviewed under the powers conferred by section 9 of the Tribunals, Courts and Enforcement Act 2007. If it is decided not to review the decision, or the decision is reviewed but no action is taken on the review, the tribunal must then consider whether to give permission to appeal in relation to part or all of the decision. Permission to appeal will be given if the application raises an arguable point of law which might affect the outcome of the appeal or if there is an arguable case of procedural unfairness, but permission will be refused if the only ground for challenging the decision is disagreement with the tribunal's findings of fact.

32.12 If permission to appeal is given, the appellant must give notice of appeal to the Upper Tribunal, in accordance with rule 23 of the Upper Tribunal Procedure Rules.[13] If permission to appeal is refused, rule 38 requires the tribunal to give reasons for the refusal and for the appellant to be notified of the right to make an application to the Upper Tribunal for permission to appeal, together with the time limits for making the application and how the application should be made. The tribunal can give permission to appeal on limited grounds, but it must then comply with these requirements in relation to any grounds of appeal in respect of which it has refused permission to appeal.

Application for permission to appeal in Scotland and in assessment appeals in Northern Ireland

32.13 The procedure for applying for permission to appeal to the Upper Tribunal in Scotland and for applying for permission to appeal to the Upper Tribunal (in assessment cases) in Northern Ireland is the same. Under rule 24 of the Scotland and Northern Ireland Procedure Rules, an application for permission to appeal against a tribunal decision must be in writing and signed by the applicant or by the applicant's appointed representative if the applicant has given the representative written authority to make the application on their behalf. The application must give sufficient particulars of the decision under appeal to enable it to be identified and give particulars of the grounds on which the applicant intends to rely.

32.14 An application for permission to appeal must be received no later than 42 days from the date on which the statement of reasons was given or sent to the appellant,[14] but there is power to extend the time limit by up to 1 year if there are

---

13 See para **32.22**.

14 England and Wales Procedure Rules, r 36(2).

special reasons for doing so. If the application is made late, it must state the grounds for seeking late acceptance.

32.15 If an application for permission to appeal is made by the Secretary of State, a copy must be sent to the claimant, who can then make written representations within 1 month of the date on which the application is sent. The representations must be taken into account when the application is determined. The determination must be recorded in writing and a copy sent to both parties.

APPLYING TO THE UPPER TRIBUNAL FOR PERMISSION TO APPEAL

32.16 If an application for permission to appeal has been refused or has not been admitted by the First-tier Tribunal in England and Wales or the Pensions Appeal Tribunal in Scotland, a renewed application for permission to appeal can be made to the Upper Tribunal. In assessment appeals in Northern Ireland, a renewed application for permission to appeal is also made to the Upper Tribunal.

32.17 The procedure for making a renewed application to the Upper Tribunal for permission to appeal is governed by rule 21 of the Upper Tribunal Procedure Rules. The application must be in writing[15] and must be made so that it is received by the Upper Tribunal no later than 1 month after the date on which notification of the refusal to give permission or to admit the application was sent to the appellant by the First-tier Tribunal or Pensions Appeal Tribunal.[16] Under rule 21(4), the application must state:

(a) the name and address of the appellant;
(b) the name and address of the representative (if any) of the appellant;
(c) an address where documents for the appellant may be sent or delivered;
(d) details (including the full reference) of the decision challenged;
(e) the grounds on which the appellant relies; and
(f) whether the appellant wants the application to be dealt with at a hearing.

Under rule 21(5), the appellant must provide with the application a copy of:

(a) the written record of the decision being challenged;
(b) any separate written statement of reasons for that decision; and
(c) … the notice of refusal of permission to appeal, or notice of refusal to admit the application for permission to appeal … .

---

15 The application is normally made on Form UT1, obtainable from tribunal offices.

16 Upper Tribunal Procedure Rules, r 21(3)(b).

32.18 Under rule 21(6) of the Upper Tribunal Procedure Rules, a late application for permission to appeal must include a request for an extension of time and give the reason why the application was not made in time. The Upper Tribunal can then extend the time for making the application under rule 5(3)(a), but if it refuses to do so it must not admit the application.

32.19 If the First-tier Tribunal or the Pensions Appeal Tribunal refused to admit the application for permission to appeal because the application itself or the application for a written statement of reasons was made late, the application to the Upper Tribunal for permission to appeal must include the reason why the application to the First-tier Tribunal for permission to appeal, or the application for the statement of reasons, was not made in time. The Upper Tribunal must only admit the application in those circumstances if it is satisfied that it is in the interests of justice to do so.[17]

32.20 Rule 22(2) of the Upper Tribunal Procedure Rules provides that if the Upper Tribunal gives permission to appeal, it must send each party written notice of the permission and of the reasons for any limitations or conditions on the permission. The application for permission to appeal then stands as the notice of appeal and the appeal proceeds in the same way as in cases where permission to appeal has been given by the tribunal below (see paras **32.24–32.45**).

32.21 Under rule 22(1) of the Upper Tribunal Procedure Rules, if the Upper Tribunal refuses permission to appeal, it must send the appellant written notice of the refusal and of the reasons for the refusal.

APPEALING TO THE UPPER TRIBUNAL

32.22 As stated above, if the Upper Tribunal gives permission to appeal, the application for permission to appeal stands as a notice of appeal and the appellant need take no further action to initiate the appeal. Under rule 23(2) of the Upper Tribunal Procedure Rules, an appellant who has been given permission to appeal by the First-tier Tribunal or by the Pensions Appeal Tribunal must provide the Upper Tribunal with a notice of appeal so that it is received no later than 1 month after the date on which notice was sent to the appellant of the grant of permission to appeal. The notice of appeal must give the same information as an application for permission to appeal (see para **33.6**) except that it is not necessary for the applicant to state whether he wants an oral hearing of the application for permission to appeal (since permission to appeal will already have been given). Copies of the following documents must also be provided:

---

17 Upper Tribunal Procedure Rules, r 21(7).

(i) the decision notice of the decision under appeal;
(ii) the statement of reasons for the decision if it is in a separate document;
(iii) the notice giving permission to appeal.

Unless an appellant wishes to add further grounds of appeal, it is usual for appellants to send the Upper Tribunal the same documents as were submitted when applying for permission to appeal to the tribunal below.

32.23 Under rule 23(5) of the Upper Tribunal Procedure Rules, if a notice of appeal has been sent late and an extension of time has not previously been granted, the notice of appeal must include a request for an extension of time and the reason why the notice has not been sent in time. If the Upper Tribunal does not extend the time for appealing, it must not admit the appeal.

PROCEEDINGS BEFORE THE UPPER TRIBUNAL

32.24 The Upper Tribunal possesses case management powers and powers in relation to the striking out of appeals, withdrawals, non-disclosure or non-publication of documents and other information, and evidence and submissions which are broadly similar to those of the First-tier Tribunal. Upper Tribunal judges in England and Wales exercise case management powers actively in order to give effect to the overriding objective in rule 2 of the England and Wales Procedure Rules.[18] Upper Tribunal judges in England and Wales are assisted by Registrars who can also give case management directions.

32.25 Following receipt of an application for permission to appeal or a notice of appeal (in cases where permission to appeal has been granted by the tribunal below), the Upper Tribunal obtains the tribunal file, which contains the Statement of Case. The Upper Tribunal then constructs its own case file and the case is referred to a judge to decide whether to give permission to appeal in cases where permission to appeal was refused by the tribunal below, or to give case management directions in cases where permission to appeal has been given by the tribunal. A judge granting permission to appeal will give case management directions at the same time. The judge to whom the appeal is allocated at this stage generally retains the case until it has been finally decided.

32.26 Judges frequently identify legal issues at this stage (whether or not raised by the parties) which they consider call for submissions from the Secretary of State. If the decision of the tribunal appears to the judge to be clearly wrong in

---

18 See para **27.2**.

law, the respondent may be invited to consider consenting to a decision without reasons allowing the appeal under rule 40(3) of the Upper Tribunal Procedure Rules, and in such cases the judge may suggest the terms of a decision disposing of the appeal. In other relatively straightforward cases, the judge may direct a simultaneous exchange of written submissions by the parties, but in the majority of cases where the Secretary of State is the respondent the judge will direct the respondent to provide a written response to the appeal within a specified time (usually 1 month), and the appellant to provide a written reply to the response within a further specified period.

32.27 Under rule 24 of the Upper Tribunal Procedure Rules, the respondent to the appeal is required to provide a written response to the appeal stating whether the appeal is opposed, the grounds of opposition, and whether an oral hearing is requested. In the majority of cases, the response is prepared by a senior Veterans UK official and sets out the position of the Secretary of State with regard to each of the issues identified by the judge as calling for a response in giving permission to appeal or in the case management directions. The response is sent to the appellant to make written submissions in reply if desired and to state whether or not an oral hearing of the appeal is requested.

32.28 On receipt of the response and any reply, the appeal is again referred to the judge, who will consider whether any further submissions are required and whether to direct an oral hearing of the appeal.

Oral hearings

32.29 Rule 34 of the Upper Tribunal Procedure Rules allows the Upper Tribunal to make any decision without a hearing, but under rule 34(2) regard must be had to any view expressed by the parties when deciding whether a hearing should be directed. If the appeal is ready for determination, the judge will proceed to decide the case. The majority of cases in the Upper Tribunal are dealt with 'on paper' but oral hearings are comparatively common in war pensions and armed forces compensation cases.

32.30 Rule 36 of the Upper Tribunal Procedure Rules requires the parties to be given reasonable notice of the time and place of the hearing (including any adjourned or postponed hearing) and of any changes. The period of notice must be at least 14 days unless the parties consent to a shorter period of notice or there are urgent or exceptional circumstances. Rule 37 provides that all hearings must be held in public, but under rule 37(2) the Upper Tribunal may direct that part or all of a hearing is to be held in private and, if it does so, who can attend the hearing. Under rule 35, an appellant can always attend a hearing, even when it is in private, unless the appellant has been excluded as the result of a direction under rule 37(4). Rule 37(4) allows the Upper Tribunal to exclude from part or all of a hearing:

(a) any person whose conduct the Upper Tribunal considers is disrupting or is likely to disrupt the hearing;
(b) any person whose presence the Upper Tribunal considers is likely to prevent another person from giving evidence or making submissions freely;
(c) any person who the Upper Tribunal considers should be excluded in order to give effect to a direction under rule 14(2) (withholding information likely to cause harm);
(d) any person where the purpose of the hearing would be defeated by the attendance of that person.

32.31 The procedure at oral hearings in the Upper Tribunal is flexible and will often depend on whether the parties are represented. However, it is usual for judges to clarify the issues in an appeal and to help unrepresented appellants to play a full part in the proceedings. Appellants are frequently represented before the Upper Tribunal by Royal British Legion and other service charity representatives, or by representatives acting *pro bono.* In cases raising difficult issues of law, the Secretary of State may be represented by counsel.

POWERS OF THE UPPER TRIBUNAL

32.32 The powers of the Upper Tribunal if it decides that the decision under appeal involved the making of an error on a point of law are set out in section 12 of the Tribunals, Courts and Enforcement At 2007, which is applied to appeals from Pensions Appeal Tribunals by section 6A(4A) of the Pensions Appeal Tribunals Act 1943. So far as material, section 12 of the 2007 Act provides:

(2) The Upper Tribunal—

(a) may (but need not) set aside the decision of the First-tier Tribunal, and
(b) if it does, must either—

(i) remit the case to the First-tier Tribunal with directions for its reconsideration, or
(ii) re-make the decision.

(3) In acting under subsection (2)(b)(i), the Upper Tribunal may also—

(a) direct that the members of the First-tier Tribunal who are chosen to reconsider the case are not to be the same as those who made the decision that has been set aside;

(b) give procedural directions in connection with the reconsideration of the case by the First-tier Tribunal.

(4) In acting under subsection (2)(b)(ii), the Upper Tribunal—

(a) may make any decision which the First-tier Tribunal could make if the First-tier Tribunal were re-making the decision, and

(b) may make such findings of fact as it considers appropriate.

32.33 Section 12(7)(2)(a) of the Tribunals, Courts and Enforcement Act 2007 gives the Upper Tribunal a discretion not to set aside a tribunal decision which it considers to have been erroneous in law, and it may be appropriate not to set aside a tribunal's decision if doing so would not achieve any practical benefit. In *CAF/4780/2014*,[19] Judge Knowles declined to set aside the decision of a tribunal which had erred in law in deciding whether a Service Pensions Order award should be backdated on the ground of official error because that was the only decision which the tribunal could have reached even if it had applied the law correctly. However, in cases where there may be a continuing entitlement to benefit it may be relevant to consider whether legally erroneous reasons for a decision might affect the exercise of review powers in the future if the decision is allowed to stand.

32.34 The Upper Tribunal will use its power under section 12(2)(b)(ii) of the Tribunals, Courts and Enforcement Act 2007 to re-make the decision under appeal itself if the facts of the case are not in doubt or have been properly found by the tribunal below, or if a further hearing would serve no useful purpose, for example, because there have been full submissions and the appellant would be unlikely to be present or represented at any future hearing. Section 12(4)(b) allows the Upper Tribunal to make such findings of fact as it considers appropriate, but if the case requires fresh or further findings of fact to be made in the light of the Upper Tribunal's decision on questions of law, it will be relevant to consider whether those findings should be made by a tribunal which includes a medical and a service member.

32.35 If the Upper Tribunal exercises its power under section 12(2)(b) of the Tribunals, Courts and Enforcement Act 2007 to remit the case to the First-tier Tribunal, it should identify in its directions the issues of law and fact which the new tribunal should consider, since otherwise the new tribunal may be unclear about its role (see *Secretary of State for Work and Pensions v Menary-Smith*[20]). It is common for directions given by Upper Tribunal judges when allowing an

---

19 Unreported.

20 [2006] EWCA Civ 1751, [2006] All ER (D) 199 (Dec).

appeal to make it clear that the directions can be supplemented or varied by a First-tier Tribunal judge. Section 12(3)(a) requires a specific direction to be given if the re-hearing is to take place before a tribunal which is not composed of members of the tribunal whose decision has been set aside.

DECISIONS

32.36 Rule 40(1) of the Upper Tribunal Procedure Rules allows a decision of the Upper Tribunal to be given orally at a hearing, but final decisions must also be given in writing. Rule 40(2) requires the Upper Tribunal to issue to each of the parties as soon as reasonably practicable after making a final decision a decision notice stating the tribunal's decision and notifying the parties of any rights of review or appeal against the decision, and the time and manner in which such rights can be exercised.

32.37 Subject to any direction under rule 14 of the Upper Tribunal Procedure Rules preventing the disclosure or publication of documents or information, rule 40(3) requires the Upper Tribunal to give written reasons for a final decision, unless:

(a) the decision was made with the consent of the parties; or
(b) the parties have consented to the Upper Tribunal not giving written reasons.

32.38 Rule 39 of the Upper Tribunal Procedure Rules allows the Upper Tribunal to make a consent order disposing of the proceedings at the request of the parties if it considers it appropriate to do so without holding an oral hearing.

CORRECTING, SETTING ASIDE AND REVIEW OF DECISIONS

32.39 The Upper Tribunal has the same powers to correct and set aside decisions as the First-tier Tribunal, and the procedures for doing so are also the same (see paras **31.1**, **31.2** and **31.3**).

32.40 On receiving an application for permission to appeal against one of its decisions, the Upper Tribunal can review the decision under section 9 of the Tribunals, Courts and Enforcement Act 2007, but under rule 45 it can do so only if:

(a) when making its decision the Upper Tribunal overlooked a legislative provision or binding authority which could have had a material effect on its decision; or

(b) since the Upper Tribunal's decision a court has made a decision which is binding on the Upper Tribunal and which, had it been made before the Upper Tribunal's decision, could have had a material effect on the decision.

33.41 Rule 46(2) provides that the tribunal must notify the parties in writing of the outcome of a review and of the rights of appeal against the review decision. Under rule 46(3), if the tribunal takes any action in relation to a decision following a review without first giving every party an opportunity to make representations, the notification of the outcome must state that any party that did not have the opportunity to make representations may apply for the action taken on the review to be set aside and for the decision to be reviewed again.

ONWARD APPEALS

32.42 Section 13 of the Tribunals, Courts and Enforcement Act 2007 gives a right of appeal to the 'relevant appellate court' on any point of law arising from a decision made by the Upper Tribunal, other than an excluded decision. Permission to appeal must be obtained from the Upper Tribunal or from the appellate court, and under section 13(5) an application for permission to appeal can only be made to the appellate court if the Upper Tribunal has refused permission. Section 13(7) provides that before the Upper Tribunal decides an application for permission to appeal, it must specify the court that is to be the relevant appellate court, i.e. the Court of Appeal in England and Wales, the Court of Session in Scotland, or the Court of Appeal in Northern Ireland, whichever is the most appropriate.

32.43 Section 13(8) specifies as 'excluded decisions' certain review decisions and decisions taken following a review, and also a decision to refuse permission to appeal from the First-tier Tribunal (but not a Pensions Appeal Tribunal) to the Upper Tribunal. A decision refusing permission to appeal from the First-tier Tribunal to the Upper Tribunal can therefore only be challenged by means of judicial review.

32.44 Under section 13(6) of the Tribunals, Courts and Enforcement Act 2007 and the Appeals from the Upper Tribunal to the Court of Appeal Order 2008,[21] permission to appeal to the Court of Appeal in England and Wales can be given only if the Upper Tribunal or the relevant appellate court considers:

(a) that the proposed appeal would raise some important point of principle or practice; or

---

21 SI 2008/2834.

(b) that there is some other compelling reason to hear the appeal.

This does not apply where the appeal to the Upper Tribunal was from a Pensions Appeal Tribunal in Scotland or Northern Ireland, due to the terms of section 13(6) and (6A).[22]

32.45 The procedure for bringing an appeal against a decision of the Upper Tribunal is governed by rules 44 and 45 of the Upper Tribunal Procedure Rules. The powers of the appellate court in relation to such appeals are set out in section 14 of the Tribunals, Courts and Enforcement Act 2007.

---

22 *Clarise Properties v Rees* [2015] EWCA Civ 1118.

Chapter 33

Appeals to the Northern Ireland Pensions Appeal Commissioners

33.1 Appeals in Northern Ireland against decisions of the Pensions Appeal Tribunal in entitlement and specified decision cases (including armed forces compensation appeals) are dealt with by the Social Security Commissioners in Northern Ireland, who are referred to as Pensions Appeal Commissioners when exercising this jurisdiction. These appeals are governed by the Pensions Appeal Commissioners (Procedure) (Northern Ireland) Regulations 2005[1] (Pensions Appeal Commissioners Procedure Regulations).

RENEWING AN APPLICATION FOR LEAVE TO APPEAL

33.2 If an application for permission to appeal to the Pensions Appeal Commissioners has been refused by the Pensions Appeal Tribunal, the application may be renewed to the Pensions Appeal Commissioners, but the application must be made to the Pensions Appeal Tribunal first. Under regulation 8 of the Pensions Appeal Commissioners Procedure Regulations, the application must be made within 1 month of the date on which notice of the refusal of leave to appeal or rejection of the application was sent to the appellant, but there is power to extend the time if the appellant failed to seek leave to appeal from the tribunal in time, but did so within 13 months from the date when the decision or statement of reasons was sent to the applicant, provided that there are special reasons for doing so.

33.3 Under regulation 9 of the Pensions Appeal Commissioners Procedure Regulations, the application for leave to appeal must be in writing and give the following information:

---

1 SI 2005/965.

(a) the name and address of the applicant;
(b) the grounds on which the applicant intends to rely;
(c) if the application is made late, the grounds for seeking late acceptance; and
(d) an address for sending notices and other documents to the applicant.

The applicant must send with the application copies of:

(a) the decision against which leave to appeal is sought;
(b) if separate, the written statement of the appeal tribunal's reasons for it; and
(c) the notice of refusal or rejection sent to the applicant by the appeal tribunal.

If an application for leave to appeal is made by the Secretary of State, the claimant must be sent a copy of the notice of application and any documents sent with it when they are sent to the Commissioners.

33.4 Under regulation 10(1) of the Pensions Appeal Commissioners Procedure Regulations, when the application for leave to appeal has been determined, the parties must be sent written notice of the determination. If leave to appeal is given, the notice of application for leave to appeal is treated as the appeal and the appeal is deemed to have been sent on the date when notice of the determination was sent to the parties. If a Commissioner gives leave to appeal, the application may with the consent of the parties be treated as the appeal.

APPEALS TO THE PENSIONS APPEAL COMMISSIONERS

33.5 Under regulation 11 of the Pensions Appeal Commissioners Procedure Regulations, an appellant who has been given leave to appeal by the Pensions Appeal Tribunal brings the appeal by giving notice in writing, which must contain the following information:

(a) the name and address of the appellant;
(b) the date on which the appellant was notified that leave to appeal has been granted;
(c) the grounds on which the appellant intends to rely;
(d) if the appeal is made late, the grounds for seeking late acceptance; and
(e) an address for sending notices and other documents to the appellant.

The appellant must send with the notice of appeal copies of:

(a) the notice informing the appellant that leave to appeal has been granted;

(b) the decision against which leave to appeal has been granted; and
(c) if separate, the written statement of the appeal tribunal's reasons for it.

Regulation 12 of the Pensions Appeal Commissioners Procedure Regulations provides that the notice of appeal will only be valid if it is sent within 1 month of the date on which the appellant was sent notice that leave to appeal had been granted, but a late appeal may be accepted if there are special reasons for doing so.

PROCEDURE

Written observations

33.6 Regulation 15 of the Pensions Appeal Commissioners Procedure Regulations provides for the respondent to the appeal to make observations within 1 month, including saying whether or not the appeal is opposed and the grounds on which the respondent proposes to rely. The practice of the Pensions Appeal Commissioners is to invite observations from Veterans UK in every case. Regulation 16 provides for the appellant to send written observations in reply within 1 month of being sent the respondent's observations. If each of the parties expresses the view that in their observations the decision under appeal was wrong in law, the Commissioner can set aside the decision without any further observations being required.

Directions

33.7 Under regulation 17 of the Pensions Appeal Commissioners Procedure Regulations, a Commissioner can direct further particulars of an application or appeal or direct further written observations, or direct the tribunal to provide a statement of facts, or give any such direction as the Commissioner considers necessary for the proper determination of the application or appeal. Either party may apply in writing for a direction to be given.

33.8 Regulation 23 of the Pensions Appeal Commissioners Procedure Regulations allows a Commissioner to waive or take steps to remedy any irregularity resulting from non-compliance with any of the rules of procedure.

Harmful evidence

33.9 Regulation 18(1) of the Pensions Appeal Commissioners Procedure Regulations provides that if the evidence before the Commissioner includes evidence relating to a person which has not been disclosed to the person and which would in the Commissioner's opinion be harmful to the health of the person if it were disclosed, the evidence is not to be disclosed to the person or to the person's representative. The provision extends to cases where the evidence relates to the disability of a person other than the appellant, but does not prevent the evidence from being taken into account by the Commissioner.

Withdrawal

33.10 Regulation 22 of the Pensions Appeal Commissioners Procedure Regulations allows an applicant to withdraw an application for leave to appeal or an appeal by written notice at any time before the application or appeal is determined. Under regulation 22(3), a Commissioner can give leave for an application or appeal which has been withdrawn to be reinstated, and can give directions about the future conduct of the proceedings.

Hearings

33.11 Under regulation 19 of the Pensions Appeal Commissioners Procedure Regulations, a Commissioner may determine proceedings without a hearing, but a hearing must be directed if requested by either party, unless the Commissioner is satisfied that the proceedings can be properly determined without a hearing. If a request for a hearing is refused, written notice of the refusal must be given. A Commissioner can direct a hearing without an application at any stage of the proceedings, but in such cases the Commissioner will usually direct final submissions from each party before deciding the case.

33.12 Regulation 20 of the Pensions Appeal Commissioners Procedure Regulations requires reasonable notice of the time and place of a hearing to be given, which must be at least 14 days, unless the parties agree to a shorter period.

33.13 Regulation 20(5) of the Pensions Appeal Commissioners Procedure Regulations provides that any hearing must be in public, unless the Commissioner for special reasons directs otherwise. If a party has been sent notice of a hearing but fails to attend, Regulation 20(4) allows the hearing to take place in the party's absence. Regulation 14 allows appellants to conduct their case themselves, with assistance from any other person, or to be represented by any person appointed for that purpose. Under regulation 20(9), any person entitled to attend a hearing may address the Commissioner and, with the leave of the Commissioner, give evidence, call witnesses and put questions directly to any person called as a witness. Regulation 20(8) allows hearings to be conducted by means of a live video-link and other forms of technology may also be used (see para **28.14**).

SUMMONING WITNESSES

33.14 Regulation 21 of the Pensions Appeal Commissioners Procedure Regulations gives a Commissioner power to summon a witness to answer questions or produce documents at a hearing, but the witness must be given 14 days' notice of the hearing, unless the witness accepts shorter notice. A person who has been summoned under this regulation may apply for the summons to be set aside.

POWERS OF THE PENSIONS APPEAL COMMISSIONERS

33.15 Section 6A of the Pensions Appeal Tribunals Act 1943 provides:

> (3) If each of the parties to an appeal under this section to a Northern Ireland Social Security Commissioner expresses the view that the decision appealed against was erroneous in point of law, the Commissioner may set aside the decision and refer the case to a Pensions Appeal Tribunal for Northern Ireland with directions for its determination.
>
> (4) Where an appeal is made to a Northern Ireland Social Security Commissioner and the Commissioner holds that the decision appealed against was erroneous in point of law, he shall set it aside and—
>
> (a) he shall have power—
>
> (i) to give the decision which he considers the Pensions Appeal Tribunal for Northern Ireland should have given, if he can do so without making fresh or further findings of fact; or
>
> (ii) if he considers it expedient, to make such findings and give such decision as he considers appropriate in the light of them; and
>
> (b) in any other case he shall refer the case to a Pensions Appeal Tribunal for Northern Ireland with directions for its determination.

Under section 6D(5) of the Pensions Appeal Tribunals Act 1943, the Chief Social Security Commissioner can direct that an application or appeal is dealt with by a tribunal of two or more Pensions Appeal Commissioners if it involves a question of law of special difficulty.

DECISIONS

33.16 Regulation 24 of the Pensions Appeal Commissioners Procedure Regulations requires any determination of an application for permission to appeal and any decision on an appeal to be in writing and signed by the Commissioner, although a Commissioner may announce the determination or decision orally at the end of a hearing. Reasons for a decision on an appeal must be given, unless the decision was given by consent under section 6A(3) of the Pensions Appeal Tribunals Act 1943 (see para **33.15**).

CORRECTION AND SETTING ASIDE OF DECISIONS

33.17 Regulation 25 of the Pensions Appeal Commissioners Procedure Regulations allows the Commissioner who gave a decision to correct accidental errors in the decision or record of a decision. Notice of the correction must be sent to the parties.

33.18 Regulation 26 of the Pensions Appeal Commissioners Procedure Regulations allows a party to apply to set aside a decision within 1 month from the date on which the decision was sent to the party making the application on the ground that:

(a) a document relating to the proceedings was not sent to, or was not received at an appropriate time by the Commissioner;
(b) a party or his representative was not present at a hearing before the Commissioner.

Unless the Commissioner considers that it is unnecessary, notice of the application must be sent to the other party. Notice of the determination of the application and the reasons for it must be sent to the parties.

ONWARD APPEALS

33.19 Regulation 28 of the Pensions Appeal Commissioners Procedure Regulations provides that an application for leave to appeal from a decision of a Commissioner to an appellate court (the Northern Ireland Court of Appeal) must be in writing and must state the grounds of appeal. The procedure for appealing to the Court of Appeal in Northern Ireland is by case stated. The time limit for applying for leave to appeal is 3 months from the date on which notice of the decision was sent to the appellant, or 3 months from the date when the appellant was sent notice of correction of a decision, or notice of a refusal to set the decision aside, except where the application to set aside was refused because it was late.

Appendix 1

Schedule 1 to the Naval, Military and Air Forces Etc. (Disablement and Death) Service Pensions Order 2006 (SI 2006/606) (as amended)

SCHEDULE 1 — Article 3(1)

DISABLEMENT DUE TO SERVICE IN THE ARMED FORCES

PART I
GROUPING OF MEMBERS OF THE ARMED FORCES ACCORDING TO RANK OR STATUS

1. In this Schedule—

(a) references to a Group shall be construed as references to those members of the armed forces who hold the rank or status listed under that Group; and

(b) the amount of any award in respect of that Group is that amount shown in the following Parts of this Schedule against that Group.

2. The Groups referred to in the foregoing paragraph comprise:—

GROUP 1:—

Royal Navy	Rear-Admiral
Royal Marines	Major-General
Army	Major-General
	Chief Controller
RAF	Air Vice-Marshal

GROUP 2:—

Army	Brigadier-General
RAF	Air Commodore disabled as a result of service during the 1914 World War

GROUP 3:—

Navy	Commodore 1st or 2nd Class
	Captain with 6 or more years seniority whose service terminated on or after 1st April 1970.
Royal Marines	Colonel-Commandant
	Colonel whose service terminated on or after 1st April 1970.
WRNS	Commandant
	Member with status of Commodore
Army	Brigadier
	Senior Controller
	Member with status of Brigadier
RAF	Air Commodore
	Air Commandant
	Member with status of Air Commodore

GROUP 4:—

Navy	Captain of less than 6 years seniority or whose service terminated before 1st April 1970.
Royal Marines	Colonel 2nd Commandant
	Colonel whose service terminated before1st April 1970
	Lieutenant-Colonel and corresponding ranks, Temporary
	Marine Officer relinquishing commission etc. prior to 1st April 1919 to be included in Group 5
WRNS	Superintendent
	Member with status of Captain RN
Army	Colonel
	Controller
	Member with status of Colonel
RAF	Group Captain
	Group Officer
	Member with status of Group Captain

GROUP 5:—

Navy	Commander
Royal Marines	Major and corresponding ranks, Temporary Marine Officer relinquishing commission etc. prior to 1st April 1919 to be included in Group 6
WRNS	Chief Officer
	Member with status of Commander RN
Army	Lieutenant-Colonel
	Chief Commander
	Member with status of Lieutenant-Colonel

RAF	Wing Commander Wing Officer Member with status of Wing Commander

GROUP 6:—

Navy	Lieutenant-Commander
Royal Marines	Captain and corresponding ranks, Temporary Marine Officer relinquishing commission etc. prior to 1st April 1919, to be included in Group 7
WRNS	First Officer Member with status of Lieutenant-Commander RN
Army	Major Senior Commander Member with status of Major
RAF	Squadron Leader Squadron Officer Member with status of Squadron Leader

GROUP 7:—

Navy	Lieutenant
Royal Marines	Lieutenant with 4 years commissioned service or over
WRNS	Second Officer Member with status of Lieutenant RN
Army	Captain Junior Commander Member with status of Captain
RAF	Flight Lieutenant Flight Officer Member with status of Flight Lieutenant

GROUP 8:—

Navy	Sub-Lieutenant Acting Sub-Lieutenant Senior Commissioned Officer (Branch List) Commissioned Officer from Warrant Rank >Midshipman (A) Midshipman or Cadet where service terminated on or after 1st January 1957
Royal Marines	Lieutenant with under 4 years commissioned service 2nd Lieutenant Senior Commissioned Officer (Branch List) Commissioned Officer from Warrant Rank and corresponding ranks

WRNS	Third Officer
	Woman member with status below Lieutenant RN
Army	Lieutenant (Quartermasters, Assistant Pay Masters and Inspectors of Army Stores)
	Second Lieutenant
	Subaltern
	Second Subaltern
	Member with status below Captain
RAF	Flying Officer
	Pilot Officer
	Acting Pilot Officer
	Section Officer
	Assistant Section Officer
	Member with status below Flight Lieutenant

GROUP 9:—

Navy	Commissioned Officer (Branch List)
	Warrant Officer
	Midshipman
	Cadet after completion of shore training where, in the case of any of these ranks, service terminated before 1st January 1957
	Naval Cadet (Serving with the Fleet)
Royal Marines	Commissioned Officer (Branch List)
	Warrant Officer and corresponding ranks

GROUP 10:—

Navy	Fleet Chief Petty Officer
	Fleet Chief Wren
	Member of a Voluntary Aid Detachment serving as an uncertificated Nurse Grade 1
Royal Marines	Regimental Sergeant-Major
Army	Warrant Officer Class 1
RAF	Warrant Officer
	Airman Class A
	Member of a Voluntary Aid Detachment serving as an uncertificated Nurse Grade 1

GROUP 11:—

Royal Marines	Quartermaster Sergeant
Army	Warrant Officer Class II
	Non-Commissioned Officer Class I
RAF	Warrant Officer 2nd Class
	Airman Class B

GROUP 12:—

Navy	Chief Petty Officer
	Chief Wren
Royal Marines	Colour Sergeant
Army	Staff Sergeant
	Non-Commissioned Officer Class II
RAF	Flight Sergeant
	Airman Class C

GROUP 13:—

Navy	Petty Officer
	Petty Officer Wren
Royal Marines	Sergeant
Army	Sergeant
	Non-Commissioned Officer Class III
RAF	Sergeant
	Airman Class D

GROUP 14:—

Navy	Leading Rating
	Leading Wren
Royal Marines	Corporal
Army	Corporal
	Non-Commissioned Officer Class IV
RAF	Corporal
	Airman Class E

GROUP 15:—

Navy	A B Rating
	Ordinary Rating
	Boy
	Wren
Royal Marines	Marine
Army	Private etc. Class V
RAF	Senior Aircraftman
	Leading Aircraftman
	Aircraftsman
	Airman Class F
	Senior Aircraftwoman
	Leading Aircraftwoman
	Aircraftwoman

PART II
RATES OF RETIRED PAY, PENSIONS, GRATUITIES AND ALLOWANCES

1. [WEEKLY RATES OF PENSIONS FOR DISABLED MEMBERS OF THE ARMED FORCES IN GROUPS 10–15 OF PART I OF THIS SCHEDULE

2. YEARLY RATES OF RETIRED PAY AND PENSIONS FOR DISABLED MEMBERS OF THE ARMED FORCES IN GROUPS 1–9 OF PART I OF THIS SCHEDULE

Degree of Disablement Per Cent	*Weekly Rate £*	*Yearly Rate £*
100	178.20	9,298
90	160.38	8,369
80	142.56	7,439
70	124.74	6,509
60	106.92	5,579
50	89.10	4,649
40	71.28	3,719
30	53.46	2,790
20	35.64	1,860]

AMENDMENT

Pt II Table substituted by The Naval, Military and Air Forces Etc. (Disablement and Death) Service Pensions (Amendment) Order 2015 (SI 2015/208), art 1(1), Sch 1

PART III
GRATUITIES PAYABLE FOR MINOR INJURIES

[Table 1 GRATUITIES PAYABLE FOR SPECIFIED MINOR INJURIES

Description of Injury ***For the loss of:***	***Assessments*** ***Per cent***	***Groups 1–15*** ***£***
A. FINGERS		
Index finger—		
More than 2 phalanges including the loss of whole finger	14	8,474
More than 1 phalanx but not more than 2 phalanges	11	6,780
1 phalanx or part thereof	9	5,649
Guillotine amputation of tip without loss of bone	5	3,381
Middle finger—		
More than 2 phalanges including loss of whole finger	1	27,341
More than 1 phalanx but not more than 2 phalanges	9	5,649
1 phalanx or part thereof	7	4,517
Guillotine amputation of tip without loss of bone	4	2,822
Ring or little finger—		
More than 2 phalanges including loss of whole finger	7	4,517
More than 1 phalanx but not more than 2 phalanges	6	3,959
1 phalanx or part thereof	5	3,381
Guillotine amputation of tip without loss of bone	2	1,693
B. TOES		
Great toe—		
Through metatarso-phalangeal joint	14	8,474
Part, with some loss of bone	3	2,253
1 other toe—		
Through metatarso-phalangeal joint	3	2,253
Part, with some loss of bone	1	1,136
2 toes, excluding great toe—		
Through metatarso-phalangeal joint	5	3,381
Part, with some loss of bone	2	1,693
3 toes, excluding great toe—		
Through metatarso-phalangeal joint	6	3,959
Part, with some loss of bone	3	2,253
4 toes, excluding great toe—		
Through metatarso-phalangeal joint	9	5,649
Part, with some loss of bone	3	2,253

Table 2 GRATUITIES PAYABLE TO MEMBERS OF THE ARMED FORCES FOR DISABLEMENT ASSESSED AT LESS THAN 20 PER CENT NOT BEING A MINOR INJURY SPECIFIED IN TABLE 1

	Assessment of degree of disablement		
Groups 1–15	1 to 5 per cent £2,834	6 to 14 per cent £6,300	15 to 19 per cent £11,018]

AMENDMENT

Pt III Tables 1, 2 substituted by The Naval, Military and Air Forces Etc. (Disablement and Death) Service Pensions (Amendment) Order 2015 (SI 2015/208), art 1(1), Sch 2

PART IV
[Table RATES OF ALLOWANCES PAYABLE IN RESPECT OF DISABLEMENT AND EARNINGS OR INCOME THRESHOLDS

Description of Allowance	***Rate*** ***Groups 1–9***	***Groups 10–15***
1. Constant attendance allowance under article 8—		
(a) under article 8—		
(i) the part day rate of constant attendance allowance under article 8(2)	£1,753 per annum	£33.60 per week
(ii) the full day rate of constant attendance allowance under article 8(3)	£3,506 per annum	£67.20 per week
(iii) the intermediate rate of constant attendance allowance under article 8(4)	£5,260 per annum	£100.80 per week
(iv) the exceptional rate of constant attendance allowance under article 8(5)	£7,013 per annum	£134.40 per week
(b) under article 71(4)—		
(i) the rate under paragraph 4(a)	£3,506 per annum*	£67.20 per week*
(ii) the rate under paragraph 4(b)	£7,013 per annum*	£134.40 per week*
2. Exceptionally severe disablement allowance under article 9	£3,506 per annum	£67.20 per week
3. Severe disablement occupational allowance under article 10	£1,753 per annum	£33.60 per week
4. Allowance for wear and tear of clothing under article 11	£230 per annum	£230 per annum
5. Unemployability allowances—		
(a) personal allowance under article 12(1)(a)	£5,745 per annum	£110.10 per week
(b) additional allowances for dependants by way of—		
(i) increase of allowances in respect of a spouse, civil partner, adult dependant, dependant living as a spouse or dependant living as a civil partner under article 12(6)(a)	£3,193 per annum*	£61.20 per week*
(ii) increase of allowance under article 12(6)(b)—		

(aa)	in respect of the only, elder or eldest child of a member	£741 per annum	£14.20 per week
(bb)	in respect of each other child of a member	£874 per annum	£16.75 per week
(cc)	where the child does not qualify for child benefit under the Social Security Contributions and Benefits Act 1992, or under any legislation in Northern Ireland or the Isle of Man corresponding to that Act	£874 per annum	£16.75 per week

For decisions made on or after 9th April 2001

[(c) the annual earnings figure for the purposes of article 12(4) is £5,590]
(d) the weekly income figure for the purposes of article 12(6)(a)(i) is £73.10

6. Invalidity allowance under article 13—

(a) if—

(i)	the relevant date fell before 5th July 1948;		
(ii)	on the relevant date the member was under the age of 35; or	£1,138 per annum	£21.80 per week
(iii)	on the relevant date the member was under the age of 40 and had not attained the age of 65, in the case of a member being a man, or 60, in the case of that person being a woman, before 6th April 1979 and the period in respect of which payment of the allowance is to relate begins on or after 6th April 1979		

(b) if head (a) does not apply and—

(i)	on the relevant date the member was under the age of 45; or		
(ii)	on the relevant date the member was under the age of 50 and had not attained the age of 65, in the case of a member being a man, or 60, in the case of that person being a woman,	£741 per annum	£14.20 per week

before 6th April 1979 and the period in respect of which payment of the allowance is to relate begins on or after 6th April 1979		
(c) if heads (a) and (b) do not apply and on the relevant date the member was a man under the age of 60 or a woman under the age of 55	£370 per annum	£7.10 per week
7. Comforts allowance—		
(a) under article 14(1)(a)	£1,508 per annum	£28.90 per week
(b) under article 14(1)(b)	£754 per annum	£14.45 per week
8. Allowance for lowered standard of occupation under article 15	£3,506 per annum*	£67.20 per week*
9. Age allowance under article 16 where the degree of pensioned disablement is—		
(a) 40 to 50 per cent	£624 per annum	£11.95 per week
(b) over 50 per cent, but not exceeding 70 per cent	£958 per annum	£18.35 per week
(c) over 70 per cent, but not exceeding 90 per cent	£1,362 per annum	£26.10 per week
(d) over 90 per cent	£1,915 per annum	£36.70 per week
10. Part-time treatment allowance under article 19	£81.75 per day*	£81.75 per day*
11. Mobility supplement under article 20	£3,347 per annum	£64.15 per week

* maximum.]

AMENDMENT

Pt IV Table substituted by The Naval, Military and Air Forces Etc. (Disablement and Death) Service Pensions (Amendment) Order 2015 (SI 2015/208), art 1(1), Sch 3

Item 5(c) substituted by The Naval, Military and Air Forces Etc. (Disablement and Death) Service Pensions (Amendment) Order 2016 (SI 2016/374), art 10

PART V
ASSESSMENT OF DISABLEMENT CAUSED BY SPECIFIED INJURIES AND OF CERTAIN OTHER DISABLEMENTS

Description of Injury	***Assessment***
Amputation Cases – Upper Limbs	*per cent*
Loss of both hands or amputation at higher sites	100
Forequarter amputation	100
Amputation through shoulder joint	90
Amputation below shoulder with stump less than 20.5 centimetres from tip of acromion	80
Amputation from 20.5 centimetres from tip of acromion to less than 11.5 centimetres below tip of olecranon	70
Amputation from 11.5 centimetres below tip of olecranon	60
Loss of thumb	30
Loss of thumb and its metacarpal bone	40
Loss of 4 fingers	50
Loss of 3 fingers	30
Loss of 2 fingers	20
Loss of terminal phalanx of thumb	20
Amputation Cases – Lower Limbs	*per cent*
Double amputation through thigh, or through thigh on one side and loss of other foot, or double amputation below thigh to 13 centimetres below knee	100
Double amputation through leg lower than 13 centimetres below knee	100
Amputation of one leg lower than 13 centimetres below knee and loss of other foot	100
Amputation of both feet resulting in end-bearing stumps	90
Amputation through both feet proximal to the metatarso-phalangeal joint	80
Loss of all toes of both feet through the metatarso-phalangeal joint	40
Loss of all toes of both feet proximal interphalangeal joint	30
Loss of all toes of both feet distal to the proximal interphalangeal joint	20
Hindquarter amputation	100
Amputation through hip joint	90
Amputation below hip with stump not exceeding 13 centimetres in length measured from tip of great trochanter	80
Amputation below hip and above knee with stump exceeding 13 centimetres in length measured from tip of great trochanter, or at knee not resulting in end-bearing stump	70

Amputation at knee resulting in end-bearing stump, or below knee with stump not exceeding 9 centimetres	60
Amputation below knee with stump exceeding 9 centimetres but not exceeding 13 centimetres	50
Amputation below knee with stump exceeding 13 centimetres	40
Amputation of one foot resulting in end-bearing stump	30
Amputation through one foot proximal to the metatarso-phalangeal joint	30
Loss of all toes of one foot proximal to the proximal interphalangeal joint, including amputations through the metatarso-phalangeal joint.	20

Other Specific Injuries	*per cent*
Loss of a hand and a foot	100
Loss of one eye, without complications, the other being normal	40
Loss of vision of one eye, without complications or disfigurement of the eyeball, the other being normal	30
Loss of sight	100

Other Disablements	*per cent*
Very severe facial disfigurement	100
Absolute deafness	100
[Mesothelioma	100]

Note:– Where the scheduled assessment for a specified injury involving multiple losses differs from the sum of the assessments for the separate injuries, the former is the appropriate assessment.

AMENDMENT

Words in square brackets in Pt 5 Table inserted by The Naval, Military and Air Forces Etc. (Disablement and Death) Service Pensions (Amendment) Order 2009 (SI 2009/706), arts 1(1), 15(d) (with art 18)

PART VI
ASSESSMENT OF DISABLEMENT IN RESPECT OF NOISE INDUCED SENSORINEURAL HEARING LOSS

Average of hearing losses (db) at 1, 2 and 3 kHz frequencies	*Degree of Disablement per cent*
50 – 53 dB	20
54 – 60 dB	30
61 – 66 dB	40
67 – 72 dB	50
73 – 79 dB	60
80 – 86 dB	70
87 – 95 dB	80
96 – 105 dB	90
106 dB or more	100

Appendix 2

Schedule 2 to the Naval, Military and Air Forces Etc. (Disablement and Death) Service Pensions Order 2006 (SI 2006/606) (as amended)

SCHEDULE 2 **Article 3(1)**

DEATH DUE TO SERVICE IN THE ARMED FORCES

PART I

GROUPING OF MEMBERS OF THE ARMED FORCES ACCORDING TO RANK OR STATUS

1. In this Schedule—

(a) references to a Group shall be construed as references to those members of the armed forces who held the rank or status listed under that Group; and

(b) the amount of any award in respect of that Group is the amount shown in the following Parts of this Schedule against that Group.

2. The Groups referred to in the foregoing paragraph comprise:—

GROUP 1:—

Royal Navy	Admiral of the Fleet
Army	Field Marshal
Royal Air Force	Marshal of the Royal Air Force

GROUP 2:—

Royal Navy	Admiral
Royal Marines	General
Army	General
Royal Air Force	Air Chief Marshal

GROUP 3:—

Royal Navy	Vice-Admiral
Royal Marines	Lieutenant-General
Army	Lieutenant-General
Royal Air Force	Air Marshal

GROUP 4:—

Royal Navy	Rear-Admiral
Royal Marines	Major-General
Army	Major-General
Royal Air Force	Air Vice-Marshal

GROUP 5:—

Royal Navy	Commodore
	Commodore 1st or 2nd Class
	Captain with 6 or more years seniority whose service terminated on or after 1st April 1970
Royal Marines	Brigadier-General
	Colonel-Commandant
	Colonel whose service terminated on or after 1st April 1970
Army	Brigadier-General
	Brigadier
Royal Air Force	Air Commodore

GROUP 6:—

Royal Navy	Captain where death is due to service in the Navy during the 1914 World War
	Captain of less than 6 years seniority or whose service terminated before 1st April 1970
Royal Marines	Colonel: where death is due to service in the Army during the 1914 World War, Colonel means a Colonel who has been employed as a substantive Colonel if a combat officer, or in the rank of Colonel if a medical, veterinary or departmental officer
	Colonel 2nd Commandant
	Colonel whose service terminated before 1st April 1970
	Lieutenant-Colonel
Army	Colonel: where death is due to service in the Army during the 1914 World War, Colonel means a Colonel who has been employed as a substantive Colonel if a combat officer, or in the rank of Colonel if a medical, veterinary or departmental officer
Royal Air Force	Group Captain

GROUP 7:—

Royal Navy	Commander
Royal Marines	Major
Army	Lieutenant-Colonel including a Colonel not employed as such where death is due to service in the Army during the 1914 World War
Royal Air Force	Wing Commander

GROUP 8:—

Royal Navy	Lieutenant-Commander
Royal Marines	Captain
Army	Major
Royal Air Force	Squadron Leader

GROUP 9:—

Royal Navy	Lieutenant
Royal Marines	Lieutenant with 4 years commissioned service or over
Army	Captain
Royal Air Force	Flight Lieutenant

GROUP 10:—

Royal Navy	Sub-Lieutenant
	Acting Sub-Lieutenant
	Senior Commissioned Officer (Branch List)
	Commissioned Officer from Warrant rank Midshipman (A) and, where service terminated on or after 1st January 1957, Midshipman or Cadet
Royal Marines	Lieutenant with less than 4 years commissioned service
	2nd Lieutenant
	Senior Commissioned Officer (Branch List)
	Commissioned Officer from Warrant rank
	Quartermaster
Army	Lieutenant and where death is due to service in the Army during the 1914 World War, Quartermasters, Assistant Paymasters andInspectors of Army Schools, not holdingpermanent commissions in the Regular Forcesmay be treated as Lieutenants
	2nd Lieutenant
Royal Air Force	Flying (or Observer) Officer
	Pilot Officer
	Acting Pilot Officer

GROUP 11:—

Royal Navy	Commissioned Officer (Branch List)
	Midshipman
	Cadet where in the case of any of these ranks, service terminated before 1st January 1957
	Warrant Officer
Royal Marines	Commissioned Officer (Branch List)
	Warrant Officer

GROUP 12:—

Royal Navy	Fleet Chief Petty Officer
Royal Marines	Regimental Sergeant-Major
	Marine Warrant Officer, Class 1
Army	Warrant Officer Class II
Royal Air Force	Warrant Officer
	Airman Class A

GROUP 13:—

Royal Marines	Quartermaster Sergeant
	Marine Warrant Officer, Class II
	Warrant Officer Class II
Army	Non-Commissioned Officer Class I
Royal Air Force	Warrant Officer 2nd Class
	Airman Class B

GROUP 14:—

Royal Navy	Chief Petty Officer
Royal Marines	Colour Sergeant
	Staff Sergeant
Army	Staff Sergeant
	Non-Commissioned Officer Class II
Royal Air Force	Flight Sergeant
	Airman Class C

GROUP 15:—

Royal Navy	Petty Officer
	First Class Petty Officer (OS)
	Petty Officer (NS)
Royal Marines	Sergeant
Army	Sergeant
	Non-Commissioned Officer Class III
Royal Air Force	Sergeant
	Airman Class D

GROUP 16:—

Royal Navy	Second Class Petty Officer
	Leading Rating
Royal Marines	Corporal
Army	Corporal
	Non-Commissioned Officer Class IV
Royal Air Force	Corporal
	Airman Class E

GROUP 17:—

Royal Navy	AB Rating
	Ordinary Rating
Royal Marines	Marine
Army	Private, etc. Class V
Royal Air Force	Senior Aircraftman
	Leading Aircraftman
	Aircraftman
	Airman Class F

PART II
RATES OF PENSIONS AND ALLOWANCES

[Table 1 YEARLY RATES OF PENSIONS FOR SURVIVING SPOUSES AND SURVIVING CIVIL PARTNERS OF OFFICERS WHO WERE MEMBERS OF THE ARMED FORCES BEFORE 14 AUGUST 1914 OR AFTER 30 SEPTEMBER 1921

PENSIONS OTHER THAN PENSIONS AWARDED UNDER ARTICLE 11(1) OR (2) OF THE 1921 (OFFICERS) ORDER OR ARTICLE 11(1) OF THE 1921 (WARRANT OFFICERS) ORDER, OF THE 1920 WARRANT OR OF THE 1921 ORDER

Group (1)	*Yearly Rate (2) £*
1	8,141
2	7,851
3	7,665
4	7,499
5	7,430
6	7,279
7	7,241
8	7,187
9	7,160
10	7,130
11	7,088

Table 2 WEEKLY RATES OF PENSIONS FOR SURVIVING SPOUSES AND SURVIVING CIVIL PARTNERS OF RATINGS, SOLDIERS OR AIRMEN

Group (1)	*Weekly Rate (2) £*
12)	135.15
13)	
14)	
15)	
16)	
17)	

Table 3 EARLY RATES OF PENSIONS FOR SURVIVING SPOUSES AND SURVIVING CIVIL PARTNERS OF OFFICERS WHO WERE MEMBERS OF THE ARMED FORCES BEFORE 14 AUGUST 1914 OR AFTER 30 SEPTEMBER 1921

PENSIONS AWARDED UNDER ARTICLE 11(1) OR (2) OF THE 1921 (OFFICERS) ORDER OR ARTICLE 11(1) OF THE 1921 (WARRANT OFFICERS) ORDER, OF THE 1920 WARRANT OR OF THE 1921 ORDER

Group (1)	*Yearly Rate (2) £*
1	8,323
2	7,956
3	7,774
4	7,589
5	7,447
6	7,297
7	7,255
8	7,187
9	7,160
10	7,130
11	7,088

Table 4 YEARLY RATES OF PENSIONS FOR SURVIVING SPOUSES AND SURVIVING CIVIL PARTNERS OF OFFICERS WHO WERE MEMBERS OF THE ARMED FORCES BEFORE 14 AUGUST 1914 OR AFTER 30 SEPTEMBER 1921

Group(1)	*Yearly Rate (2) £*
1	8,141
2	7,851
3	7,665
4	7,499
5	7,430
6	7,279
7	7,241
8	2,496
9	2,226
10	1,958
11	1,732

Table 5 WEEKLY RATES OF PENSION FOR CHILDLESS SURVIVING SPOUSES AND SURVIVING CIVIL PARTNERS AGED UNDER 40 BEING SURVIVING SPOUSES OR SURVIVING CIVIL PARTNERS OF RATINGS, SOLDIERS OR AIRMEN

Group (1)	*Weekly Rate (2) £*
12)	32.37
13)	
14)	
15)	
16)	
17)	

Table 6 YEARLY RATE OF SUPPLEMENTARY PENSION FOR SURVIVING SPOUSES AND SURVIVING CIVIL PARTNERS OF OFFICERS WHO WERE MEMBERS OF THE ARMED FORCES AND WHOSE SERVICE TERMINATED ON OR BEFORE 31 MARCH 1973

Group (1)	*Yearly Rate (2) £*
(1–11)	4,717.59

Table 7 WEEKLY RATE OF SUPPLEMENTARY PENSION FOR SURVIVING SPOUSES AND SURVIVING CIVIL PARTNERS OF RATINGS, SOLDIERS AND AIRMEN WHO WERE MEMBER OF THE ARMED FORCES AND WHOSE SERVICE TERMINATED ON OR BEFORE 31 MARCH 1973

Group (1)	*Weekly Rate (2) £*
(12–17)	90.41]

AMENDMENT

Pt II Tables 1–7 substituted by The Naval, Military and Air Forces Etc. (Disablement and Death) Service Pensions (Amendment) Order 2015 (SI 2015/208), art 1(1), Sch 4

PART III

[Table RATES OF PENSIONS, OTHER THAN SURVIVING SPOUSES' AND SURVIVING CIVIL PARTNERS' PENSIONS AND ALLOWANCES PAYABLE IN RESPECT OF DEATH

Description of Pension or Allowance	*Rates* Groups 1–11	*Groups 12–17*
1. Pension under article 24 to dependant who lived as a spouse or dependant who lived as a civil partner	£6,930 per annum*	£132.80 per week*
2. Rent allowance under article 25	£2,656 per annum*	£50.90 per week*
3. Elderly persons allowance under article 26—		
(a) if aged 65 or over but under 70	£804 per annum	£15.40 per week
(b) if aged 70 or over but under 80	£1,545 per annum	£29.60 per week
(c) if aged 80 or over	£2,291 per annum	£43.90 per week
4. Allowances in respect of children—		
(a) under article 28(2)(a)—		
(i) in respect of the only, elder or eldest child of a member	£1,106 per annum	£21.20 per week
(ii) in respect of each other child of a member	£1,239 per annum	£23.75 per week
(iii) where the child does not qualify for child benefit under the Social Security Contributions and Benefits Act 1992 or any legislation in Northern Ireland or the Isle of Man corresponding to that Act	£1,239 per annum	£23.75 per week
(b) under article 28(2)(b)—		
(i) in respect of the only, elder or eldest child of a member	£1,265 per annum	£24.25 per week
(ii) in respect of each other child of a member	£1,385 per annum	£26.55 per week
(iii) where the child does not qualify for child benefit under the Social Security Contributions and	£1,385 per annum	£26.55 per week

Benefits Act 1992 or any legislation in Northern Ireland or the Isle of Man corresponding to that Act		
5. Pension under article 29 to a child of a member who has no parent living and has not attained the child's age limit—		
(a) in respect of the only, elder or eldest child of a member	£1,265 per annum	£24.25 per week
(b) in respect of each other child of a member	£1,385 per annum	£26.55 per week
(c) where the child does not qualify for child benefit under the Social Security Contributions and Benefits Act 1992 or any legislation in Northern Ireland or the Isle of Man corresponding to that Act	£1,385 per annum	£26.55 per week
6. Allowance under article 30(2)(b) to or in respect of a child who has attained the child's age limit	£5,419 per annum*	£103.85 per week*

* maximum.]

AMENDMENT

Pt III Table substituted by The Naval, Military and Air Forces Etc. (Disablement and Death) Service Pensions (Amendment) Order 2015 (SI 2015/208), art 1(1), Sch 5

Appendix 3

Schedule 3 to the Armed Forces and Reserve Forces (Compensation Scheme) Order 2011 (SI 2011/517) (as amended)

SCHEDULE 3 — Article 15(2)

THE TARIFF AND SUPPLEMENTARY AWARDS

PART 1

DESCRIPTORS, TARIFF LEVELS AND AMOUNTS – "THE TARIFF"

[Table 1 – Burns(*)

Item	*Column (a) Level*	*Column (b) Description of injury and its effects ("descriptor")*
1	4	Burns, with partial, deep or full thickness burns affecting 70% or more of whole body surface area.
2	5	Burns, with partial, deep or full thickness burns affecting 50 to 69.9% of whole body surface area.
3	5	Burns, with partial, deep or full thickness burns to the face or face and neck including one or more of the following: loss of or very severe damage to chin, ear, lip or nose, resulting in or expected to result in residual scarring and poor cosmetic result despite treatment and camouflage.
4	6	Burns, with partial, deep or full thickness burns affecting 15 to 49.9% of whole body surface area.
5	7	Burns, with partial, deep or full thickness burns to the face or face and neck resulting in, or expected to result in, residual scarring and poor cosmetic result despite treatment and camouflage.
6	8	Burns, with partial, deep or full thickness burns affecting 9 to 14.9% of whole body surface area.

7	9	Burns, with partial, deep or full thickness burns to face or face and neck resulting in, or expected to result in, residual scarring and satisfactory cosmetic result with camouflage.
8	11	Burns, with partial, deep or full thickness burns affecting 4.5 to 8.9% of whole body surface area.
9	12	Burns, with partial, deep or full thickness burns affecting less than 4.5 of whole body surface area.
10	12	Burns, with superficial burns affecting more than 15% of whole body surface area.
11	13	Burns, with superficial burns to the face or face and neck.
12	14	Burns, with superficial burns affecting 4.5 to 15% of whole body surface area.
13	15	Burns, with superficial burns affecting 1 to 4.4% of whole body surface area.

(*) Awards for all burns include compensation for any residual scarring or pigmentation and take into account any skin grafting.
(*) Awards for partial, deep or full thickness burns include compensation for actual or expected metabolic or cardiovascular consequences.]

AMENDMENT

Table 1 substituted by The Armed Forces and Reserve Forces (Compensation Scheme) (Amendment) Order 2014 (SI 2014/412), arts 1(1), 3, Sch

Table 2 – Injury, Wounds and Scarring(*)

Item	*Column (a)* *Level*	*Column (b)* *Description of injury and its effects ("descriptor")*
[A1	2	Bilateral complex injury to both upper limbs including hand on only one side and only from above elbow on the other, causing permanent total or virtually total functional limitation or restriction.]
1	5	Complex injury covering all or most of the area from thigh to ankle or shoulder to wrist, with complications, causing permanent significant functional limitation or restriction.
2	5	Loss of both kidneys or chronic renal failure.
3	6	Complex injury covering all or most of the area from thigh to knee, knee to ankle, shoulder to elbow or elbow to wrist, with complications, causing permanent significant functional limitation or restriction.
4	6	Injury covering all or most of the area from thigh to ankle or shoulder to wrist, with complications, causing permanent significant functional limitation or restriction.
5	6	Complex injury to chest, with complications, causing permanent significant functional limitation or restriction.

6	7	Complex injury covering all or most of the area from thigh to ankle or shoulder to wrist, causing permanent significant functional limitation or restriction.
7	7	Injury covering all or most of the area from thigh to knee, knee to ankle, shoulder to elbow or elbow to wrist, with complications, causing permanent significant functional limitation or restriction.
8	7	Injury to chest, with complications, causing permanent significant functional limitation or restriction.
9	7	Complex injury to chest causing permanent significant functional limitation or restriction.
10	7	Complex injury to abdomen, including pelvis or perineum, or both, with complications, causing permanent significant functional limitation or restriction.
11	[6]	Severe facial lacerations including one or more of the following: loss of or very severe damage to chin, ear, lip or nose, which have required, or are expected to require, operative treatment, but with poor cosmetic result despite camouflage.
12	7	[High energy transfer gunshot wound, deeply penetrating missile fragmentation or other penetrating injury (or all or any combination of these)] with clinically significant damage to bone, soft tissue structures and vascular or neurological structures of the head and neck, torso or limb, with complications, which have required, or are expected to require, operative treatment with residual permanent significant functional limitation or restriction.
13	8	Injury covering all or most of the area from thigh to ankle or shoulder to wrist, causing permanent significant functional limitation or restriction.
14	8	Complex injury covering all or most of the area from thigh to knee, knee to ankle, shoulder to elbow or elbow to wrist, causing permanent significant functional limitation or restriction.
15	[7]	Severe facial lacerations which have required, or are expected to require, operative treatment, but with poor cosmetic result despite camouflage.
16	8	Injury to abdomen, including pelvis or perineum, or both, with complications, causing permanent significant functional limitation or restriction.
17	8	Complex injury to abdomen, including pelvis or perineum, or both, causing permanent significant functional limitation or restriction.
18	8	Injury to chest, causing permanent significant functional limitation or restriction.
19	9	Injury to abdomen, including pelvis or perineum, or both, causing permanent significant functional limitation or restriction.

20	9	Injury covering all or most of the area from thigh to knee, knee to ankle, shoulder to elbow or elbow to wrist, causing permanent significant functional limitation or restriction.
21	9	Complex injury covering all or most of the hand, with complications, causing permanent significant functional limitation or restriction.
22	9	[High energy transfer gunshot wound, deeply penetrating missile fragmentation or other penetrating injury (or all or any combination of these)] with clinically significant damage to soft tissue structures and vascular or neurological structures of the head and neck, torso or limb, which have required, or are expected to require, operative treatment with residual permanent significant functional limitation or restriction.
[22A	9	Non-freezing cold injury in the feet, hands or both, with small fibre neuropathy diagnosed clinically and by appropriate tests with continuing neuropathic pain and severely compromised mobility or dexterity beyond 26 weeks.]
23	10	Severe facial lacerations which have required, or are expected to require, operative treatment with a good cosmetic result with camouflage.
24	10	Complex injury covering all or most of the area from thigh to ankle or shoulder to wrist, with complications, which has caused, or is expected to cause, significant functional limitation or restriction at 26 weeks, with substantial recovery beyond that date.
25	10	Complex injury to chest, with complications, which has caused, or is expected to cause, significant functional limitation or restriction at 26 weeks, with substantial recovery beyond that date.
26	10	Complex injury covering all or most of the foot, with permanent significant functional limitation or restriction.
27	…	
28	11	Complex injury covering all or most of the area from thigh to ankle or shoulder to wrist, which has caused, or is expected to cause, significant functional limitation or restriction at 26 weeks, with substantial recovery beyond that date.
29	11	Traumatic damage to spleen which has required splenectomy and where there is, or where there is a high risk of, overwhelming post-splenectomy infection.
30	[10]	Severe facial scarring which produces a poor cosmetic result despite camouflage.
31	11	[High energy transfer gunshot wound, deeply penetrating missile fragmentation or other penetrating injury (or all or any combination of these)] with clinically significant damage to soft tissue structures of the head and neck, torso or limb, which have required, or are expected to require,

		operative treatment with residual permanent significant functional limitation or restriction.
32	11	Complex injury covering all or most of the area from thigh to knee, knee to ankle, shoulder to elbow or elbow to wrist, with complications, which has caused, or is expected to cause, significant functional limitation or restriction at 26 weeks, with substantial recovery beyond that date.
33	11	Injury covering all or most of the area from thigh to ankle or shoulder to wrist, with complications, which has caused, or is expected to cause, significant functional limitation or restriction at 26 weeks, with substantial recovery beyond that date.
34	11	Complex injury to chest, which has caused or is expected to cause, significant functional limitation or restriction at 26 weeks, with substantial recovery beyond that date.
35	11	Complex injury to abdomen, including pelvis or perineum, or both, with complications, which has caused, or is expected to cause, significant functional limitation or restriction at 26 weeks, with substantial recovery beyond that date.
36	11	Complex injury covering all or most of the hand, with complications, which has caused or is expected to cause significant functional limitation or restriction at 26 weeks, with substantial recovery beyond that date.
37	12	Complex injury covering all or most of the area from thigh to knee, knee to ankle, shoulder to elbow or elbow to wrist, which has caused, or is expected to cause, significant functional limitation or restriction at 26 weeks, with substantial recovery beyond that date
38	12	Severe scarring of face, or face and neck, or neck, scalp, torso or limb, where camouflage produces a good cosmetic result.
39	12	Injury to chest, with complications, which has caused or is expected to cause, significant functional limitation or restriction at 26 weeks, with substantial recovery beyond that date.
40	12	Injury covering all or most of the area from thigh to ankle or shoulder to wrist, which has caused or is expected to cause, significant functional limitation or restriction at 26 weeks, with substantial recovery beyond that date.
41	12	[High energy transfer gunshot wound, deeply penetrating missile fragmentation or other penetrating injury (or all or any combination of these)] to the head and neck, torso or limb which have required, or are expected to require, operative treatment with substantial functional recovery.
42	12	Traumatic injury to external genitalia requiring treatment resulting in severe permanent damage or loss.
43	12	Injury covering all or most of the area from thigh to knee, knee to ankle, shoulder to elbow or elbow to wrist, with complications, which has caused, or is expected to cause

		significant functional limitation or restriction at 26 weeks, with substantial recovery beyond that date.
44	12	Complex injury to abdomen, including pelvis or perineum, or both, which has caused or is expected to cause significant functional limitation or restriction at 26 weeks, with substantial recovery beyond that date.
45	12	Complex injury covering all or most of the foot, with complications, which has caused, or is expected to cause, significant functional limitation or restriction at 26 weeks, with substantial recovery beyond that date.
46	13	Injury to abdomen, including pelvis or perineum, or both, with complications, which has caused, or is expected to cause, significant functional limitation or restriction at 26 weeks, with substantial recovery beyond that date.
47	13	Injury to all or most of the area from thigh to knee, knee to ankle, shoulder to elbow or elbow to wrist, which has caused, or is expected to cause, significant functional limitation or restriction at 26 weeks, with substantial recovery beyond that date.
48	13	Injury to chest, which has caused, or is expected to cause, significant functional limitation or restriction at 26 weeks, with a substantial recovery beyond that date.
49	13	Moderate facial scarring where camouflage produces a good cosmetic result.
50	13	Lung damage due to toxic fumes, smoke inhalation or blast, where symptoms have continued, or are expected to continue beyond 6 weeks and where the claimant has made or is expected to make a substantial recovery within 26 weeks.
51	13	Traumatic tension or open pneumothorax.
52	13	Superficial shrapnel fragmentation or one or more puncture wounds (or both such injuries) to head and neck, torso or limb which have required, or are expected to require, operative treatment.
53	13	Fractured tooth which has required, or is expected to require, root resection.
54	13	Loss of two or more front teeth.
[55	13	Non-freezing cold injury which has caused neuropathic pain in the feet, hands or both, with significant functional limitation or restriction at 26 weeks and substantial recovery beyond that time. Continuing cold sensitivity may be present beyond 26 weeks.]
[55B	13	Blunt trauma resulting in soft tissue injury to head and neck, torso or limb, which has required, or is expected to require, operative treatment.]
[55A	13	Freezing cold injury including skin, nail and soft tissue damage, which has caused, or is expected to cause,

		significant functional limitation or restriction at 26 weeks, with substantial resolution of symptoms beyond that date.]
56	14	Injury to abdomen including pelvis or perineum, or both, which has caused, or is expected to cause, significant functional limitation or restriction at 26 weeks, with substantial recovery beyond that date.
57	14	Moderate scarring of scalp, neck, torso or limbs where camouflage produces a good cosmetic result.
58	14	Minor facial scarring.
59	14	Flesh wound which has required, or is expected to require, operative treatment.
60	14	Traumatic injury to external genitalia requiring treatment resulting in moderate permanent damage.
61	14	Damage to one front tooth which has required, or is expected to require, a crown or root canal surgery.
62	14	Damage to two or more teeth other than front which have required, or are expected to require, crowns or root canal surgery.
63	14	Loss of one front tooth.
64	14	Loss of two or more teeth other than front.
65	14	Non-freezing cold injury which has caused pain in the feet, hands or both, with functional limitation or restriction at 6 weeks and substantial recovery by 12 weeks. Continuing cold sensitivity may be present beyond 12 weeks
[65A	14	Freezing cold injury including skin, nail and soft tissue damage, which has caused, or is expected to cause, significant functional limitation or restriction at 6 weeks, with substantial resolution of symptoms beyond that date.] (a)
66	15	Minor scarring of scalp, neck, torso or limbs.
67	15	Injury to abdomen, including pelvis, or both, which has caused, or is expected to cause significant functional limitation or restriction at 13 weeks, with substantial recovery within 26 weeks.
68	15	Shrapnel fragmentation or one or more puncture wounds (or both such injuries) to head and neck, torso or limb not requiring operative treatment.

(*) When applied to a limb injury the expression "complex injury" means that the injury affects all or most of the following structures: skin, subcutaneous tissues, muscle, bone, blood vessels and nerves.

(*) When applied to a limb injury the expression "with complications" means that the injury is complicated by at least one of septicaemia, osteomyelitis, clinically significant vascular or neurological injury, avascular necrosis, gross shortening of the limb, mal-united or non-united fracture, or the fact that the claimant has required, or is expected to require, a bone graft.

(*) When applied to a limb injury, the expression "injury covering all or most of the area" means external injury causing direct damage to contiguous areas

of the limb circumference. In the case of a lower limb this may include direct damage to the buttocks.
(*) When applied to an injury to the torso the expression "complex injury" means that there is clinically significant damage to vital structures and organs including two or more of the following: trachea, lungs, heart, gastrointestinal tract, great vessels, major nerves, diaphragm, chest or abdominal wall, pelvic floor, liver, pancreas, kidneys, bladder, spleen or ovaries.
(*) When applied to an injury to the torso the expression "with complications" means that management of the injury has required two or more of the following: resuscitation, ventilation, thoracic or abdominal drainage, a laparotomy with repair and/or removal of organs and structures.
(*) When applied to an injury in this Table, the term "torso" means any part of the chest, back or abdomen including pelvis and perineum.
(*) When applied to any injury, the expression "vital structures" includes major nerve or blood vessels.
(*) An award for injury to a limb or the torso includes compensation for related scarring and damage to, or removal of structures (including skin, subcutaneous tissue, muscle, bone, tendons, ligaments, blood vessels, lymphatics and nerves).
[(*) A non-freezing cold injury must be diagnosed by a non-treating consultant neurologist.]
[(*) Neuropathic pain is pain initiated or caused by a primary lesion or disorder of the nervous system.]
[(*) A descriptor for a freezing cold injury refers to either unilateral or bilateral damage to the upper or lower extremities.]
(a) [In items 55A and 65A, a descriptor] for a [freezing cold or] non-freezing cold injury refers to either unilateral or bilateral damage to the upper or lower extremities.

AMENDMENT

Last three items in footnote to Table 2 inserted by The Armed Forces and Reserve Forces (Compensation Scheme) (Amendment) Order 2016 (SI 2016/557), art *3(f)*

Words in footnote to Table 2 substituted by The Armed Forces and Reserve Forces (Compensation Scheme) (Amendment) Order 2014 (SI 2014/412), arts 1(1), 4(g)

Words in footnote (a) inserted by The Armed Forces and Reserve Forces (Compensation Scheme) (Amendment) Order 2012 (SI 2012/1573), arts 1(1), 7(a)(iii) (with art 8)

Item A1 inserted by The Armed Forces and Reserve Forces (Compensation Scheme) (Amendment) Order 2016 (SI 2016/557), art *3(a)*

Word in item 11 substituted by The Armed Forces and Reserve Forces (Compensation Scheme) (Amendment) Order 2014 (SI 2014/412), arts 1(1), 4(a)

Words in item 12 substituted by The Armed Forces and Reserve Forces (Compensation Scheme) (Amendment) Order 2014 (SI 2014/412), arts 1(1), 4(d)

Word in item 15 substituted by The Armed Forces and Reserve Forces (Compensation Scheme) (Amendment) Order 2014 (SI 2014/412), arts 1(1), 4(b)

Words in item 22 substituted by The Armed Forces and Reserve Forces (Compensation Scheme) (Amendment) Order 2014 (SI 2014/412), arts 1(1), 4(d)

Item 22A inserted by The Armed Forces and Reserve Forces (Compensation Scheme) (Amendment) Order 2016 (SI 2016/557), art *3(b)*
Item 27 deleted by The Armed Forces and Reserve Forces (Compensation Scheme) (Amendment) Order 2016 (SI 2016/557), art *3(c)*
Word in item 30 substituted by The Armed Forces and Reserve Forces (Compensation Scheme) (Amendment) Order 2014 (SI 2014/412), arts 1(1), 4(c)
Words in item 31 substituted by The Armed Forces and Reserve Forces (Compensation Scheme) (Amendment) Order 2014 (SI 2014/412), arts 1(1), 4(d)
Words in item 41 substituted by The Armed Forces and Reserve Forces (Compensation Scheme) (Amendment) Order 2014 (SI 2014/412), arts 1(1), 4(e)
Item 55 substituted by The Armed Forces and Reserve Forces (Compensation Scheme) (Amendment) Order 2016 (SI 2016/557), art *3(d)*
Item 55B inserted "after item 55" by The Armed Forces and Reserve Forces (Compensation Scheme) (Amendment) Order 2014 (SI 2014/412), arts 1(1), 4(f)
Item 55A inserted by The Armed Forces and Reserve Forces (Compensation Scheme) (Amendment) Order 2012 (SI 2012/1573), arts 1(1), 7(a)(i) (with art 8)
Item 65 substituted by The Armed Forces and Reserve Forces (Compensation Scheme) (Amendment) Order 2016 (SI 2016/557), art *3(e)*
Item 65A inserted by The Armed Forces and Reserve Forces (Compensation Scheme) (Amendment) Order 2012 (SI 2012/1573), arts 1(1), 7(a)(ii) (with art 8)

Table 3 – Mental disorders(*)

Item	*Column (a)* *Level*	*Column (b)* *Description of injury and its effects ("descriptor")*
1	6	Permanent mental disorder, causing severe functional limitation or restriction.[1]
2	8	Permanent mental disorder, causing moderate functional limitation or restriction.[2]
3	10	Mental disorder, causing functional limitation or restriction, which has continued, or is expected to continue for 5 years.
4	12	Mental disorder, which has caused, or is expected to cause functional limitation or restriction at 2 years, from which the claimant has made, or is expected to make, a substantial recovery within 5 years.
5	13	Mental disorder, which has caused, or is expected to cause, functional limitation or restriction at 26 weeks, from which the claimant has made, or is expected to make, a substantial recovery within 2 years.
6	14	Mental disorder, which has caused or is expected to cause, functional limitation or restriction at 6 weeks, from which the claimant has made, or is expected to make, a substantial recovery within 26 weeks.

(*) In assessing functional limitation or restriction in accordance with article 5(6) account is to be taken of the claimant's psychological, social and occupational function.
[(*) Mental disorders must be diagnosed by a clinical psychologist or psychiatrist at consultant grade."]
1 Functional limitation or restriction is severe where the claimant is unable to undertake work appropriate to experience, qualifications and skills at the time of onset of the illness and over time able to work only in less demanding jobs.
2 Functional limitation or restriction is moderate where the claimant is unable to undertake work appropriate to experience, qualifications and skills at the time of onset of the illness but able to work regularly in a less demanding job.

AMENDMENT

Footnote to Table 3 substituted by The Armed Forces and Reserve Forces (Compensation Scheme) (Amendment) Order 2014 (SI 2014/412), arts 1(1), 5

Table 4 – Physical disorders – illnesses and infectious diseases(*)

Item	*Column (a) Level*	*Column (b) Description of physical disorder and its effects ("descriptor")*
1	6	Physical disorder causing severe functional limitation or restriction where life expectancy is less than 5 years.
[1A	6	Physical disorder causing permanent very severe functional limitation or restriction.]
2	7	Physical disorder causing severe functional limitation or restriction where life expectancy is reduced, but is more than 5 years.
3	[8]	Physical disorder causing permanent severe functional limitation or restriction.
4	11	Physical disorder which has caused, or is expected to cause, severe functional limitation or restriction at 26 weeks from which the claimant has made, or is expected to make, a substantial recovery beyond that date.
5	11	Physical disorder causing permanent moderate functional limitation or restriction.
6	12	Permanent physical disorder where symptoms and functional effects are well controlled by regular medication.
7	13	Physical disorder which has caused, or is expected to cause, severe functional limitation or restriction at 6 weeks, from which the claimant has made, or is expected to make, a substantial recovery within 26 weeks.
8	13	Physical disorder which has caused, or is expected to cause, moderate functional limitation or restriction at 26 weeks,

		from which the claimant has made, or is expected to make, a substantial recovery beyond that date.
9	14	Physical disorder which has caused, or is expected to cause, severe functional limitation or restriction at 6 weeks, from which the claimant has made, or is expected to make, a substantial recovery within 13 weeks.
10	14	Physical disorder which has caused, or is expected to cause, moderate functional limitation or restriction at 13 weeks, from which the claimant has made, or is expected to make, a substantial recovery within 26 weeks.
11	15	Physical disorder which has caused, or is expected to cause, moderate functional limitation or restriction at 6 weeks, from which the claimant has made, or is expected to make, a substantial recovery within 13 weeks.

(*) This Table relates to diseases and related physical health problems included in the World Health Organisation International Classification of Diseases and Related Health Problems. Mental and behavioural disorders and traumatic and accidental physical injuries are excluded.
[(*) Permanent functional limitation or restriction is very severe when the claimant is unable to undertake work appropriate to experience, qualifications and skills, following best practice treatment, and at best thereafter is able to undertake work only sporadically and in physically undemanding jobs.
(*) Permanent functional limitation or restriction is severe where the claimant is unable to undertake work appropriate to experience, qualifications or skills at the time of onset of the disorder and over time able to work in only physically less demanding jobs.]

AMENDMENT

Item 1A inserted by The Armed Forces and Reserve Forces (Compensation Scheme) (Amendment) Order 2014 (SI 2014/412), arts 1(1), 6(a)

Word in item 3 substituted by The Armed Forces and Reserve Forces (Compensation Scheme) (Amendment) Order 2014 (SI 2014/412), arts 1(1), 6(b)

Words in footnote inserted by The Armed Forces and Reserve Forces (Compensation Scheme) (Amendment) Order 2014 (SI 2014/412), arts 1(1), 6(c)

Table 5 – Amputations(*)

Item	*Column (a)* *Level*	*Column (b)* *Description of injury and its effects ("descriptor")*
1	1	Loss of both legs (above or below knee) and both arms (above or below elbow).
2	1	Loss of both eyes or sight in both eyes and loss of either both legs (above or below knee), or both arms (above or below elbow).

3	1	Total deafness and loss of either both legs (above or below knee) or both arms (above or below elbow).
4	1	Loss of both arms where one loss is a shoulder disarticulation or forequarter loss, and the loss of the other arm is at any level.[1]
5	1	Loss of both arms above or below elbow (not shoulder disarticulation or forequarter) and one leg (above or below knee).
6	1	Loss of one arm, above or below elbow, and one leg, above or below knee, with total loss of use of another limb due to traumatic injury involving vital structures.[2]
7	2	Loss of both arms where one loss is at or above elbow (trans-humeral or elbow disarticulation) and the loss of the other arm is at, above or below elbow.
8	2	Loss of one arm above elbow (shoulder disarticulation or forequarter).[1]
9	2	Loss of both legs where one loss is at hip disarticulation or hindquarter loss, and the loss of the other leg is at any level.[1]
10	2	Loss of both legs above or below knee (not hip disarticulation or hemipelvectomy) and one arm (above or below elbow).
11	3	Loss of both arms below elbow (trans-radial).
12	3	Loss of both legs where one loss is at or above knee (trans-femoral or knee disarticulation) and the loss of the other is at any level.
13	3	Loss of one leg above knee (hip disarticulation or hemipelvectomy).[1]
14	4	Loss of one arm at or above elbow (trans-humeral or elbow disarticulation).
15	4	Loss of both legs below knee (trans-tibial).
16	4	Loss of both hands (wrist disarticulation) or where amputation distal to that site has led to permanent total loss of use of both hands.
17	5	Loss of one arm below elbow (trans-radial).
18	5	Loss of one leg at or above knee (trans-femoral or knee disarticulation).
19	5	Loss of both feet at ankle distal to the calcaneum.
20	6	Loss of one leg below knee (trans-tibial).
21	6	Loss of one hand (wrist disarticulation) or where amputation distal to that site has led to permanent total loss of use of one hand.
22	7	Loss of both thumbs.
23	8	Loss of one foot at ankle distal to the calcaneum.
24	10	Loss of both great toes.
25	10	Loss of thumb.
26	10	Loss of both index fingers.

27	10	Loss of two or more fingers, other than thumb or index finger, from each hand.
28	10	Partial loss of thumb and index finger from each hand.
29	11	Loss of two or more fingers, other than thumb or index finger, from one hand.
30	12	Loss of great toe.
31	12	Loss of two or more toes, other than great toe, from each foot.
32	12	Loss of index finger from one hand.
33	12	Partial loss of thumb and index finger from one hand.
34	12	Partial loss of two or more fingers, other than thumb or index finger, from each hand.
35	12	Loss of one finger, other than thumb or index finger, from each hand.
36	12	Partial loss of thumb or index finger from each hand.
37	12	Persistent phantom limb pain.
38	12	Stump neuroma with trigger point stump pain.
39	13	Loss of two or more toes, other than great toe, from one foot.
40	13	Partial loss of each great toe.
41	13	Partial loss of one finger, other than thumb or index finger, from each hand.
42	13	Loss of one finger, other than thumb or index finger, from one hand.
43	13	Partial loss of two or more fingers, other than thumb or index finger, from one hand.
44	13	Partial loss of thumb or index finger from one hand.
45	14	Partial loss of great toe from one foot.
46	14	Loss of one toe, other than great toe, from each foot.
47	14	Partial loss of one finger, other than thumb or index finger, from one hand.
48	14	Partial loss of two or more toes, other than great toe, from one foot.
49	15	Loss of one toe, other than great toe, from one foot.

(*) Loss of one or both legs below knee includes loss of foot with loss of all or part of calcaneum (heel).

(*) Loss of a finger or thumb means that amputation has taken place at the metacarpophalangeal joint.

(*) Loss of a toe means that amputation has taken place at the metatarsophalangeal joint.

1 These descriptors also apply to circumstances where stump length or condition precludes satisfactory fitting of prosthesis.

2 "Total loss of use of another limb" means the total loss of the physical capacity or power to carry out its expected functions as compared with a normal healthy person of the same age and sex.

Table 6 – Neurological disorders, including spinal, head or brain injuries(*)

Item	*Column (a)* *Level*	*Column (b)* *Description of injury and its effects ("descriptor")*
1	1	Cervical spinal cord injury where the claimant requires ventilatory support and there is complete tetraparesis.
2	1	Cervical spinal cord injury with minimal upper limb function and complete or near complete paraparesis.
3	1	Complete brachial plexus injury with avulsion of the roots from the spinal cord, resulting in complete flaccid paralysis and sensory loss, with persistent severe central pain.
4	1	Brain injury with persistent vegetative state.
5	1	Brain injury resulting in major loss or limitation of responsiveness to the environment, including absence or severe impairment of language function, and a requirement for regular professional nursing care.
6	2	Cervical spinal cord injury with some useful upper limb function and complete or near complete paraparesis.
7	2	Thoracic spinal cord injury with complete paraparesis.
8	2	Injury to conus medullaris or cauda equina giving rise to complete paraparesis.
9	2	Complete brachial plexus injury with avulsion of the roots from the spinal cord, resulting in complete flaccid paralysis and sensory loss, without persistent severe central pain.
10	2	Partial brachial plexus injury in which spontaneous recovery or operative treatment has led to some restoration of useful function in the arm at the shoulder and elbow, but with no restoration of useful function in the hand.
11	2	Brain injury where the claimant has some limitation of response to the environment; substantial physical and sensory problems; and one or more of cognitive, personality or behavioural problems, requiring some professional nursing care and likely to require considerable regular support from other health professionals.
12	3	Injury to conus medullaris or cauda equina giving rise to partial paraparesis or severe monoparesis.
13	3	Thoracic spinal cord injury with partial paraparesis.
14	4	Injury to conus medullaris or cauda equina giving rise to partial asymmetric paraparesis.
15	4	Uncontrolled post head injury epilepsy.
16	4	Traumatic spinal injury with partial spinal cord, conus or cauda equina damage causing paraparesis of upper or lower limbs, or both, with some recovery and restoration of upper limb motor and sensory function, but no useful manual dexterity or ability to walk.

17	4	Brain injury where the claimant has moderate physical or sensory problems; one or more of cognitive, personality or behavioural problems and requires regular help from others with activities of everyday living, but not professional nursing care or regular help from other health professionals.
18	5	Partial brachial plexus injury in which spontaneous improvement or operative treatment has led to restoration of some useful function in the arm and hand.
19	5	Hemiplegia.
20	6	Injury to conus medullaris or cauda equina giving rise to partial monoparesis.
21	7	Traumatic spinal injury resulting in partial paresis of lower or upper limbs, or both, with substantial recovery, restoration of lower and upper limb motor and sensory function, including a useful ability to walk.
[21A	7	Brain injury, with substantial recovery of sensory and cognitive function, some useful recovery of upper and/or lower limb motor and sensory function, but with some residual motor deficit in upper or lower limbs or both.]
22	8	Brain injury from which the claimant has made a substantial recovery and is able to undertake some form of employment and social life, has no major physical or sensory deficits, but one or more of residual cognitive deficit, behavioural change or change in personality.[1]
23	8	Mild brachial plexus injury with substantial recovery of arm and hand function resulting in good restoration of manual dexterity.
24	9	Permanent isolated damage to one cranial nerve.
25	10	Permanent foot or wrist drop.
26	11	Minor traumatic head injury which has caused, or is expected to cause, functionally limiting or restricting post traumatic syndrome for more than 52 weeks.[2]
27	11	Brain or traumatic head injury with persistent balance symptoms and other functionally limiting neurological damage including permanent sensorineural hearing loss of less than 50dB averaged over 1, 2 and 3kHz.
28	12	Cerebral infarction due to vascular injury in the neck, resulting in persisting impairment of function and restriction of activities.
29	12	Controlled post head injury epilepsy.
30	12	Permanent substantial peripheral motor sensory or autonomic nerve damage.
31	12	Entrapment neuropathy which has not responded to treatment.
32	13	Permanent facial numbness including lip.
33	13	Entrapment neuropathy which has responded, or is expected to respond, to treatment.

34	13	Minor traumatic head injury which has caused, or is expected to cause, functionally limiting or restricting impaired balance or post-traumatic syndrome for more than 6 weeks, with substantial recovery beyond that date.
35	14	Permanent facial numbness which does not include the lip.
36	15	Permanent minor peripheral sensory nerve damage.

(*) An award for brain injury in levels 1, 2 or 4 includes compensation for associated sexual dysfunction, incontinence of the bowel and bladder, and epilepsy.
(*) An award for a spinal injury including a spinal cord, conus medullaris or cauda equina injury, complete or partial, at any tariff level, includes compensation for associated sexual dysfunction and incontinence of the bowel and bladder.
(*) The descriptors for a brachial plexus injury are for a unilateral injury.
1 The claimant is unable to undertake work appropriate to experience, qualifications and skills at the time of onset of the illness, but able to work regularly in a less demanding job.
2 The diagnosis and prognosis of post traumatic syndrome must be determined by a consultant neurologist.

AMENDMENT

Item 21A inserted by The Armed Forces and Reserve Forces (Compensation Scheme) (Amendment) Order 2014 (SI 2014/412), arts 1(1), 7

Table 7 – Senses(*)

Item	*Column (a) Level*	*Column (b) Description of injury and its effects ("descriptor")*
1	1	Total deafness and loss of both eyes, or total deafness and total blindness in both eyes, or total deafness and loss of one eye and total blindness in the other eye.
2	2	Loss of eyes.
3	2	Total blindness in both eyes.
4	2	Loss of one eye and total blindness in the other eye.
5	2	Total deafness in both ears.
6	5	Loss of one eye and permanent damage to the other eye, where visual acuity is correctable to 6/36.
7	5	Blast injury to ears or acute acoustic trauma due to impulse noise with permanent bilateral sensorineural hearing loss of more than 75dB averaged over 1, 2 and 3kHz.
8	6	Severe binocular visual field loss.
9	6	Blast injury to ears or acute acoustic trauma due to impulse noise with permanent sensorineural hearing loss of 50–75dB averaged over 1, 2 and 3kHz in one ear and more than 75dB loss averaged over 1, 2 and 3kHz in the other.

10	6	Bilateral permanent hearing loss of more than 75dB averaged over 1, 2 and 3kHz.[1]
11	7	Blast injury to ears or acute acoustic trauma due to impulse noise with permanent bilateral sensorineural hearing loss of 50–75dB averaged over 1, 2 and 3kHz.
12	8	Total deafness in one ear.
13	8	Bilateral permanent hearing loss of 50–75dB averaged over 1, 2 and 3kHz.[1]
14	8	Loss of one eye or total blindness in one eye.
15	9	Partial loss of vision where visual acuity is correctable to 6/60.
16	9	Permanent and inoperable cataracts in both eyes.
17	10	Partial loss of vision where visual acuity is correctable to better than 6/60 and at least 6/36.
18	10	Detached retina in both eyes.
19	10	Blast injury to ears or acute acoustic trauma due to impulse noise with permanent sensorineural hearing loss in one ear of more than 75dB averaged over 1, 2 and 3kHz.
20	10	Acute physical trauma to ear causing conductive or permanent sensorineural hearing loss in one ear of more than 75dB averaged over 1, 2 and 3kHz.
21	11	Partial loss of vision where visual acuity is correctable to better than 6/36 and at least 6/18.
22	11	Blast injury to ears or acute acoustic trauma due to impulse noise with permanent sensorineural hearing loss in one ear of 50–75dB averaged over 1, 2 and 3kHz.
23	11	Acute physical trauma to ear causing conductive or permanent sensorineural hearing loss in one ear of 50–75dB averaged over 1, 2 and 3kHz.
24	12	Partial loss of vision where visual acuity is correctable to better than 6/18 and at least 6/12.
25	12	Permanent and inoperable cataract in one eye.
26	12	Operable cataracts in both eyes.
27	12	Moderate binocular visual field loss.
28	12	Detached retina in one eye.
29	12	Secondary glaucoma.
[29A	12	Traumatic uveitis.]
30	13	Significant penetrating, or blunt injury, to both eyes.
31	13	Retinal damage (not detached) to both eyes.
32	13	Partial loss of vision where visual acuity is correctable to better than 6/12.
33	13	Dislocation of lens in one eye.
34	13	Degeneration of optic nerve in both eyes.
35	13	Permanent diplopia.
36	13	Blast injury to ears or acute acoustic trauma due to impulse noise.

37	13	Acute physical trauma to ear causing conductive or permanent sensorineural hearing loss in one ear.
38	14	Diplopia which is present, or is expected to be present, at 13 weeks, from which the claimant has made, or is expected to make, a substantial recovery beyond that date.
39	14	Operable cataract in one eye.
40	14	Corneal abrasions in both eyes.
41	14	Hyphaema in both eyes which has required, or is expected to require, operative treatment.
42	14	Retinal damage (not detached) in one eye.
43	14	Significant penetrating, or blunt, injury in one eye.
44	14	Degeneration of optic nerve in one eye.
45	14	Slight binocular visual field loss.
46	14	Traumatic mydriasis.
47	15	Diplopia which is present, or is expected to be present, at 6 weeks, from which the claimant has made, or is expected to make, a substantial recovery beyond that date.
48	15	Corneal abrasions in one eye.
49	15	Hyphaema in one eye which has required, or is expected to require, operative treatment.

(*) For the purposes of this table the following definitions apply:—
"Total blindness in both eyes" means that the claimant must have been diagnosed as being blind by an accredited medical specialist;
"Total blindness in one eye" means that the claimant must have been diagnosed by an accredited medical specialist as having visual acuity of 3/60 or worse in the affected eye;
"Total deafness" means that the claimant's bilateral average hearing threshold level is 90dB or more, averaged over 1, 2 and 3kHz, as measured by appropriately calibrated equipment meeting British Standards, operated by trained staff, and using quality assured pure tone audiometry;
"Total deafness in one ear" means that the average hearing threshold is 90dB or more averaged over 1, 2 and 3kHz as measured by appropriately calibrated equipment meeting British Standards, operated by trained staff, and using quality assured pure tone audiometry.
(*) All awards for hearing loss, including blast injury to ears and acute acoustic trauma, include compensation for associated tinnitus, and no separate award is payable for tinnitus alone.
(*) Degree of visual field loss must be assessed by reference to an accredited specialist physician report which includes reasons.
1 These descriptors apply to bilateral hearing loss caused otherwise than by blast injury or acute acoustic trauma due to impulse noise.

AMENDMENT

Item 29A inserted by The Armed Forces and Reserve Forces (Compensation Scheme) (Amendment) Order 2012 (SI 2012/1573), arts 1(1), 7(b) (with art 8)

Table 8 – Fractures and dislocations(*)

Item	*Column (a) Level*	*Column (b) Description of injury and its effects ("descriptor")*
1	9	Fracture of one femur, tibia, humerus, radius or ulna, with complications, causing permanent significant functional limitation or restriction.
2	9	Fracture or dislocation of one hip, knee, ankle, shoulder, elbow, or wrist, which has required, or is expected to require, arthrodesis, osteotomy or total joint replacement.
3	10	Fractured heels of both feet causing permanent significant functional limitation or restriction.
4	10	Fractures or dislocations of both hips, both knees, both ankles, both shoulders, both elbows or both wrists causing permanent significant functional limitation or restriction.
5	10	Multiple face fractures causing permanent significant cosmetic effect and functional limitation or restriction despite treatment.
6	11	Fractures or dislocations of both hips, both knees, both ankles, both shoulders, both elbows or both wrists which have caused, or are expected to cause, significant functional limitation or restriction beyond 26 weeks.
7	11	Fractured heel of one foot causing permanent significant functional limitation or restriction.
8	11	Fractured heel of both feet which has caused, or is expected to cause, significant functional limitation or restriction beyond 26 weeks.
9	11	Fracture of pelvis which has caused, or is expected to cause, significant functional limitation or restriction beyond 26 weeks.
10	11	Fracture or dislocation of great toe of both feet, which has caused, or is expected to cause, significant functional limitation or restriction beyond 26 weeks.
11	11	Fractured tarsal bones of both feet which have caused, or are expected to cause, significant functional limitation or restriction beyond 26 weeks.
12	11	Fractures of both femurs, both tibiae, both humeri, both radii or both ulnae which have caused, or are expected to cause, significant functional limitation or restriction beyond 26 weeks.
13	11	Fracture of one femur, tibia, humerus, radius or ulna causing permanent significant functional limitation or restriction.
14	11	Fracture of one femur, tibia, humerus, radius or ulna, with complications, which has caused, or is expected to cause, significant functional limitation or restriction beyond 52 weeks.

15	11	Multiple fractures to face, or face and neck where treatment has led, or is expected to lead, to a good cosmetic and functional outcome.
16	11	Fracture or dislocation of one hip, knee, ankle, shoulder, elbow or wrist causing permanent significant functional limitation or restriction.
[17	11	Shoulder joint instability which has required or is expected to require operative treatment with permanent significant functional limitation or restriction.]
[17A	12	Shoulder joint instability which has required or is expected to require operative treatment with substantial recovery.]
18	12	Fracture of one femur, tibia, humerus, radius or ulna, which has caused, or is expected to cause, significant functional limitation or restriction beyond 26 weeks.
19	12	Fracture of mandible or maxilla, which has required, or is expected to require, operative treatment and which has caused, or is expected to cause, significant functional limitation or restriction beyond 26 weeks.
20	12	Fracture of both hands which has caused, or is expected to cause, significant functional limitation or restriction beyond 26 weeks.
21	12	Fractures of both clavicles, or both scapulae, which have caused, or are expected to cause, significant functional limitation or restriction beyond 26 weeks.
22	12	Fracture of the skull with sub-dural or extra-dural haematoma which has required evacuation, from which the claimant has made, or is expected to make, a substantial recovery within 26 weeks.
23	12	Fracture or dislocation of thumb of both hands which has caused, or is expected to cause, significant functional limitation or restriction beyond 26 weeks.
24	12	Fracture or dislocation of one hip, knee, ankle, shoulder, elbow or wrist, which has caused, or is expected to cause, significant functional limitation or restriction beyond 26 weeks.
25	12	Fracture or dislocation of index finger on both hands which has caused, or is expected to cause, significant functional limitation or restriction beyond 26 weeks.
26	12	Fracture or dislocation of great toe on one foot which has caused, or is expected to cause, significant functional limitation or restriction beyond 26 weeks.
27	12	Fractured tarsal bones on one foot which have caused, or are expected to cause, significant functional limitation or restriction beyond 26 weeks.
28	12	Fractured heel of one foot which has caused, or is expected to cause, significant functional limitation or restriction beyond 26 weeks.

29	12	Fractured heel of both feet from which the claimant has made, or is expected to make, a substantial recovery within 26 weeks.
30	12	Fractured or dislocated patella on both knees which has caused, or is expected to cause, significant functional limitation or restriction beyond 26 weeks.
31	12	Fractured metatarsal bones on both feet which have caused, or are expected to cause, significant functional limitation or restriction beyond 26 weeks.
32	12	Fractures of both femurs, both tibiae, both humeri, both radii or both ulnae, from which the claimant has made, or is expected to make a substantial recovery within 26 weeks.
33	12	Depressed skull fracture requiring operative treatment.
34	13	Fractured tarsal or metatarsal bones on both feet from which the claimant has made, or is expected to make, a substantial recovery within 26 weeks.
35	13	[Fracture or dislocation of metatarsal bones on one foot which has caused, or is expected to cause, significant functional limitation or restriction beyond 26 weeks.]
36	13	Fracture or dislocation of great toe of both feet from which the claimant has made or is expected to make a substantial recovery within 26 weeks.
37	13	Fracture of one femur, tibia, humerus, radius or ulna from which the claimant has made, or is expected to make a substantial recovery within 26 weeks.
38	13	Fracture of skull with intracranial, extracerebral haematoma that has not required evacuation.
39	13	Fracture of ethmoid which has required or is expected to require operative treatment.
40	13	Fracture of zygoma which has caused, or is expected to cause, significant functional limitation or restriction beyond 26 weeks.
41	13	Fracture or dislocation of one hip, knee, ankle, shoulder, elbow or wrist from which the claimant has made, or is expected to make, a substantial recovery within 26 weeks.
42	13	Fracture of one hand which has caused, or is expected to cause, significant functional limitation or restriction beyond 26 weeks.
43	13	Fractured heel of one foot, from which the claimant has made, or is expected to make a substantial recovery within 26 weeks.
44	13	Fracture of both hands from which the claimant has made, or is expected to make, a substantial recovery within 26 weeks.
45	13	Blow-out fracture of orbit which has required, or is expected to require, operative treatment.

46	13	Dislocated jaw which has caused, or is expected to cause, significant functional limitation or restriction beyond 26 weeks.
47	13	Fracture of one scapula or one clavicle which has caused, or is expected to cause, significant functional limitation or restriction beyond 26 weeks.
48	13	Fracture of both clavicles or both scapulae from which the claimant has made, or is expected to make, a substantial recovery within 26 weeks.
49	13	Fracture of pelvis from which the claimant has made, or is expected to make, a substantial recovery within 26 weeks.
50	13	Fracture of sternum which has, or is expected to have, symptoms continuing beyond 26 weeks.
51	13	Subluxed dislocated acromio or sterno-clavicular joint, which has caused, or is expected to cause, significant functional limitation or restriction beyond 26 weeks.
52	13	Fractures or dislocations of two or more toes, other than great, of both feet which have caused, or are expected to cause, significant functional limitation or restriction beyond 26 weeks.
53	13	Fracture or dislocation of thumb on one hand which has caused, or is expected to cause, significant functional limitation or restriction beyond 26 weeks.
54	13	Fracture or dislocation of thumb of both hands which has caused, or is expected to cause, significant functional limitation or restriction at 13 weeks from which the claimant has made, or is expected to make a substantial recovery within 26 weeks.
55	13	Fractures or dislocations of index finger on both hands, which have caused, or are expected to cause, significant functional limitation or restriction at 13 weeks, from which the claimant has made, or is expected to make, a substantial recovery within 26 weeks.
56	13	Fractures or dislocations of two or more fingers, other than index, on both hands, which have caused, or are expected to cause, significant functional limitation or restriction beyond 26 weeks.
57	13	Fracture or dislocation of index finger on one hand which has caused, or is expected to cause, significant functional limitation or restriction beyond 26 weeks.
58	13	Fractured or dislocated patella of one knee which has caused, or is expected to cause significant functional limitation beyond 26 weeks.
59	13	Shoulder joint instability not requiring operative treatment.
60	14	Dislocated jaw from which the claimant has made, or is expected to make, a substantial recovery within 26 weeks.

61	14	Fractured zygoma from which the claimant has made, or is expected to make a substantial recovery within 26 weeks.
62	14	Fractured ethmoid which has not, or is not expected to require, operative treatment.
63	14	Fracture of mandible or maxilla from which the claimant has made, or is expected to make, a substantial recovery within 26 weeks.
64	14	Fracture of one hand from which the claimant has made, or is expected to make, a substantial recovery within 26 weeks.
65	14	Deviated nasal septum requiring corrective surgery.
66	14	Displaced fracture of nasal bones.
67	14	Simple skull fracture.
68	14	Fractured fibula which has caused, or is expected to cause, significant functional limitation or restriction beyond 26 weeks.
69	14	Fracture or dislocation of thumb on one hand which has caused, or is expected to cause, significant functional limitation or restriction at 13 weeks, from which the claimant has made, or is expected to make, a substantial recovery within 26 weeks.
70	14	Fracture or dislocation of index finger, on one hand, which has caused, or is expected to cause, significant functional limitation or restriction at 13 weeks, from which the claimant has made, or is expected to make, a substantial recovery within 26 weeks.
71	14	Fracture or dislocation of one finger, other than index, on both hands, which has caused, or is expected to cause, significant functional limitation or restriction beyond 26 weeks.
72	14	Fractures or dislocations of two or more fingers, other than index, on one hand, which have caused, or are expected to cause significant functional limitation or restriction beyond 26 weeks.
73	14	Fractures or dislocations of two or more fingers, other than index, on both hands which have caused, or are expected to cause, significant functional limitation or restriction beyond 13 weeks from which the claimant has made, or is expected to make, a substantial recovery within 26 weeks.
74	14	Fractures or dislocations of two or more toes, other than great toe, on one foot, which have caused, or are expected to cause, significant functional limitation or restriction beyond 26 weeks.
75	14	Fractures or dislocations of one toe other than great toe, on both feet, which have caused, or are expected to cause, significant functional limitation or restriction beyond 26 weeks.

76	14	Fractures or dislocations of two or more toes, other than great toe, on both feet, from which the claimant has made, or is expected to make, a substantial recovery within 26 weeks.
77	14	Fracture or dislocation of great toe on one foot from which the claimant has made, or is expected to make, a substantial recovery within 26 weeks.
78	14	Fracture or dislocation of index finger on both hands, from which the claimant has made, or is expected to make, a substantial recovery within 13 weeks.
79	14	Fracture or dislocation of thumb on both hands, from which the claimant has made, or is expected to make, a substantial recovery within 13 weeks.
80	14	Subluxed dislocated acromio or sterno-clavicular joint from which the claimant has made, or is expected to make, a substantial recovery within 26 weeks.
81	14	Fracture of coccyx from which the claimant has made, or is expected to make, a substantial recovery within 26 weeks.
82	14	Fracture of clavicle or scapula from which the claimant has made, or is expected to make, a substantial recovery within 26 weeks.
83	14	Fracture of sternum from which the claimant has made, or is expected to make, a substantial recovery within 26 weeks.
84	14	Fractured tarsal or metatarsal bones on one foot which have caused, or are expected to cause, significant functional limitation or restriction at 13 weeks from which the claimant has made, or is expected to make, a substantial recovery within 26 weeks.
85	14	Fractured or dislocated patella of both knees which has caused, or is expected to cause, significant functional limitation or restriction at 6 weeks, from which the claimant has made, or is expected to make, a substantial recovery within 26 weeks.
86	14	Stress fracture where symptoms have lasted, or are expected to last, for more than 6 weeks.
87	15	Fracture of mastoid.
88	15	Undisplaced fracture of nasal bones.
89	15	Deviated nasal septum which has not required, or is not expected to require, operative treatment.
90	15	Fractured or dislocated patella of one knee which has caused, or is expected to cause, significant functional limitation or restriction at 6 weeks, from which the claimant has made, or is expected to make, a substantial recovery within 26 weeks.
91	15	Fracture of three or more ribs.
92	15	Fractures or dislocations of two or more toes, on one foot, which have caused, or are expected to cause significant

		functional limitation or restriction at 13 weeks, from which the claimant has made, or is expected to make, a substantial recovery within 26 weeks.
93	15	Fractures or dislocations of one toe, other than great toe, on both feet, which have caused, or are expected to cause significant functional limitation or restriction at 13 weeks, from which the claimant has made, or is expected to make, a substantial recovery within 26 weeks.
94	15	Fracture or dislocation of thumb on one hand from which the claimant has made, or is expected to make, a substantial recovery within 13 weeks.
95	15	Fractured tarsal or metatarsal bone on one foot, which has caused, or is expected to cause, significant functional limitation or restriction at 6 weeks, from which the claimant has made, or is expected to make, a substantial recovery within 13 weeks.
96	15	Fracture or dislocation of two or more fingers, other than index, on one hand which have caused, or are expected to cause, significant functional limitation or restriction at 13 weeks, from which the claimant has made, or is expected to make, a substantial recovery within 26 weeks.
97	15	Fracture or dislocation of two or more fingers, other than index, on both hands, from which the claimant has made, or is expected to make, a substantial recovery within 13 weeks.
98	15	Fracture or dislocation of one finger, other than index, on both hands, which has caused, or is expected to cause, significant functional limitation or restriction at 13 weeks, from which the claimant has made, or is expected to make, a substantial recovery within 26 weeks.
99	15	Fracture or dislocation of index finger on one hand, from which the claimant has made, or is expected to make, a substantial recovery within 13 weeks.
100	15	Fracture or dislocation of one finger, other than index, on one hand, which has caused or is expected to cause significant functional limitation or restriction beyond 26 weeks.
101	15	Fractured fibula from which the claimant has made, or is expected to make, a substantial recovery within 26 weeks.
102	15	Fracture of three vertebral transverse or spinous processes.

[(*) In this table, shoulder includes acromio-clavicular and sterno-clavicular joints.]

(*) An award for an injury in this table includes compensation for any expected consequential osteoarthritis.

(*) An award for dislocation includes ligament and other soft tissue damage not requiring operative treatment.

(*) Where a fracture results in a dislocation only one award is payable.
[(*) In this table, "with complications" means that the injury is complicated by at least one of septicaemia, osteomyelitis, clinically significant vascular or neurological injury, avascular necrosis, gross shortening of the limb, mal-united or non-united fracture, or the fact that the claimant has required, or is expected to require, a bone graft.]

AMENDMENT

Item 17 substituted by The Armed Forces and Reserve Forces (Compensation Scheme) (Amendment) Order 2011 (SI 2011/2552), arts 1(1), 9(1)(a) (with art 10)

Item 17A inserted by The Armed Forces and Reserve Forces (Compensation Scheme) (Amendment) Order 2011 (SI 2011/2552), arts 1(1), 9(1)(b)(ii) (with art 10)

Words in item 35 substituted by The Armed Forces and Reserve Forces (Compensation Scheme) (Amendment) Order 2015 (SI 2015/413), arts 1(1), 9

Footnote to Table 8 inserted by The Armed Forces and Reserve Forces (Compensation Scheme) (Amendment) Order 2014 (SI 2014/412), arts 1(1), 8

First item in footnote to Table 8 inserted by The Armed Forces and Reserve Forces (Compensation Scheme) (Amendment) Order 2016 (SI 2016/557), art 4

Table 9 – Musculoskeletal disorders(*)

Item	*Column (a) Level*	*Column (b) Description of injury and its effects ("descriptor")*
1	9	Permanent severely impaired grip in both hands.
2	9	Septic arthritis or other pathology requiring arthrodesis [, osteotomy] or total joint replacement.
[2A	9	Traumatic back injury resulting in vertebral or intervertebral disc damage and medically verified neurological signs, which has required, or is expected to require, operative treatment and which is expected to result in permanent significant functional limitation or restriction.]
3	10	Ligament injury which has resulted in full thickness rupture, affecting both knees, ankles, shoulders, elbows or wrists, causing permanent significant functional limitation or restriction.
4	11	Ligament injury which has resulted in full thickness rupture, affecting one [hip,] knee, ankle, shoulder, elbow or wrist, causing permanent significant functional limitation or restriction.
[5A	11	Full thickness muscle or tendon unit rupture causing permanent significant functional limitation or restriction.]
5	11	Ligament injury which has resulted in full thickness rupture, affecting both knees, ankles, shoulders, elbows, wrists which has caused, or is expected to cause, significant

		functional limitation or restriction at 26 weeks, from which the claimant is expected to make a substantial recovery beyond that date.
6	11	Traumatic back injury (with medically verified neurological signs and vertebral damage) extending over several levels of vertebrae, which has required, or is expected to require, operative treatment and which has caused, or is expected to cause, significant functional limitation or restriction beyond 13 weeks.
7	11	Radiologically confirmed juxta-articular aseptic necrosis of hip or shoulder.
8	11	Ligament injury short of full thickness rupture, to both knees, ankles, shoulders, elbows or wrists, causing permanent significant functional limitation or restriction.
9	11	Permanent severely impaired grip in one hand.
10	11	Radiologically confirmed osteoarthritis of both hips, both knees, both ankles, both shoulders, both elbows or both wrists (caused by a repetitive or attrition injury), causing permanent significant functional limitation or restriction.
11	12	Two frozen shoulders, or other shoulder pathology, which have caused, or are expected to cause, significant functional limitation or restriction beyond 26 weeks.
12	12	Ligament injury short of full thickness rupture, to both knees, ankles, shoulders, elbows or wrists, which has caused, or is expected to cause, significant functional limitation or restriction at 26 weeks, from which the claimant has made or is expected to make a substantial recovery beyond that date.
[13	12	Ligament injury, short of full thickness rupture, to one knee, ankle, foot, shoulder, elbow or wrist causing permanent significant functional limitation or restriction.]
[14	12	Ligament injury, which has resulted in full thickness rupture, affecting one knee, ankle, foot, shoulder, elbow or wrist which has caused, or is expected to cause, significant functional limitation or restriction at 26 weeks from which the claimant has made, or is expected to make, a substantial recovery beyond that date.]
15	12	Full thickness muscle or tendon unit rupture which has caused, or is expected to cause, significant functional limitation or restriction beyond 26 weeks.
16	12	Traumatic back injury (with medically verified neurological signs and vertebral damage), extending over several levels of vertebrae which has caused, or is expected to cause, significant functional limitation or restriction beyond 13 weeks.
[16A	12	Traumatic back injury with one or more intervertebral disc prolapses or vertebral body or facet joint fractures which has

		required, or is expected to require, operative treatment and which has caused, or is expected to cause, significant functional limitation or restriction beyond 13 weeks.]
17	13	Frozen shoulder, or other shoulder pathology, which has caused, or is expected to cause, significant functional limitation or restriction beyond 26 weeks.
18	13	Two frozen shoulders, or other shoulder pathology, which have caused or are expected to cause significant functional limitation at 6 weeks, from which the claimant has made, or is expected to make, a substantial recovery within 26 weeks.
19	13	Ligament injury short of full thickness rupture, to both knees, ankles, shoulders, elbows or wrists from which the claimant has made, or is expected to make, a substantial recovery within 26 weeks.
20	13	Muscle or tendon unit injury short of full thickness rupture, which has caused, or is expected to cause, significant functional limitation or restriction beyond 26 weeks.
21	13	Two muscle or tendon unit injuries, short of full thickness rupture, from which the claimant has made, or is expected to make, a substantial recovery within 26 weeks.
22	13	Full thickness muscle or tendon unit rupture, from which the claimant has made, or is expected to make a substantial recovery within 26 weeks.
23	13	Ligament injury short of full thickness rupture, to one knee, shoulder, ankle, elbow or wrist which has caused, or is expected to cause, significant functional limitation or restriction at 26 weeks with substantial recovery beyond that date.
24	13	Traumatic back injury with one or more intervertebral disc prolapses or vertebral body or facet joint fractures which has caused or is expected to cause, significant functional limitation or restriction beyond 13 weeks.
[25	13	Radiologically confirmed osteoarthritis of hip, knee, ankle, back, shoulder, elbow or wrist (caused by repetitive or attrition injury) causing permanent significant functional limitation or restriction.]
26	13	Overuse injury of lower limb requiring, or expected to require, operative treatment.
27	13	Hip, [pelvis,] knee, ankle, shoulder, elbow or wrist strain, sprain or overuse injury, which has required, or is expected to require, operative treatment.
28	14	Frozen shoulder, or other shoulder pathology, which has caused, or is expected to cause, significant functional limitation or restriction at 6 weeks, from which the claimant has made, or is expected to make, a substantial recovery within 26 weeks.
29	14	Ligament injury short of full thickness rupture to one knee, ankle, shoulder, elbow or wrist, which has caused or is

		expected to cause, significant functional limitation or restriction at 13 weeks, from which the claimant has made, or is expected to make, a substantial recovery within 26 weeks.
30	14	Muscle or tendon unit injury short of full thickness rupture, which has caused or is expected to cause significant functional limitation or restriction at 13 weeks, from which the claimant has made, or is expected to make, a substantial recovery within 26 weeks.
31	14	Tendon or ligament rupture of finger, thumb or toe which has required, or is expected to require, operative treatment.
32	14	Back sprain or strain, with one or more intervertebral disc prolapses which has caused, or is expected to cause significant functional limitation or restriction beyond 13 weeks.
33	14	Low back or neck pain syndrome.
34	14	Anterior knee pain syndrome in both knees which has caused, or is expected to cause, significant functional limitation or restriction at 6 weeks, from which the claimant has made, or is expected to make, a substantial recovery beyond that date.
35	14	Overuse injury of foot or heel, which has required or is expected to require operative treatment.
36	15	Knee meniscus injury which has caused, or is expected to cause, significant functional limitation or restriction at 6 weeks, from which the claimant has made, or is expected to make, a substantial recovery within 26 weeks.
37	15	Anterior knee pain syndrome in one knee which has caused, or is expected to cause, significant functional limitation or restriction at 6 weeks, from which the claimant has made, or is expected to make, a substantial recovery beyond that date.
38	15	… hernia which has required operative treatment.
39	15	Frozen shoulder which has caused, or is expected to cause, significant functional limitation or restriction at 6 weeks, from which the claimant has made, or is expected to make, a substantial recovery within 13 weeks.
40	15	Ligament injury short of full thickness rupture, to one knee, ankle, shoulder, elbow or wrist which has caused, or is expected to cause, significant functional limitation or restriction at 6 weeks, from which the claimant has made, or is expected to make, a substantial recovery within 13 weeks.

(*) An award for an injury in this table includes compensation for any expected consequential osteoarthritis.

(*) An award for dislocation includes ligament and other soft tissue damage not requiring operative treatment.

[(*) References to back in this table include cervical, thoracic, lumbar and sacral vertebral segments or coccyx."]

AMENDMENT

Words in item 2 inserted by The Armed Forces and Reserve Forces (Compensation Scheme) (Amendment) Order 2011 (SI 2011/2552), arts 1(1), 9(1)(c)(i) (with art 10)

Item 2A substituted by The Armed Forces and Reserve Forces (Compensation Scheme) (Amendment) Order 2014 (SI 2014/412), arts 1(1), 9(a)

Word in item 4 inserted by The Armed Forces and Reserve Forces (Compensation Scheme) (Amendment) Order 2014 (SI 2014/412), arts 1(1), 9(b)

Item 5A inserted by The Armed Forces and Reserve Forces (Compensation Scheme) (Amendment) Order 2015 (SI 2015/413), arts 1(1), 10(a)

Item 13 substituted by The Armed Forces and Reserve Forces (Compensation Scheme) (Amendment) Order 2015 (SI 2015/413), arts 1(1), 10(b)

Item 14 substituted by The Armed Forces and Reserve Forces (Compensation Scheme) (Amendment) Order 2015 (SI 2015/413), arts 1(1), 10(c)

Item 16A inserted by The Armed Forces and Reserve Forces (Compensation Scheme) (Amendment) Order 2011 (SI 2011/2552), arts 1(1), 9(1)(c)(ii) (with art 10)

Item 25 substituted by The Armed Forces and Reserve Forces (Compensation Scheme) (Amendment) Order 2014 (SI 2014/412), arts 1(1), 9(c)

Word in item 27 inserted by The Armed Forces and Reserve Forces (Compensation Scheme) (Amendment) Order 2011 (SI 2011/2552), arts 1(1), 9(1)(c)(iii) (with art 10)

Word in item 38 omitted by virtue of The Armed Forces and Reserve Forces (Compensation Scheme) (Amendment) Order 2011 (SI 2011/2552), arts 1(1), 9(1)(c)(iv) (with art 10)

Footnote to Table 9 substituted by The Armed Forces and Reserve Forces (Compensation Scheme) (Amendment) Order 2014 (SI 2014/412), arts 1(1), 9(d)

Table 10 – Tariff amounts

Column (a) *Level*	*Column (b)* *Amount*
1	£570,000
2	£470,000
3	£380,000
4	£290,000
5	£175,000
6	£140,000
7	£90,000
8	£60,000
9	£40,000
10	£27,000
11	£15,500
12	£10,000
13	£6,000
14	£3,000
15	£1,200

PART 2
SUPPLEMENTARY AWARDS

Supplementary award following traumatic physical damage

1. —(1) Subject to the provisions in this article a supplementary award is payable where—

(a) an injury is a traumatic physical injury; [and]
(b) the injury is described by a descriptor in Table 2 of the tariff.

(2) Subject to sub-paragraph (3), the supplementary award is £60,000 where the injury is accompanied by—

(i) incontinence of the bowel or bladder, or both;
(ii) impotence;
(iii) infertility; or
(iv) physical disfigurement due to an injury to external genitalia.

(3) Where an injury is accompanied by more than one of the effects specified in paragraphs (i) to (iv) of sub-paragraph (2) a supplementary award of £60,000—

(a) is payable for each of the paragraphs which apply; but
(b) for each condition is payable once only.

(4) The supplementary award is £40,000 where the injury—

(a) results in the loss of one kidney, or
(b) treatment for the injury requires a kidney to be removed,

in either case without the development of chronic renal failure.

AMENDMENT

Words in para 1(1)(a) inserted by The Armed Forces and Reserve Forces (Compensation Scheme) (Amendment) Order 2011 (SI 2011/2552), arts 1(1), 9(2) (with art 10)

Other supplementary awards

2. —(1) A supplementary award of £3,000 is payable where—

(a) an injury is a limb injury, including a fracture of a limb;
(b) the injury is described by a descriptor in Table 2 or Table 8 of the tariff; and
(c) the injury is accompanied by acute compartment syndrome requiring operative treatment.

(2) A supplementary award of £1,000 is payable where—

(a) an injury is blast injury to ears;
(b) the injury is described by a descriptor in Table 7 of the tariff; and
(c) the tympanic membrane of one ear is perforated.

(3) A supplementary award of £1,000 is payable where—

(a) an injury is a fracture;
(b) the injury is described by a descriptor in Table 8 of the tariff; and
(c) the fracture is an open fracture.

(4) Where sub-paragraph (2) applies and the tympanic membrane of both ears is perforated two supplementary awards of £1,000 are payable.

Index

References are to page numbers. AFCS and WPS refer to the Armed Forces Compensation Scheme and the War Pensions Scheme, respectively. The index entries for the overarching themes of the book are short; details are covered in entries for narrower topics.